Studies in Renaissance Literature

Volume 40

PITY AND IDENTITY IN THE AGE OF SHAKESPEARE

Studies in Renaissance Literature

ISSN 1465-6310

General Editors
Raphael Lyne
Sean Keilen
Matthew Woodcock
Jane Grogan

Studies in Renaissance Literature offers investigations of topics in English literature focussed in the sixteenth and seventeenth centuries; its scope extends from early Tudor writing, including works reflecting medieval concerns, to the Restoration period. Studies exploring the interplay between the literature of the English Renaissance and its cultural history are particularly welcomed.

Proposals or queries should be sent in the first instance to the editors, or to the publisher, at the addresses given below; all submissions receive prompt and informed consideration.

Dr Raphael Lyne, Murray Edwards College, Cambridge, CB3 0DF

Professor Sean Keilen, Literature Department, UC Santa Cruz, 1156 High St, Santa Cruz, CA 95064, USA

Professor Matthew Woodcock, School of Literature and Creative Writing, University of East Anglia, Norwich, NR4 7TJ

Dr Jane Grogan, School of English, Drama and Film, University College Dublin, Belfield, Dublin 4

Boydell & Brewer Limited, PO Box 9, Woodbridge, Suffolk, IP12 3DF

Previously published volumes in this series are listed at the back of this volume

PITY AND IDENTITY IN THE AGE OF SHAKESPEARE

Toria Johnson

D. S. BREWER

© Toria Johnson 2021

All Rights Reserved. Except as permitted under current legislation
no part of this work may be photocopied, stored in a retrieval system,
published, performed in public, adapted, broadcast,
transmitted, recorded or reproduced in any form or by any means,
without the prior permission of the copyright owner

The right of Toria Johnson to be identified as
the author of this work has been asserted in accordance with
sections 77 and 78 of the Copyright, Designs and Patents Act 1988

First published 2021
D. S. Brewer, Cambridge

ISBN 978-1-84384-574-4

D. S. Brewer is an imprint of Boydell & Brewer Ltd
PO Box 9, Woodbridge, Suffolk IP12 3DF, UK
and of Boydell & Brewer Inc.
668 Mt Hope Avenue, Rochester, NY 14620–2731, USA
website: www.boydellandbrewer.com

A catalogue record for this title is available
from the British Library

The publisher has no responsibility for the continued existence or accuracy of URLs
for external or third-party internet websites referred to in this book, and does not
guarantee that any content on such websites is, or will remain, accurate or appropriate

This publication is printed on acid-free paper

For my parents

CONTENTS

Acknowledgements	ix
Textual Note	xiii
Introduction	1
1. 'My name is Pity': Mediated Emotion and *King Lear*	35
2. Violent Spectacle and Violent Feeling in Early Modern Lucrece Narratives	75
3. Dramatic Reworkings of Poetic Pity	117
4. Theorising Humanity Through Pity	153
Conclusion	195
Bibliography	201
Index	219

ACKNOWLEDGEMENTS

In the years it has taken to write this book I have accumulated many debts, not least from the family, friends, and colleagues who have offered support and inspiration along the way. It is a very great pleasure to have the opportunity to offer my heartfelt thanks, though now that the moment is upon me it feels almost inevitable that I will forget someone. To start, then, I should like to say that I could not have been better supported in this process, and I'm very grateful to everyone who has contributed in ways both big and small to getting me here. Any remaining errors in this work are entirely my own.

My parents, Keith and Nicola Johnson, are my first, best, and longest-serving teachers, and have done the most to shape the way I look at the world. Their love and support make everything possible, and it is my great privilege to be their daughter. This book is dedicated to them.

I have a great debt to a long run of truly inspired teachers who appeared earlier in my education, particularly at Colgate University. My thanks especially go to Margaret Darby, David Dudrick, Robert Garland, and Doug Johnson. At Washington State University, Will Hamlin, Todd Butler, and Michael Hanly all had a profound impact on this work in its early stages, and each has helped me better understand what good teaching and scholarship looks like.

The aims of this book changed fundamentally because of the visiting fellowship I held at the Australian Research Council's Centre for the History of Emotions (Grant Number CE110001011). I'm grateful to everyone at the Adelaide node, and to Merridee Bailey in particular, for helping me clarify the intervention this work represents.

I had the great fortune to be at the University of St Andrews as a PhD student and as a teaching fellow, and I cannot conceive of a better place to be. Particularly bright spots in the landscape, for me, included: Christina Alt, Katie Garner, Clare Gill, Rachel Holmes, Lorna Hutson, Kristine Johanson, Ian Johnson, Tom Jones, Rhiannon Purdie, Christine Rauer, Anindya Raychaudhuri, Abi Shinn, and Louise Wilson. Neil Rhodes has been a long-time champion of this project and my work more generally, and continues to be the very definition of a generous mentor and scholar.

Acknowledgements

Thanks are also due to the friends, colleagues, and mentors who have come from the broader academic community, and have for many years supplied support and inspiration: Katharine Craik, Derek Dunne, Katherine Ibbett, Eric Langley, Kristine Steenbergh, and Emma Whipday.

I finished this book at the University of Birmingham, where I have been supported in many ways by very many people. This is a big department and School, with too many true and generous colleagues to list here, but here's a start: Hugh Adlington, Sally Delbeke, Michael Dobson, Andrzej Gasiorek, Miranda Jones, Tom Lockwood, Deborah Longworth, Rebecca Mitchell, Chris Mourant, Sophia Robertshaw, Liv Robinson, Asha Rogers, Will Sharpe, Antonia Parker Smith, Tiffany Stern, Erin Sullivan, Rachel Sykes, Will Tattersdill, Rebecca White, Emily Wingfield, and Sara Wood. Countless other colleagues have offered good cheer and solidarity in key moments, and I feel very lucky to work with such wonderful people, including those at the Cadbury Research Library and the Shakespeare Institute Library. The postgraduate students in Page Breaks have given me some of the happiest professional hours of my career, and have done much more than they realise to keep spirits high in the final months of writing.

At UoB, two colleagues have gone so far above and beyond in their support that I am hardly able to capture it. Dorothy Butchard has cheerfully seen me through the day-to-day writing of this book and has managed, in a year of national lockdown, to make normal research activity seem possible. Gillian Wright has read countless chapter drafts, each time with a truly remarkable level of engagement and care, and has been a true and seemingly tireless mentor. Both have pushed my thinking, and talked me through conceptual bumps, and this book would not have been possible without them.

My sincere thanks to everyone involved in the production of this book, including my series editors, Jane Grogan, Sean Keilen, Raphael Lyne, and Matthew Woodcock; and at Boydell & Brewer, Elizabeth McDonald and Caroline Palmer. My anonymous readers provided careful and considered perspectives that allowed me to reframe the project on more ambitious terms. I am also grateful to The Metropolitan Museum of Art (NY), and The Huntington Library (CA) for image use.

I would be remiss not to mention friends and family who have, for years now, indulged me in conversations about Shakespeare and emotion. They have made this work possible and life more broadly enjoyable in lots of ways. At the very top of this list is Joanne Dalston, but it also includes: Lauren Clark, the Dalston family, Maria Dalton, Aasta and John EikCaffery, Dustin and Patrick Frazier-Wood, Robert Gelb, Taylor Gouge, Amanda Hahn, Ole Hjortland, Carley Hollis, Sarah Howie, Nikki Khanna, Lucy Knisley, Lisa Jones, Simon May, Malcolm and Naomi McLeod, Lara Meischke, Kate

Acknowledgements

Smith, Jesse Tomalty, Amy Wallace, Michael Weh, the Wilkie family, and of course, the Page, Clark, and Tooley families.

Alex Davis has done the most to influence my thinking on this project, and my thinking more broadly as a scholar. I'm certain his will always be the standard of work I push towards, and I hope these pages will honour in some small way the many years of careful guidance he's invested in me. Thank you, Alex.

The words that are most difficult to find are for Jamie Page. No one could have been more steadfast, or could have done more for me and our boy. What is here, and what will follow, is all for you and Will.

TEXTUAL NOTE

I have silently regularised early modern textual conventions such as long -*s* and consonantal *i* and *u* in accordance with modern usage. Initial citations will be accompanied by a full bibliographic footnote, with subsequent references provided parenthetically. Unless otherwise noted, all references to the works of William Shakespeare are from the Arden Shakespeare *Complete Works*, ed. by Richard Proudfoot, Ann Thompson, David Scott Kastan, and H.R. Woudhuysen (London: Thomas Nelson and Sons Ltd., 1998).

INTRODUCTION

The Weakest Creature God Hath Made
Man is the weakest creature God hath made,
For where all else, by heav'nly *Providence*,
Have bodyes arm'd 'gainst Foes that them invade,
And rage of Times by Natures muniments,
Man onely *Vertue* hath for his defence,
This gentle vertue, sweet humanity,
With loving kind and tender heart, from whence
Flow *Pitie, Mercy, Love, Benignity*,
Whereby we mutuall helpes to others heere supply.[1]

This is a book about the social and emotional vulnerabilities of humankind, and the ways in which early modern English subjects in particular thought about, wrote about, and coped with those vulnerabilities in the context of their own subjectivity. It is about what made them feel weak and emotionally exposed as individuals, how they attempted to manage those weaknesses in social, communal terms, and how literary writing helped them explore, test, and better understand their feelings. It is a central contention of this book that early modern literary depictions of pity – and in particular those written for the early modern stage – bear witness to an impressive range of emotional thinking. I argue that in turning to contemporary literary accounts of pity – many of which explicitly attempt to reconcile the instinct for fellow-feeling with broader notions of personal vulnerability and social obligation – we are able to access a more complex and thorough vision of that period's overarching emotional landscape. That landscape, I suggest, places emotional agency squarely at the intersection of personal subjectivity and social identity. Beyond clarifying a crucial era in a single emotion's history, this way of looking at emotion in print and in practice also opens up important possibilities in the broader field of history of emotions studies.

---

[1] Robert Aylett, *Peace with her foure garders* (London: 1622), sig. C6ʳ, emphasis in original.

Both as a concept and as an emotional practice, pity fundamentally influenced early modern subjectivity, defining the boundaries of humanity and individual agency even as it also sometimes eroded them. Published in 1622, the poet Robert Aylett's *Peace with her foure garders* offers a clear vision of this emotionally inflected subjectivity, in which both emotion and identity are framed in collaborative terms. Aylett describes the human as 'the weakest creature God hath made', a being predominantly stripped of physical defences.[2] Whereas he suggests that the rest of God's creatures 'by heav'nly Providence | Have bodyes arm'd 'gainst Foes that them invade', for humankind he sees only one protection: 'sweet humanity'. This humanity he describes as the 'loving kind and tender heart, from whence | Flow *Pitie, Mercy, Love, Benignity*'. It is this tender heart of humanity that drives humans to offer 'mutual helpes to others'; this community of 'mutual helpes', for humankind, represents its own particular defence system.

In many ways, Aylett looks to be offering a standard description of human compassion: this is an uncomplicated, positive vision of humankind's emotional impulses, one which suggests that humans are predisposed – purposely designed even – to offer help to those who need it. It is also a description that conveniently ignores the darker, more selfish impulses that might be considered 'natural' to humanity: Aylett fails to acknowledge, for example, that humans are generally most in need of defence against *other* humans. Nonetheless, even in this simple description there is much to see. The passage's ultimate focus, of course, is compassionate humanity, this vision of the human heart, overflowing with pity, love, mercy, and benignity. The first description, however, is one of vulnerability. Judged alongside other creatures, humankind is remarkable because of its weakness, its utter lack of physical defences. As the account develops, however, it becomes clear that the strength of Aylett's individual is not an individual characteristic at all, but rather, a social one: humankind is made strong, is protected, by its collective impulse towards pity and compassion. But of course, in the face of a physical threat it is not *one's own* impulse to pity, to feel love and offer mercy, that protects – it is rather the assumption of, or reliance on this impulse in other humans, those who will rush to offer 'mutual helpes' or be compelled to intervene in pity or mercy. Aylett's singular, vulnerable, 'weakest' creature is, crucially, only protected in that precise moment in which the individual subject of the passage becomes the 'we' of the last

[2]   In cases such as these, where 'man' is clearly a reference to 'humankind', rather than a reference to biological sex or gender, I have preferred to use the more inclusive term, 'human' or 'humankind' in my analysis. In instances where the materials do reference pity's association as a particularly masculine or feminine trait I have preserved gender-specific terms.

Introduction

line, the 'we' united in compassionate humanity, looking out from the isolated, defenceless self towards the 'others' in need of help. The emotional impulses described here create communities: the people Aylett describes are connected through emotion, through their emotional obligation to one another. In this passage Aylett transitions between the defenceless subject – the 'I' – and the fortified 'we' seamlessly: the moment passes without comment or fanfare. Nonetheless, in this book I argue that in early modern England, fluid movement between the 'I' and the 'we' felt anything but easy and unremarkable, precisely because of the weight and impact of the type of emotional obligation assumed in the passage above. This book argues that the key to understanding this tense and complex relationship between the early modern 'I' and the early modern 'we' is the first 'benevolent' emotion that Aylett references: pity.

This book interrogates the early modern English relationship with social and emotional vulnerability by scrutinising that period's relationship with pity, and in particular its use of pity in contemporary drama. In bringing together artistic, social, and cultural depictions of pity, *Pity and Identity in the Age of Shakespeare* traces a complex and at times convoluted system of belief concerning a specific type of emotional response, in order to place early modern England definitively in a broader, longer timeline of emotional subjectivity. Variously understood as evidence of one's humanity, a source of social comfort, and a dangerous marker of vulnerability, for early modern subjects there was perhaps no single emotion that more effectively raised the problems of placing the emotional self within society. In what follows, I argue that this problem of emotionally situating the self within society was a defining challenge of being a human in early modern England.

DEFINING PITY

One of the primary aims of this book is to introduce a stronger sense of 'messiness' into our understandings of both early modern emotion and early modern subjectivity; this is one reason that pity represents such a natural case study for the bringing together of these two discourses. Considered on a broader spectrum of emotion, pity is a particularly messy – and slippery – emotion. When we talk of pity, we may be referencing an offer of pity (e.g. 'I pity you'), but that statement is anything but straightforward. What does it mean to pity someone? Is it a positive (or even desirable) offer? Does it bring two people, the subject of pity and the pitier, together in compassion, or is it a way of creating distance between them? Beyond the struggle for a stable value judgement – is pity a good thing, or a bad thing? – there are myriad points of disagreement. Are all humans susceptible to pity, or just certain kinds of people? How does the emotion register on the body?

Pity and Identity in the Age of Shakespeare

Who benefits from pity? Is pity a natural instinct, or rather entangled in a complex set of social and cultural rules? Where (if anywhere) is the power in this kind of emotional exchange? What are the conditions needed to be able to offer someone pity? What are the conditions required to receive it? Can you ask for pity, or must it be freely given? Add to this the distinction between *pity*, a transactional emotion that requires at least two subjects (the focus of the present study), and the more narcissistic *self-pity*, and it is easy to see why this particular emotion has attracted so many philosophers and writers – not just in early modern England, but across history – to its study.[3] As a philosophical, cultural, and social concept, the emotion has a long and complicated history of its own, with each era seemingly reworking its understanding of what pity is, and what it means to encounter it.

Even if we restrict an overview of the philosophical tradition on pity to the most commonly associated thinkers, we take in a vast expanse of history that begins with Aristotle, resurfaces in every major philosophical era and remains, in the work of contemporary philosophers like Martha Nussbaum, a rich field of modern philosophical enquiry. Still one of the most prominent figures in pity's history, Aristotle defined pity as 'a perturbation of the mind, arising from the apprehension of hurt, or trouble to another that doth not deserve it, and which he thinks may happen to himself or his.'[4] Aristotle's identification of the emotion as a 'perturbation' suggests first and foremost that the emotion registers as an agitation or a disturbance to the person offering it; there is an emotional cost. There are also elements of

---

[3]   As David Punter has pointed out, there may be elements of self-identification that make outwardly-facing pity possible; this self-identification, Punter claims, means that 'it may be that pity and self-pity may not be as fully distinguishable as we might like to believe' (p. 4). Nonetheless, given the present work's interest in social emotion, I will follow Anna Wierzbicka in preserving a distinction between 'pity' and 'self-pity'. As she writes, 'the focus of *pity* [...] is on the other person (the one to whom bad things have happened) rather than on oneself [...]. '*Self-pity*', she notes 'is not a special case of *pity*, but rather, something like *pity* [...] a misapplication and distortion of *pity*' (p. 101). David Punter, *The Literature of Pity* (Edinburgh: Edinburgh University Press, 2014); Anna Wierzbicka, *Emotions across Languages and Cultures: Diversity and Universals* (Cambridge: Cambridge University Press, 1999).

[4]   Aristotle, *A Briefe of the Art of Rhetorique*, unnamed translator (London: 1637), sig. D12ʳ. All other references to the *Rhetoric* are to this edition, unless otherwise noted. This particular edition of the *Rhetoric* does not name its translator. However, 'an abridgement containing the most useful part of Aristotle's Rhetoric' (sig. A3ᵛ) also appears in a 1681 collection attributed to Thomas Hobbes; Hobbes both includes the material on pity and compassion, and preserves the language of the 1637 translation's definition verbatim. See: Thomas Hobbes, *The Art of Rhetoric, with A Discourse of the Laws of England* (London: 1681), sig. E7ᵛ–E8ʳ.

Introduction

judgement and imagination here: to offer pity is to 'apprehend' the hurt, or to recognise it, to judge that trouble undeserved, and also to imagine one's self or one's family as equally vulnerable to comparable circumstances.

Aristotle's description might look similar to the impulse later imagined by Aylett, but it is complicated by the imagined process of feeling here. What Aristotle describes is something more akin to a sequence: regardless of how quickly pity materialises in practice, for Aristotle it comes at the end of a process involving many steps. Whereas Aylett transitions smoothly between feeling and action – the pity of his passage ends in 'mutual helpes' – Aristotle says nothing of what follows on from pity: he only details the process of arriving at the emotion. Aristotle's pity is also considerably more conditional than Aylett's: 'because it appertaines to Pitty to thinke that he, or his may fall into the misery he pitties in others', Aristotle writes, some are more disposed to the emotion than others. His imagined company of the compassionate is an interesting one, including: those 'who have passed through Misery; and old men; and weake men; and Timorous men; and learned; and such as have Parents, wife and children; and such as thinke there be honest men' (sig. D12ʳ). Those *less* inclined toward compassion include those 'who are in great despaire; who are in great prosperity; and they that are Angry, for they consider not; and they that are very Confident, for they also consider not' (sig. D12ᵛ). The silent gaps in these lists suggest the possibility (or indeed even the probability) of pitiful misfirings – the failure of pity to materialise because the would-be pitier lacks the social, economic, or emotional conditions necessary for the emotion to flourish. This is a far cry from the pity Aylett describes. On Aristotle's view, pity might only function within a privileged (but not too privileged) group. And of course, Aristotle seems only to consider men as viable emotional agents: the women and children of this passage serve only to clarify the man's emotional position. What Aristotle does make clear, however, is pity's relational nature: although the person being pitied receives considerably less attention in Aristotle's description – the passage only offers a short list of the 'things [and] men to be pittied' – it is obvious that the 'pitiable' subject is an emotional provocateur.[5] The trouble or plight of the pitied becomes shared ground, as the pitier recognises it, judges it, and imagines it as his own. This pity is not, and cannot be, an independent emotion: it is, by its very nature, an inherently social exchange.

Although Aristotle's description offers no explicit valuation of pity, many of the conditions and influences he identifies as potential obstacles to its proper function nevertheless suggest a problematic, unreliable

---

5   'Things to be pittied' include: 'such as grieve, and withall hurt; such as destroy; and calamities of fortune, if they be great; [...] and Evill that arrives where good is expected' (sig. D12ᵛ).

Pity and Identity in the Age of Shakespeare

kind of emotional response. Additionally, the compassionate collective he imagines is hardly straightforwardly appealing: it is one thing to identify as a someone who believes that 'there be honest men'; it is quite another to face the possibility that your instinct to pity stems from your being 'old', 'weak', or 'timorous'. Aristotle's list of 'Men to be pittied' introduces another set of obstacles. He includes: 'such as are knowne to us [...]; and such as be of our owne yeares; such as are like us in manners; such as are of the same, or like stocke; and our Equalls in dignity' (sig. E1ʳ). The insistence on similarity between the pitied and the pitier pulls still farther away from the more inclusive vision presented by Aylett. With such an extensive list of conditionals and possible obstacles, Aristotelian pity looks increasingly unstable and unreliable, highlighting the emotion's capacity to be influenced by social hierarchy, power dynamics, and a whole host of other individually subjective factors.

The broader history of thought on pity suggests that Aylett's account is something of an outlier, tending instead to reflect a long-running suspicion about the emotion's capacity for instability, and a particular worry about the impact on those who *offer* pity. Seneca described pity as 'a weakness, though many times mistaken for a virtue', and called the emotion 'a kind of moral sickness, contracted from other people's misfortune'.[6] As one critic summarises the Senecan position, 'The sage never pities (*miseretur*) because pity is necessarily accompanied by misery (*miseria*) of the mind. It does not require pity to come to the aid of those in trouble'.[7] Pity on this view is something quite distinct from (and unnecessary to) the instinct to offer help. The emotional cost of pity – specifically, its ability to permeate and weaken the pitier – is a recurring theme in philosophical explorations of pity, where writers often considered pity's capacity to negatively impact the individual.

The revival of Stoicism in early modern Europe saw the return of these ideas.[8] The Flemish neo-Stoic philosopher Justus Lipsius, whose treatise *De Constantia* was translated into English by Sir John Stradling in 1595, and subsequently was circulated widely in England between the sixteenth and

---

[6] Lucius Annaeus Seneca, *Seneca's Morals*, trans. by Sir Roger L'Estrange (Philadelphia, PA: Gregg and Elliot, 1834), p. 314.

[7] David Konstan, 'Senecan Emotions', in Shadi Bartsch and Alessandro Schiesaro (eds.), *The Cambridge Companion to Seneca* (Cambridge: Cambridge University Press, 2015), pp. 174–186 (p. 180).

[8] For more on the revival of Stoicism in early modern Europe, see: Freya Sierhuis, 'Autonomy and Inner Freedom: Lipsius and the Revival of Stoicism', in Quentin Skinner and Martin Van Gelderen (eds.), *Freedom and the Construction of Europe*, 2 vols (Cambridge: Cambridge University Press, 2013), II (2013), pp. 46–64.

Introduction

eighteenth centuries, was also unequivocal in his condemnation of pity. Lipsius argues that pity 'must be despised of him that is wise and constant'.[9] This sort of man, he notes, should be marked by 'steddinesse and stedfastnes of courage', two core qualities which, for Lipsius, a man 'cannot retaine, if he be cast downe not only with his owne mishaps, but also at other mens'.[10] The emotion was, for Lipsius, 'defined to be the fault of an abject and base mind', not least because of its intrusive capacity to destabilise more desirable qualities.[11] 'Pitty', Lipsius warns, 'intrudeth herselfe unto thee'.[12] To indulge in pity, therefore, one must be weak enough to yield. Cast in opposition to these permeable natures is the early modern ideal of masculine temperance, the 'steddinesse and stedfastnes of courage' that Lipsius references. Philosophical anxiety about pity's threat to selfhood is prevalent throughout the early modern period, although contemporary literature largely suggests a more obvious indulgence in the emotion's seductive, penetrating appeal. Nonetheless, the masculine relationship with pity specifically remained fraught, not least because of the potential consequences of losing's one's judgement, or compromising an otherwise temperate nature.[13] As Baruch Spinoza wrote:

> He who is easily touched by the emotion of pity and is moved by another's distress or tears often does something which he later regrets, both because from emotion we do nothing that we certainly know to be good and because we are easily deceived by false tears.[14]

More than the risk of emotional penetration, Spinoza further highlights the possibility of deception and regret: it is not just that in pity we are made vulnerable to another person's feelings – as in Aylett, Aristotle, Seneca, and Lipsius – it is that pity might also be a conduit for manipulation, a social tool that adds another layer of vulnerability.

Nonetheless, it is possible to find more straightforwardly positive philosophical assessments of pity. In the eighteenth century, Rousseau strongly advocated for pity in *Emile*, writing that, 'A man who knew nothing of suffering would be incapable of tenderness towards his fellow-creatures and ignorant of the joys of pity; he would be hard-hearted, unsocial, a very

---

[9]   Justus Lipsius, *Two Bookes of Constancie* (London: 1595), sig. E3^r.

[10]   Ibid., sig. E3^r.

[11]   Ibid., sig. E3^r.

[12]   Ibid., sig. E3^r.

[13]   On the relationship between early modern masculinity and emotional vulnerability, see: Jennifer C. Vaught, *Masculinity and Emotion in Early Modern English Literature* (Aldershot: Ashgate, 2007).

[14]   Baruch Spinoza, *Complete Works*, ed. by Michael L. Morgan, trans. Samuel Shirley (Indianapolis, IN: Hackett Publishing, 2002), pp. 346–347.

monster among men'.[15] Like Aylett long before him, Rousseau firmly aligned pity with basic human nature, classifying the absence of the emotion as a sort of defect. Moreover, this description imagines the associated suffering of pity as both vital and beneficial: a constructive pain. Rousseau's later assertion that 'whether we will or not, we pity the unfortunate', touches on the earlier elements to which the Stoics objected, insofar as it imagines pity's overriding influence on human agents. Nonetheless, for Rousseau pity is beyond a person's control, powerfully felt even against his/her own judgement, and present even in the worst specimens of humanity. 'Even the most depraved are not wholly without this instinct', he notes.[16] There is a connective quality here, an imagined community built not just on the practice of pity, but the common capacity for it. Rousseau cites many of the same characteristics raised in opposition to the emotion – its prevalence across humanity, humankind's apparent inability to suppress it – but nonetheless champions the emotion as evidence of a common thread of human goodness, rather than a potentially damaging weakness.

Rousseau's contemporary Adam Smith also spoke at some length about the universality of pity:

> How selfish soever man may be supposed, there are evidently some principles in his nature, which interest him in the fortune of others, and render their happiness necessary to him, though he derives nothing from it except the pleasure of seeing it. Of this kind is pity or compassion, the emotion which we feel for the misery of others, when we either see it, or are made to conceive it in a very lively manner. That we often derive sorrow from the sorrow of others, is a matter of fact too obvious to require any instances to prove it; for this sentiment, like all the other original passions of human nature, is by no means confined to the virtuous and humane, though they perhaps may feel it with the most exquisite sensibility. The greatest ruffian, the most hardened violator of the laws of society, is not altogether without it.[17]

Arguments such as these move away from considerations of pity's personal effect, and only acknowledge the emotion as a fundamental characteristic of humanity. For Smith the connective possibilities inherent in pity are most prominent, as he extends his conception to include even 'the greatest ruffian'. In these descriptions of pity, the problem of pity typically only emerges in absence, with the lack of pity signalling the lack of humanity.

---

[15] Jean-Jacques Rousseau, *Emile* (Middlesex: Echo Library, 2007), p. 49.
[16] Ibid., pp. 236–237.
[17] Adam Smith, *The Theory of Moral Sentiments*, ed. by D.D. Raphael and A.L. Macfie (Oxford: Oxford University Press, 1976), p. 9.

Introduction

Arthur Schopenhauer also picks up on this notion of a common humanity, bound together by pity, in his own writing, arguing that whilst 'Envy reinforces the wall between Thou and I [...] pity makes it thin and transparent; indeed, it sometimes tears the wall down altogether, whereupon the distinction between I and Not-I disappears'.[18] The very capacity for blurring the boundaries between subjects – that is, the very thing some find most alarming about pity – Schopenhauer praises for bringing people together in mutual understanding; these accounts insist on pity as a positive, common ground between people, something universal and ultimately benevolent.

The conflict between these readings of pity rest largely on discrepant interpretations of vulnerability, and its value: for each of these writers, pity highlights a capacity for connection between subjects that also, invariably, produces a kind of vulnerability that might shape (or even destabilise) individual selfhood. It is easy to see therefore that discourses on pity naturally lend themselves to larger considerations of emotional obligation and human nature. From the Romantic period onward, however, other writers' discourses on pity returned to (and extended) earlier themes of pity's darker nature. William Blake imagined pity as a force that relied on social stratification: 'Pity would be no more | If we did not make somebody Poor'.[19]

Later still, Nietzsche, perhaps the most outspoken philosophical opponent of pity, explicitly denied the idea of benevolent pity. In *The Anti-Christ*, he admits pity as a fairly common sensation, acknowledging an implicit connection between the pitier and the object of pity, but he classifies any resulting connections to be damaging, and completely void of benefit to either party: 'Pity is the opposite of the tonic affects that heighten the energy of vital feelings', he writes, and 'it has a depressive effect. You lose strength when you pity [...] pity makes suffering into something infectious'.[20] Here again we find the idea of a connection facilitated through pity, though for Nietzsche it is a diseased, contagious bond, a way of unleashing emotions rather than containing or addressing them. Nietzsche also cites pity as a potentially destructive influence on identity in *Daybreak*, placing pity amongst other 'extreme states' like anger, hatred, and love. Unlike the middle or lower degrees, which 'weave the web of our character and our destiny', he

---

[18] Arthur Schopenhauer, *On the Basis of Morality*, trans. E.F.J. Payne (Providence, RI: Berghahn Books, 1995), p. 134.

[19] William Blake, 'The Human Abstract', in *The Complete Poetry and Prose of William Blake*, ed. by David V. Erdman (Berkeley, CA: University of California Press, 1982), p. 27, ll. 1–2.

[20] Friedrich Nietzsche, *The Anti-Christ*, in *The Anti-Christ, Ecco Homo, Twilight of the Idols, and Other Writings*, ed. by Aaron Ridley and Judith Norman, trans. Judith Norman (Cambridge: Cambridge University Press, 2005), p. 6.

instead suggests that extreme states like pity only 'rend the web apart'.[21] The consequences of Nietzsche's negative legacy vis-à-vis pity are still evident in the modern reticence to engage with the term. The philosopher Martha Nussbaum, for example, has openly acknowledged her reluctance to use the term 'pity', arguing that the emotion 'has recently come to have nuances of *condescension and superiority* to the sufferer that it did not have when Rousseau invoked "*pitié*".[22] Modern philosophers – Nussbaum included – prefer to use 'compassion' as a term that captures the fellow-feeling embedded in the pity, while at the same time leaving behind the baggage of social stratification, contempt, distance, and diseased connection. And yet, as this book will show, these worries about pity's destructive edge prevailed long before the modern era, and well before Rousseau.

All of that said, bringing together the major philosophical work on pity does very little to clarify definitively what pity *is* and what it *does* to human subjects. Instead, the assembled discourse shows a fractious, uneasy tradition of contradictory thinking. Nonetheless, this does successfully showcase the 'messiness' of the emotion that I find so compelling, its capacity to arouse passionate debate and disagreement. The line of enquiry I have traced here, albeit briefly, is itself a simplified version: it isolates thinking around a specific version of pity that is secular (rather than explicitly religious) and social, a version that imagines one human agent suffering and another recognising and responding to that suffering. The vivid disagreement about pity's impact and value, however – good or bad, binding or destructive – also hints at pity's appeal too, if not as a practice than as a philosophical problem, something with nuance and complexity that demands further exploration. The present study does not presume to reconcile the long history of thinking on pity but instead aims to clarify a specific moment within it, and ask how this emotion's 'messiness' helped to shape an era's understanding of selfhood.[23] By tracing the emotion's literary deployment

---

[21] *Daybreak*, in *The Nietzsche Reader*, ed. by Keith Ansell Pearson and Duncan Large (Oxford: Blackwell Publishing, 2006), pp. 197–198.

[22] Martha Nussbaum, *Upheavals of Thought: The Intelligence of Emotions* (Cambridge: Cambridge University Press, 2001), p. 301, emphasis mine. Interestingly, the *Oxford English Dictionary* only acknowledges these negative associations when pity is used as a verb: the entry there points out that the word, 'In modern use sometimes impl[ies] disdain or mild contempt for a person as intellectually or morally inferior' and re-directs to 'pitiful'. 'pity, v.'. *OED* Online. June 2006. Oxford University Press. http://www.oed.com./view/Entry/144815?rskey=6q1W8Q&result=2&isAdvanced=-false#eid (accessed 24 May 2018).

[23] On this, see also Erin Sullivan, who recently argued that it is time to acknowledge that the early modern period saw 'a more dynamic, pluralistic, and at times unpredictable model of affective selfhood than has previously been acknowledged'. Erin

Introduction

in detail, in a period in which people grappled with and gravitated toward that emotion with particular focus, I hope to deepen our understanding of how feelings about *this* feeling developed, and how they influenced lines of thought emerging from the early modern period.

Among all of this emotional 'messiness', there remains one further issue that can complicate an exploration of pity in *any* age, but requires particular clarity in a study of early modern pity: the frequent conflation of 'pity' with seemingly comparable terms. Amidst the many problems surrounding pity – concerns about what the feeling is, from whence it comes, in what context it should arise, and if there are consequences connected to its receipt or its dispensation – this regular emergence of terms that seem related (or even synonymous) is problematic not least because other words – 'sympathy' is the most obvious example – often carry very different social and emotional baggage. This is an especially pressing concern for this study, which aims to place early modern pity as a distinct emotional reflex in a broader, longer history of pity that reaches forward to the present day. There is also often a disconnect between the words used by early moderns, and the words used by modern critics when analysing early modern materials.

As I will argue, the emotional baggage of 'pity' as Shakespeare uses it in the 1590s is almost entirely different to the way Nietzsche deploys the term in the late nineteenth century. Still, it is important to ask: when people in early modern England used the word 'pity', were they talking about something *different* to (or distinct from) commonly related words, like 'mercy', 'clemency', 'sympathy', or 'compassion'? The potential for lexical uncertainty adds further confusion to an already murky concept. How can we trace a feeling that might appear under different names? Although I have focused my own examples, in this book, almost exclusively on explicit early modern references to *pity* itself, in my own analysis of the material I also use 'compassion' as an interchangeable term. To my mind, this captures the emotional tenor of the exchanges I trace in the following chapters, while also respecting the lexical habits of early modern England, and restricting any further anachronistic complications. I do want to comment briefly on this choice.

In a work focusing on the emotional climate of early modern England, I see no objections to the use of 'compassion' in relation to pity. Indeed, early modern texts often use the terms as interchangeable. The 1637 edition of Aristotle, for example, positions the terms as synonymous in Chapter 20: 'Of Pitty, or Compassion'; Florio's translation of Montaigne's *Essais* also reflects fluid movement between the terms.[24] 'I should more naturally stoop unto

---

Sullivan, *Beyond Melancholy: Sadness and Selfhood in Renaissance England* (Oxford: Oxford University Press, 2016), p. 4.

[24] Aristotle, *A briefe of the art of rhetorique*, sig. D12^r.

compassion, than bend to estimation', Montaigne wrote, before immediately following the observation with this acknowledgement: 'Yet is *pitie* held a vicious passion among the Stoickes'.[25] John Bullokar's compellingly-titled 1621 work, *An Englis[h] Expositor[:] teaching the in[ter]pretation of the harde[st] words [used] in our language* also uses pity and compassion as synonyms, to define 'commiseration'.[26] There are many similar examples that suggest a period-specific lexical flexibility in using these two terms.

However, in my view, the use of any *other* synonyms for pity unnecessarily complicates an already muddy discourse. 'Mercy' and 'clemency' are already obviously distinct, requiring a certain social hierarchy or authority contained, for example, in the relationship between a king and his subject. But 'sympathy' may seem an attractive and reasonable synonym for pity, not least because modern understandings of sympathy tend to see the emotion as a more straightforwardly positive, less complicated shared emotional connection.[27] This conflation of terms, however, is for the present study a dangerous and problematic association to make, crowding an already littered field. 'Sympathy', as a purely emotional term – the common modern usage referring to the 'quality or state of being affected by the condition of another with a feeling similar or corresponding to that of the other; the fact or capacity of entering into or sharing the feelings of another or others; fellow-feeling' – is an anachronism for the early modern period. This particular understanding of sympathy does not properly emerge in English until the Restoration, with the *Oxford English Dictionary* placing its first use in 1660, when Richard Mathews writes of the desire to share his medical knowledge 'Out of faithful and true simpathy and fellow-feeling with you'.[28]

A proper understanding of early modern sympathy requires a more expanded vision of the term which, when used before 1660, often places its emphasis on a material connection rather than a social one, 'a (real or supposed) affinity between certain things, by virtue of which they are similarly or correspondingly affected by the same influence, affect or influence one another (esp. in some occult way), or attract or tend towards

---

[25] Michel de Montaigne, *Essayes*, trans. John Florio (London: 1613), sig. B1ᵛ, emphasis mine.

[26] J.B., *An Englis[h] Expositor[:]teaching the in[ter]pretation of the harde[st] words [used] in our language* (London: 1621), sig. D8ʳ. The author of this work also uses 'pittiful' to define 'compassionate' (sig. D8ʳ), though no variant of 'pity' is defined in its own right.

[27] For a more in-depth account of early modern sympathy, see Ann E. Moyer 'Sympathy in the Renaissance', in Eric Schliesser (ed.), *Sympathy: A History* (Oxford: Oxford University Press, 2015), pp. 70–101.

[28] Richard Mathews, *The Unlearned Alchymist* (London: 1660), sig. A7ᵛ.

Introduction

each other'.[29] As Ann E. Moyer has pointed out, 'sympathy' appeared in treatises on natural philosophy, and as a way of explaining magic; in the context of Galenic medicine; and in moral philosophy. 'These categories', she writes, 'overlapped frequently in combinations that varied from one scholar to another'.[30] If 'sympathy' had an early modern emotional context, it was both inconsistent, and often inseparable from the material (typically medical) world.[31] For these reasons, and because the dramatic tradition far and away prefers 'pity' to describe the kind of emotional sensation I trace in this book, I have excluded 'sympathy' – both in my own writing and in the range of early modern examples I examine.

BUILDING A 'HISTORY' OF EMOTION

When Peter Burke commented that 'the idea that emotions have a history is not a new one', he was reflecting on a field of humanistic study that had been developing at least since Lucien Febvre's call for a greater focus on the history of the emotions in 1973.[32] Until histories of love, pity, death, and cruelty were written, Febvre insisted, 'there [would] be no real history possible'.[33] Of course, it is far easier to call for these histories than

---

[29] 'sympathy, n.' *OED Online*. December 2020. Oxford University Press. www.oed.com/view/Entry/196271 (accessed 30 June 2021). There are many pre-1660 examples to confirm that this alternate understanding of sympathy was in regular use. *An Englis[h] Expositor*, for example, defines 'sympathie' as 'A likenesse in quantitie; or a like disposition or affection of one thing to another' (sig. O4^r). John Lyly references the concept in *Euphues and his England*: 'But nature recompenced the similitude of mindes, with a Sympathy of bodies, for we were in all parts one so like the other, that it was hard to distinguish either in speach, countenaunce, or height one from the other'. See: John Lyly, *Euphues and his England* (London: 1580), sigs. C2^v–C3^r. Fellow-feeling is often referenced in pre-1660 definitions of sympathy, but again these uses seem to signal a different phenomenon to the focus of the present study. See for example Philemon Holland's translation of Pliny's *History of the World*, where 'sympathie' is defined as 'a fellow-feeling, used [...] for the agreement or amitie naturall in divers sencelesse things, as betweene yron and the loadstone'. Pliny, *The History of the World* (London: 1634), sig. A6^v.

[30] Moyer, p. 87.

[31] For an exploration of the link between sympathy and medical contagion, see Eric Langley, 'Plagued by Kindness: Contagious Sympathies in Shakespearean Drama', *Medical Humanities* 37 (2011), 103–109.

[32] Peter Burke, 'Is there a Cultural History of the Emotions?', in Penelope Gouk and Helen Hills (eds.), *Representing Emotions: New Connections in the Histories of Art, Music and Medicine* (Aldershot: Ashgate, 2005), pp. 35–48 (p. 36).

[33] Lucien Febvre, 'Sensibility and History: How to Reconstitute the Emotional Life of the Past', in *A New Kind of History: From the Writings of Febvre*, ed. by Peter Burke,

Pity and Identity in the Age of Shakespeare

to complete them. Indeed, as Barbara Rosenwein has noted, 'the topic is paradoxically very old – historians have *always* talked about emotions – and almost entirely unexplored, since for the most part such talk has been either unfocused or misguided.'[34] In the years that have followed, however, a huge volume of scholarship has emerged that forever settles the question of whether or not emotions have *remained* unexplored.[35] Nonetheless, as a field of scholarly enquiry, history of emotions scholarship has always been the particular target of methodological scrutiny, not least because there is an ever-present, seductive opportunity to universalise – to talk about 'sadness', 'happiness', or 'anger' as if these feelings *feel* the same to everyone who experiences them.[36] The constant risk for history of emotions scholars is that their subject should cease to represent a ground of enquiry, and that a critic might instead assume scholarly legibility on the basis of his or her own emotional responses. Johan Huizinga and Norbert Elias, both of whom are frequently cited as 'early' history of emotions scholars, have also been criticised for this

---

trans. K. Folca (London: Routledge and Kegan Paul, 1973), pp. 12–26 (p. 24).

[34] Barbara Rosenwein, *Emotional Communities in the Early Middle Ages* (Ithaca, NY: Cornell University Press, 2006), p. 1.

[35] Given the ever-growing nature of the field, and the number of disciplines involved, it would be impossible to offer an exhaustive list of relevant research. Some key contributions include: Jennifer Harding and Deirdre Pribram (eds.), *Emotions: A Cultural Studies Reader* (New York, NY: Routledge, 2009); Jerome Kagan, *What is Emotion?: History, Measures, and Meanings* (New Haven, CT: Yale University Press, 2007); Helena Wulff (ed.), *The Emotions: A Cultural Reader* (Oxford: Berg, 2007), Daniel M. Gross, *The Secret History of Emotion: From Aristotle's Rhetoric to Modern Brain Science* (Chicago, IL: University of Chicago Press, 2006), Keith Oatley, *Emotions: A Brief History* (Malden, MA: Blackwell, 2004), and *The Psychology of Emotions* (Cambridge: Cambridge University Press, 1992). See also Richard Meek and Erin Sullivan (eds.), *The Renaissance of Emotion: Understanding Affect in Shakespeare and His Contemporaries* (Manchester: Manchester University Press, 2015); Gail Kern Paster, Katherine Rowe and Mary Floyd-Wilson, 'Introduction: Reading the Early Modern Passions', in Gail Kern Paster, Katherine Rowe, and Mary Floyd-Wilson (eds.), *Reading the Early Modern Passions: Essays in the Cultural History of Emotion* (Philadelphia, PA: University of Pennsylvania Press, 2004), pp. 1–20; Thomas Dixon, *From Passions to Emotions: The Creation of a Secular Psychological Category* (Cambridge: Cambridge University Press, 2003); Peter Goldie, (ed.), *Understanding Emotions: Minds and Morals* (Burlington, VT: Ashgate, 2002); William M. Reddy, *The Navigation of Feeling: A Framework for the History of Emotions* (Cambridge: Cambridge University Press, 2001); Paul Ekman and Richard J. Davidson (eds.), *The Nature of Emotion: Fundamental Questions* (Oxford: Oxford University Press, 1994); Robert Solomon, *The Passions: Emotions and the Meaning of Life* (Indianapolis, IN: Hackett, 1993); and Ronald De Sousa, *The Rationality of Emotion* (Cambridge, MA: MIT Press, 1987).

[36] For a more extended discussion of this, see Andrew Ortony and Terence J. Turner, 'What's Basic About Basic Emotions?', *Psychological Review*, 97 (1990), 315–331.

Introduction

kind of overgeneralisation in their work.[37] With this in mind, many of the foundational 'methodological' texts in history of emotions scholarship have focused their attention on ways of making the most subjective concepts seem more objective, and better able to facilitate rigorous analysis.[38]

Today, emotions scholarship is anxious to keep in view the fact that its concepts are at times unstable: without question, this is why the emotions have been approached from so many angles, and by so many different types of researchers; this is why the field continues to grow. Nonetheless, within these explorations of emotion there remains a consistent attention to language. Peter and Carol Stearns, for example, traced the problems associated with the study of emotion to the impossibility of studying the *experience* of emotion itself; their solution, 'emotionology', proposed that emotions studies should focus *not* on emotion itself but rather the way a given culture *talks about* emotion.[39] A tidy way of accessing the inaccessible, the Stearnses' interest in 'emotionological filters' – the language at work in conduct manuals, letters, sermons, diaries, and other kinds of texts – still informs the majority of emotions scholarship (the present work included). Other prominent figures in emotions methodology have performed similar moves in order to render the emotions 'fit' for study, able to be discussed in concrete terms. William Reddy framed his own study of emotion in Revolutionary France in terms of 'emotives' (the speech used to describe emotion) and the 'emotional regimes' (sets of emotional rituals and practices that support political regimes) they produce; Barbara Rosenwein, whom I have already mentioned, suggested the tracing of emotional norms by identifying discrete 'emotional communities'.[40] Each of these moves responds to the same basic scholarly need identified by Peter and

---

[37] For more on this, see Barbara H. Rosenwein, 'Worrying about Emotions in History', *The American Historical Review*, 107 (2002), 821–845.

[38] For a helpful review of the problems of representation inherent in the historical study of social experience, see Stuart Airlie, 'The History of Emotions and Emotional History', *Early Medieval Europe*, 10 (2001), 235–241.

[39] Peter N. Stearns and Carol Z. Stearns, 'Emotionology: Clarifying the History of Emotions and Emotional Standards', *The American Historical Review*, 90 (1985), 813–836 (p. 824, p. 830).

[40] Reddy, *The Navigation of Feeling*. For more on 'emotional communities', see Barbara Rosenwein, 'Worrying about Emotions in History', and *Emotional Communities in the Early Middle Ages*. For an overview of recent historiographical work on emotions, see: Susan J. Matt, 'Current Emotion Research in History: Or, Doing History from the Inside Out', *Emotion Review*, 3.1 (2011), 117–124; Erin Sullivan, 'The History of Emotions: Past, Present, Future', *Cultural History*, 2.1 (2013), 93–96; and Jan Plamper, *The History of Emotions: An Introduction* (Oxford: Oxford University Press, 2015). This methodological instinct to find ways of 'containing' emotion is

Pity and Identity in the Age of Shakespeare

Carol Stearns: to find something that is 'more accessible than emotional experience' while still attempting to understand the impact and influence of emotion on individuals, their cultures, and their historical eras.[41] That said, this methodological instinct to claim stability and precision as workable outputs of emotions studies has tended to push scholars away from literary/fictional material, and toward linguistic and textual material that is sometimes imagined as more 'objective' in its recording of events (and emotions): material like legal records, chronicles, diaries, or news media. Erin Sullivan has recently commented on this in her own call to open up the field of emotional source texts, noting that 'Fenced off as [literary sources] are from many of the cultural demands of "the real" – in particular the expectation that the opinions and beliefs voiced in a text will correspond directly with a particular historical person or event – some scholars have perhaps seen them as less reliable sources.'[42] A misapprehension about what constitutes 'the real' has meant that our picture of emotion is incomplete, because it has been compiled out of only *some* of the available sources.

In the specific context of early modern emotion, critical understanding of the period's emotional intelligence has, until very recently, been utterly dominated by the idea that early moderns understood their emotions (or, less anachronistically, their 'passions') in physiological terms, using medical humoral theory.[43] Cautions against falling victim to one's feelings were fairly commonplace, and many writers of the period framed the passions as bodily functions that resulted from the bodily 'humors' (either the balance,

---

also discussed in Rachel E. Holmes and Toria A. Johnson, 'Introduction: In Pursuit of Truth', *Forum for Modern Language Studies*, 54.1 (2018), 1–16.

[41] Peter N. Stearns and Carol Z. Stearns, 'Emotionology: Clarifying the History of Emotions and Emotional Standards', p. 825.

[42] Sullivan, *Beyond Melancholy*, p. 8. On this, see also: Adela Pinch, 'Emotion and History: A Review Article', *Comparative Studies in Society and History*, 37 (1995), 100–109; Daniel Wickberg, 'What is the History of Sensibilities?: On Cultural Histories, Old and New', *The American History Review*, 112 (2007), 661–684, and Frances E. Dolan, *True Relations: Reading, Literature, and Evidence in Seventeenth-Century England* (Philadelphia, PA: University of Pennsylvania Press, 2013).

[43] The seminal work of Gail Kern Paster figures prominently in this strain of criticism, and prompted an entire generation of academics who argued that early modern emotion was understood primarily (if not exclusively) as the balance or imbalance of the four bodily humors. See, for example: Gail Kern Paster, *Humoring the Body: Emotions and Shakespeare's Stage* (Chicago, IL: University of Chicago Press, 2004); see also Mary Floyd-Wilson and Garrett A. Sullivan, Jr. (eds.), *Environment and Embodiment in Early Modern England* (Basingstoke: Palgrave, 2007); Carla Mazzio and David Hillman (eds.), *The Body in Parts: Emotions and the Shakespearean Stage* (New York, NY: Routledge, 1999), Gail Kern Paster, Katherine Rowe, and Mary Floyd-Wilson (eds.), *Reading the Early Modern Passions*.

Introduction

or more commonly, the *im*balance of these humors).[44] According to these theories, the passions were not only implicated in the physical body, but also, and perhaps more importantly, in fact produced by it. Medical writers in particular often included in their work various recommendations for maintaining one's emotional temperament through one's body. Among his pithy commendations of bodily temperance, for example, the English physician Humphrey Brooke noted that 'It moderates our Passions and Affections, and renders them easily commendable'.[45] Intemperance, meanwhile, according to Brooke, 'subjects us to our Passions, and makes them irresistible' (sig. E8^r). Both comments understand the passions as being determined by physical health.

Others offered more precise suggestions for controlling the emotional body by regulating what goes into it, as Thomas Walkington (in a forerunner of Robert Burton's *Anatomy of Melancholy*) describes in the case of the choleric man:

> A cholericke man therefore [...] knowing himselfe to be overpoizd with its predominancy, but even foreseeing his corporall nature to have a propension or inclination to this humour, hee must wisely defeate, and waine his appetite of all such honey flowing meates and hote wines as are poison to his distemperature, and which in tract of time will aggravate this humour soe much, til it generate and breede either a hecticke fever mortall consumption, yellow jaundice, or any the like disease incident to this complexion; and so concerning all the rest.[46]

Walkington assumes not only that the choleric man will be able to self-assess his irritable nature, but also that he can self-medicate (or self-regulate) through expelling the emotionally poisonous 'honey flowing meates and

---

[44] The four bodily humors are: black bile, or melancholy; blood; yellow bile, or choler; and phlegm. Peter Lowe, who served as the surgeon to the King of France, describes the four humors in the following way: blood, 'an humor hot, aerious, of good consistance, red coloured, swete tasted, most necessarie for the nourishment of the parts of our body, which are hot and humide, ingendered in the lyver, retayned in the veines, and is compared to the aire'; phlegm, 'an humor cold and humide, thyn in consistance, white coloured, [which] when it is in the veines, it nourisheth the parts cold and humide, it lubrifieth the moving of the joynts & is compared to the water'; choler, 'hot and drie, of thyn and subtill consistence, black coloured, bitter tasted, proper to nourish the parts hot and dry, it is comparrd to the fire'; and melancholy, 'cold and drie, thick in consistence, sower tasted proper to nourish the parts that are cold and dry and is compared to the earth or winter'. Peter Lowe, *The whole course of chirurgerie* (London: 1597), sig. C3^v.

[45] Humphrey Brooke, *Ugieine or A conservatory of health* (London: 1650), sig. E7^v.

[46] Thomas Walkington, *The Opticke Glasse of Humors* (London: 1607), sigs. B7^r–B7^v.

Pity and Identity in the Age of Shakespeare

hote wines' from his diet. What Walkington (and the theory of the humoral body more generally) suggests is that the emotions are located within the body, that there are physical reasons for them, and that they can, in theory, be managed in quite a straightforward way. Nonetheless, these theories do more than just reveal an early modern preoccupation with feeling and its origin: the emphasis on physicality suggests that people in this period felt especially susceptible to emotion, and conceived of it as something all-encompassing, something experienced by both the mind and the body, and most importantly, something that needed to be explained and controlled.

As I will go on to argue, to view early modern emotion only through the lens of humoral theory – as physiological events, occurrences *produced* by and *contained within* the body – is to view only one part of a much larger picture, not least because this way of thinking imagines the emotional self also, crucially, as self-contained and in isolation. Even if we revisit a classic source text like Thomas Wright's *The Passions of the Mind in Generall* (1604), we can see a more complex emotional theory at work. Wright argues, for example, that:

> The humors wait upon the Passions, as their Lords and Maisters. The Physitians therefore knowing by what Passion the maladie was caused, may well inferre what humor aboundeth, & consequently what ought to be purged, what remedy to be applied; & after, how it may be prevented.[47]

While this description seems a straightforward account of the emotional attitude I have just outlined, in which the humors and the passions are inextricably linked, there is also a social dimension here that has been unaccounted for. The language of control used in fact focuses more on the 'Physitian' than on the passions themselves: Wright implies a model of medical intervention in which the physician identifies, cures, and manages the humors – and in so doing, manages the potentially domineering emotions as well. So, rather than offering a purely self-sufficient model of producing, managing, and experiencing feeling through balancing the humors, Wright ultimately points to a social relationship as the method of managing one's passions. The passions may manifest within the individual, but it is the physician who identifies them, 'cures' them, and is able to prevent them. Here we have perhaps the smallest possible version of what Barbara Rosenwein has called an 'emotional community'.[48] The 'passionate malady' of which Wright speaks may be

---

[47] Thomas Wright, *The Passions of the Mind in Generall* (London: 1604), sig. B2ᵛ.

[48] Rosenwein calls the 'emotional community' a group 'in which people adhere to the same norms of emotional expression and value – or devalue – the same or related emotions'. See: Rosenwein, *Emotional Communities in the Early Middle Ages*, p. 2.

Introduction

located within the individual body, but there is a clear social aspect of its identification and management. One of the aims of the present study is to showcase the social dimensions of both emotion *and* selfhood in early modern England, to trace the way these two concepts come together, and to understand how the period's drama supported, challenged, and shaped a new framework for emotional humanity.

THE EARLY MODERN 'SELF'

At the core of all history of emotions work is a belief that emotion plays a central role in the life of the individual, that the feeling and expression of emotion can tell us something important about how humans function, both within themselves and within society. As William Reddy has written, 'the emotions are the most immediate, the most self-evident, and the most relevant of our orientations toward life'.[49] Katharine Craik has also outlined the ways in which emotion impacted the foundational areas of early modern life, noting that 'Emotions such as sadness, love, courage, and compassion contributed in important ways to early modern systems of ethics, morals and religious belief'.[50] Recent scholarship in early modern studies seems to echo this opinion: there has been a significant increase in studies focusing on particular emotions (such as shame or sadness), all in an attempt to access what Paul Harris has called the 'emotional universe' of the period.[51] If, as I argue in this book, we are to shift our view of early modern English emotion towards a more social model, in which emotions are understood not just as products of the body but something produced (and managed) in a community context, then this will also necessarily impact our understanding of early modern subjectivity, what it meant to be a human in this era.

---

[49] Reddy, p. 3.

[50] Katharine Craik, *Reading Sensations in Early Modern England* (Basingstoke: Palgrave Macmillan, 2007), pp. 12–13.

[51] Harris, quoted in Anna Wierzbicka, *Emotions Across Languages and Cultures*, p. 32. For emotion-specific studies, see for example: Gwynne Kennedy, *Just Anger: Representing Women's Anger in Early Modern England* (Carbondale, IL: Southern Illinois University Press, 2000); Ewan Fernie, *Shame in Shakespeare* (London: Routledge, 2002); and Erin Sullivan, *Beyond Melancholy*. Other relevant studies do not emphasise emotion exclusively, but engage with it in a central way. Abjection, for example, is a central theme of Catherine Bates, *Masculinity, Gender and Identity in the English Renaissance Lyric* (Cambridge: Cambridge University Press, 2007). Lynn Enterline also emphasises emotion in *Shakespeare's Schoolroom: Rhetoric, Discipline, Emotion* (Philadelphia, PA: University of Pennsylvania Press, 2012).

Pity and Identity in the Age of Shakespeare

For modern critics of the early modern period, however, this idea of a clear relationship between social emotion and a social model of early modern subjectivity has only recently seemed possible, much less probable. If we return briefly one final time to the Aylett passage with which I opened this introduction, it is important to acknowledge just how unusual Aylett's vision of humanity may look in comparison to the traditional – though now largely disputed – critical notion of the 'Renaissance' subject as the first example of autonomous subjectivity. This is a sharp contrast, for example, to the vision Jacob Burckhardt offers in his seminal study of Renaissance individuality in Italy. Burckhardt's Renaissance man is a true individual, representative of a marked development from the medieval model, in which:

> [B]oth sides of human consciousness – that which was turned within as that which was turned without – lay dreaming or half awake beneath a common veil [...] Man was conscious of himself only as a member of a race, people, party, family or corporation – only through some general category.[52]

Largely positioned as the antithesis of this medieval model, Burckhardt depicts the Renaissance as the time in which 'man became a spirited individual', whose 'impulse to the highest individual development' created 'the "all-sided man" – *l'uomo universale*'.[53] Although this position is now seen as transparently incorrect, both in its reading of medieval subjectivity and its depiction of a hard line between 'the medieval' and 'the early modern', Burckhardt's view remains a point against which modern criticism works; his influence is still constantly acknowledged, even as it is contested. Lorna Hutson, for example, acknowledges the continued critical 'identification of the period as "the Renaissance"', with its implicit homage to the myth of essential and universal Man coming to stand (in all his sovereign individuality) at the centre of a new world picture'.[54]

Studies that continue to take as their premise the inherent 'specialness' of the 'Renaissance' individual are increasingly unfashionable; yet even those who seek to challenge Burckhardt often continue to do so within his terms of reference. The title of Stephen Greenblatt's classic *Renaissance*

---

[52] Jacob Burckhardt, *The Civilization of the Renaissance in Italy*, trans. S.G.C. Middlemore (London: Penguin, 1990), p. 98.

[53] Ibid., p. 99; p. 101.

[54] Lorna Hutson, 'Series Editor's Preface' in James Kuzner, *Open Subjects: English Renaissance Republicans, Modern Selfhoods, and the Virtue of Vulnerability* (Edinburgh: Edinburgh University Press, 2011), p. xiii. Given my own interest in pursuing fluidity between boundaries – individual and community, historical and literary, medieval and early modern – I favour 'early modern' over 'Renaissance' in referencing the period in question.

Introduction

Self-Fashioning, for instance, clearly announces its Burckhardtian affiliations, even as his argument pushes against them: 'Autonomy is an issue,' Greenblatt writes, 'but not the sole or even the central issue: the power to impose a shape upon oneself is an aspect of the more general power to control identity – that of others at least as often as one's own.'[55] Greenblatt's idea that 'there appears to be an increased self-consciousness about the fashioning of human identity as a manipulable, artful process' during this period still remains attractive, however, and accounts of early modern identity still tend to frame subjectivity as an isolated project rather than a social process.[56] Even those studies that avoid romanticising early modern humanity have tended to emphasise interiority, focusing on the Cartesian 'I' that creates itself through rational thought; Charles Taylor has classified this tendency as 'the sense of ourselves as beings with inner depths'.[57] Jerrod Seigel's three-part theory of the self (bodily, relational, and reflective) similarly imagines the formulation of the self through focused attention, prioritising the reflective reflex as that which makes people capable of 'putting ourselves at a distance from our own being so as to examine, judge, and sometimes regulate or revise it'.[58] Katharine Eisaman Maus, to give yet another example, has argued for the pervading sense of 'inwardness' amongst early modern subjects; and Michael Schoenfeldt has traced in early modern literature 'a kind of psychological inwardness that we value deeply, and that we often associate with the most valued works of the Renaissance'.[59] All of these views contribute, in some way, to an overarching picture of people in the early modern period standing (and self-identifying) on their own, with the individual subject prioritised above all else.[60]

[55] Stephen Greenblatt, *Renaissance Self-Fashioning: From More to Shakespeare*, (Chicago, IL: University of Chicago Press, 1980), p. 1.

[56] Ibid., p. 2. For a more nuanced Burkhardtian account, see: William Kerrigan and Gordon Braden, *The Idea of the Renaissance* (Baltimore, MD: Johns Hopkins University Press, 1989).

[57] Charles Taylor, *Sources of the Self: The Making of Modern Identity* (Cambridge: Cambridge University Press, 1989), p. x.

[58] Jerrod Seigel, *The Idea of the Self: Thought and Experience in Western Europe Since the Seventeenth Century* (Cambridge: Cambridge University Press, 2005), p. 6.

[59] Katharine Eisaman Maus, *Inwardness and Theater in the English Renaissance* (Chicago, IL: University of Chicago Press, 1995). Michael C. Schoenfeldt, *Bodies and Selves in Early Modern England: Physiology and Inwardness in Spenser, Shakespeare, Herbert, and Milton* (Cambridge: Cambridge University Press, 1999), p. 1.

[60] For a refreshing contrast to this line of critical enquiry, see for example: Margreta de Grazia, Maureen Quilligan, and Peter Stallybrass (eds.), *Subject and Object in Renaissance Culture* (Cambridge: Cambridge University Press, 1996). In their introduction, the editors announce their desire to 'reconfigure' this 'obsessive teleological

Pity and Identity in the Age of Shakespeare

Moreover, these accounts make this kind of self-reflective, self-reflexive subjectivity a defining characteristic of the early modern period.

I do not wish to dispute the scholarly narrative about self-reflection and its prevalence in early modern England. Indeed, it is one of the central assumptions of this book that early moderns spent a significant amount of time thinking about their own subjectivity. I do, however, wish to challenge the sense of this reflection happening in a social vacuum. This thinking, I argue, was not only largely emotional: it also, through its emphasis on pity, prioritised a particular type of emotional *relation*. In short: the emotional thinking that shaped early modern selfhood was, ultimately and fundamentally, social in nature. By looking at the early modern relationship with pity I believe we are able to learn much more about the early modern relationship with the self: the early modern obsession with pity suggests that subjects were neither confident in their own emotional autonomy, nor were they confident in their ability to emotionally influence others. Instead, the evidence suggests a culture that was both highly emotionally aware, and one that was extremely emotionally anxious.

This book is about the moments of emotional exchange that complicate or destabilise the subject's sense of self rather than obviously bolstering it; my own findings confirm and explore Cynthia Marshall's contention that 'the contradiction between autonomy and instability *defined* the emerging subject'.[61] In a sense, my work also has a Burckhardtian debt: it is an attempt to return to Burckhardt's original emphasis upon what grew out of medieval culture, to foreground this sense of historical transition without replicating its problematic historiography, or assuming an uncomplicated trajectory of 'progress'. Of the available narratives of the early modern self, my work belongs to an ever-growing collection of scholarship that understands the early modern subject as a self within a community, an individual still very much dependent on and defined by social interactions. Natalie Zemon Davis in particular has argued for the mutually beneficial relationship between individual and community, noting that 'embeddedness did not preclude self-discovery, but rather prompted it'.[62] Nancy Selleck also notes

---

history' that, starting with Burckhardt, advances the 'sovereignty of the subject'. 'Introduction', pp. 1–13 (p. 4).

[61] Cynthia Marshall, *The Shattering of the Self: Violence, Subjectivity, and Early Modern Texts* (Baltimore, MD: Johns Hopkins University Press, 2002), p. 14.

[62] Natalie Zemon Davis, 'Boundaries and the Sense of Self in Sixteenth-Century France', in Thomas C. Heller, Morton Sosna and David E. Wellbery (eds.), *Reconstructing Individualism: Autonomy, Individuality and the Self in Western Thought* (Stanford, CA: Stanford University Press, 1986), pp. 53–63 (p. 63); For more on the influence of community on selfhood, see also Kay Stockholder, who notes that 'one's

Introduction

that 'Because the notion of subjectivity takes account of only one concrete, embodied perspective (that of the subject), it entails a one-person model of selfhood. To move beyond it involves addressing the ways that other bodies and other perspectives fashion the self'.[63] As I argue throughout this book, a turn to the theatre demonstrates Selleck's point here in important ways: dramatic material from the period confirms a sense of highly cultivated early modern 'personhood', particularly through the sheer volume of emotional exploration seen on stage. At the same time, early modern drama insistently presents the self-reflective subject in company, responding to and being shaped by the others onstage. As Timothy Reiss observes: 'Person and community, one cannot repeat too often, are in a mutually creative dialectic'.[64] In tracing early modern dramatic portrayals of social selves, we can see clearly that the individual is always created in context.

LITERARY SUBJECTS

Although scholars working in the 'history' of emotions have been relatively slow in accepting fictional material in building their own narratives of emotion, literary scholars have long been convinced of literature's capacity both to depict emotive subjects and to provoke emotion in readers and spectators.[65] Writers in the early modern period seemed particularly aware of this material's affective potential: George Puttenham, for example, memorably wrote of 'all maner of conceites that stirre up any vehement passion in a man', outlining the various ways that literature might move an audience.[66] 'To make a man angry', he wrote, 'there must be some injury or contempt offered, to make him envy there must proceede some undeserved prosperitie of his egall or inferiour, to make him pitie some miserable fortune or spectakle to behold'.[67] In a similar vein, Philip Sidney argued that in poetry we might find 'all vertues, vices, and passions, so in their own naturall seates layd to

---

place in the world was identical to one's self-definition'; 'Yet Can He Write: Reading the Silences in *The Spanish Tragedy*', *American Imago*, 47 (1990), 93–124 (p. 95).

[63] Nancy Selleck, *The Interpersonal Idiom in Shakespeare, Donne, and Early Modern Culture* (Houndsmills: Palgrave Macmillan, 2008), p. 3.

[64] Timothy Reiss, *Mirages of the Selfe: Patterns of Personhood in Ancient and Early Modern Europe* (Stanford, CA: Stanford University Press, 2003), p. 24.

[65] This connection between readers, texts, and emotions is pursued in detail by Katharine Craik, who tracks the early modern conception of 'literary experience as a resourceful, dynamic exchange between readers and writers in which emotional and physiological feelings [...] played an important part'. See Craik, p. 7.

[66] George Puttenham, *The Arte of English Poesie* (London: 1589), sig. Ii3ᵛ.

[67] Ibid., sig. Ii3ᵛ.

Pity and Identity in the Age of Shakespeare

the viewe.'[68] Sidney's image of the passions 'layd out to viewe' further evokes the possibilities opened up by literature, the chance to observe emotion at a controlled distance. In language and literature, the early moderns had what Jan Frans van Dijkhuizen has called 'a cultural laboratory': a place to explore, to express, and to cultivate their understanding of emotion.[69] Given all of this it would be impossible, in my view, to present a convincing exploration of any early modern emotion without reference to these types of texts.

In the present study, I have focused my attentions primarily on dramatic material, though not because other genres of writing stand to contribute less to an examination of literature's role in shaping affective selfhood. Of course, we have much to learn from both poetry and prose as well, but in bringing together prose *and* verse writing, and in explicitly 'lay[ing] to the viewe' its affective content, to my mind drama offers a natural place to begin an investigation of an emotion with such a profound investment in visual displays of feeling. There is, of course, also another case to be made, given the particular investment that Shakespeare seems to have in this emotion.[70] The word 'pity' appears at least once in each of Shakespeare's plays (as well as the narrative poems and the sonnets), suggesting that the emotion spans all genres and all periods of his career. Even just sampling from the Shakespearean uses reveals a number of possible contexts in which one might deploy the term 'pity'. Alcibiades, for example, marries the emotion with friendship: 'I am thy friend and pity thee, dear Timon'; Mecaenas' comment to Octavia is similarly themed, though perhaps less intimate and more publicly minded: 'Each heart in Rome does love and pity you.'[71] Remarkably, even Julia feels compelled to offer her pity to her own beloved, in his failed

---

[68] Philip Sidney, *An Apologie for Poetry* (London: 1595), sig. D4ʳ.

[69] Jan Frans van Dijkhuizen, *Pain and Compassion in Early Modern English Literature and Culture* (Cambridge: D.S. Brewer, 2012), p. 7.

[70] Given this book's specific interest in pity, there is still yet another reason to focus on drama: the influence of Aristotle's theory of tragedy based on 'pity and fear', from the *Poetics*. The early modern dramatic use of pity, however, reaches well beyond the tragic genre. For more see: Aristotle, *Poetics*, trans. D.W. Lucas (Oxford: Clarendon Press, 1968); Charles B. Daniels and Sam Scully, 'Pity, Fear, and Catharsis in Aristotle's *Poetics*', *Noûs*, 26.2 (1992), 204–217. For a more specific consideration of Aristotelian pity in Shakespeare, see: Claire McEachern, *Believing in Shakespeare: Studies in Longing* (Cambridge: Cambridge University Press, 2018).

[71] *Timon of Athens*, IV.iii.98; *Antony and Cleopatra*, III.vi.94. Unless otherwise noted, all references to Shakespeare in this chapter are taken from *The Arden Shakespeare Complete Works*, ed. by Richard Proudfoot, Ann Thompson, David Scott Kastan, and H.R. Woudhuysen (London: Thomas Nelson and Sons Ltd, 1998).

Introduction

attempt to win another woman: 'Because I love him I must pity him'.[72] And Othello credits the emotion for his successful courtship of Desdemona:

OTHELLO
My story being done,
She gave me for my pains a world of sighs:
She swore, in faith, 'twas strange, 'twas passing strange,
'Twas *pitiful*, 'twas wondrous *pitiful*:
She wish'd she had not heard it, yet she wish'd
That heaven had made her such a man: she thank'd me
And bade me, if I had a friend that loved her,
I should but teach him how to tell my story.
And that would woo her. Upon this hint I spake:
She loved me for the dangers I had pass'd,
And I loved her that she did *pity* them.[73]

In this latter instance, pity works on multiple levels: it affords a reason for the interaction between Othello and Desdemona, but also fosters the bond between them. Desdemona's pity both propels her towards Othello, and commends her to him. For all that this relationship later fails, it begins as an intimate emotional community created by pity. As I will go on to highlight in more detail in the chapters that follow, moments like these feature frequently on the early modern English stage: connection is created through pity, in part because through feeling pity we are then motivated to act in the interest of others. Through pity characters become implicated in one another's lives, both emotionally and through their actions.

Yet there are also many Shakespearean references to pity that counsel against the emotion, specifically referencing the extent to which it compromises those who prove susceptible. There is York's reminder to Bolingbroke: 'Forget to pity him, lest thy pity prove | a serpent that will sting thee to thy heart'.[74] Think too of Dionyza's warning: 'Nor let pity, which even women have cast off, melt thee, but be a soldier to thy purpose'.[75] Or the First Stranger's observation in *Timon of Athens*: 'Men must learn now with pity to dispense, for policy sits above conscience' (III.ii.90–91). In these contexts pity is a nuisance, a distraction, or a hindrance, but it is also, seemingly, a constant threat: something that should occasionally be forgotten or cast off, but which always threatens to impact social exchange. These characters suggest a certain anxiety about pity's effect on an individual's identity, goals,

---

[72] *Two Gentlemen of Verona*, IV.iv.95.
[73] *Othello*, I.iii.159–169, my emphasis.
[74] *Richard II*, V.iii.55–56.
[75] *Pericles*, IV.i.6–8.

Pity and Identity in the Age of Shakespeare

or relationships. If anything, these references do *more* to confirm pity's prevalence in early modern England than the more casual, positive uses: the emotion clearly posed a sufficient threat to require frequent warning. All of these examples – insofar as they imagine a wide range of social inter-action – must also be seen as contributing to contemporary understandings of interpersonal exchange. Even in the cases that view pity as potentially destructive, these lines assume that pity exists as part of a person's nature, and that the emotion binds people together (or tears them apart) in one way or another.

Perhaps the strongest recommendation for drama as the central generic concern of this study, however, is found in the prologue to *Romeo and Juliet*. At the risk of reprinting an already-famous passage, here it is again, in full:

> CHORUS
> Two households, both alike in dignity,
> In fair Verona, where we lay our scene,
> From ancient grudge break to new mutiny,
> Where civil blood makes civil hands unclean.
> From forth the fatal loins of these two foes
> A pair of star-crossed lovers take their life,
> Whose misadventured piteous overthrows
> Doth with their death bury their parents' strife.
> The fearful passage of their death-marked love,
> And the continuance of their parents' rage,
> Which but their children's end naught could remove,
> Is now the two hours' traffic of our stage;
> The which, if you with patient ears attend,
> What here shall miss, our toil shall strive to mend.[76]

This passage clarifies the force and impact of pity, and also positions the early modern English stage as a vital affective space; in so doing, it also captures the guiding premises of this work. The emotion word – 'piteous' is flanked on either side by another word that signals either a lack of control ('misadventured') or a scale that defies containment ('overthrows'): what we are about to see on the stage is not just big, uncontrollable action or spectacle; it is also big emotion.[77] The single emotion embedded here – pity – is also positioned as the kind of emotion capable of overcoming ancient strife: the emotional force of the spectacle and reality of 'their

---

[76] *Romeo and Juliet*, Prol. 1–14.

[77] The *OED* defines 'misadventured' as 'unfortunate' or 'hapless', pointing to Shake-speare's use here in *Romeo and Juliet* as the first use of the word with this meaning. 'misadventured, adj.'. *OED* Online. June 2002. Oxford University Press. http://www. oed.com. /view/Entry/119153 (accessed 24 May 2018).

Introduction

children's end', we are told, is the only thing capable of overcoming another deep-seated emotional current already at work.

Although the framing of pity here – as something capable of large scale, as something that defies control – aligns with the wider contemporary interpretations of this emotion's capacity for impact, what also interests me in this passage is the reference to the stage itself and the emotional labour to be undertaken by the actors. The content is explicitly marked for the stage ('now the two hours' traffic of our stage'), but the end of the prologue also recognises the relationship between the stage and its emotional content as an ongoing work-in-progress in which actor, playwright, and spectator are all implicated. The playwright provides the lines, of course, but the actors must convey them, and the audience 'with patient ears must attend'. Even so, the passage assumes (or allows for) things to be missed ('what here shall miss'), and in its final thought, 'our toil shall strive to mend', the Chorus acknowledges future performances in which the emotional impact of the play will be adjusted, enriched, or reconfigured. The relationship between the emotional content of the play and the various subjects involved (player, playwright, audience members) is shown as both intimate and changeable. This emotional landscape is an ongoing work of production that shapes (and is shaped by) its agents. This coming together of agents, emotion, and literary content is, to my mind, what positions drama so perfectly for the present study.

DIVISION OF CHAPTERS

It is a central contention of this book that early modern English subjects felt that human vulnerability – both their own, and the vulnerability of those around them – was being exposed and unleashed in new and unsettling ways. Suddenly, the suffering of others was a closer, more immediate and intimate problem. In a culture less and less convinced that the Church should formally mediate charitable action, the concept of human pity – the natural instinct of which Robert Aylett speaks – was increasingly deployed, particularly in literary texts, as an alternative way of structuring and understanding these fraught interactions. This book attends to pity's emergence as a secular concept in the literary and cultural works of early modern England, considering how (and why) these texts reinforce the idea of pity as a natural by-product of human existence and human interaction, even as they question and worry about pity's impact on individual selfhood. In these works, pity is simultaneously something vital that binds people together, and something that compromises the boundaries of their individual subjectivity. How should we understand the cultural impact of an emotion that was understood as somehow central to early modern humanity, but also damaging, undermining, unreliable, often ineffective, and all told, wholly problematic? By considering the literary development of this emotion in detail, I argue, we are better able to understand the intimate – and fractious – relationship between early modern subjectivity and social emotion more generally.

This book understands early modern England as watershed moment in pity's broader history, and through a series of case studies, demonstrates that the period's anxious attitude towards the emotion played a major – and unique – role in defining both the era and its literature. The early modern English approach to pity emphasised individual vulnerability with an intimacy and an intensity unknown to the medieval period. At the same time, the frequency with which the early moderns portrayed pity as a necessary part of being human clearly distinguishes this era from the periods that follow, in which pity grew increasingly separated from compassion, increasingly understood as an affective instinct more destructive than connective. In using dramatic texts to explore these cultural attitudes towards pity, I hope also to demonstrate once and for all the value of imaginative material in constructing a 'history' of emotion. Literature *is* our history; this is especially true when we are thinking of the history of emotional selfhood.

Chapter 1 focuses on the emergence of secular pity as a particular recurring theme in early modern English drama, tracing emotional antecedents in medieval morality plays, and using Shakespeare's *King Lear* as an illustration of the emotional shift around pity that occurs in later drama. Why are early modern authors newly preoccupied with emotional vulnerability, with the idea of the self made permeable by secular pity? Why are the social and emotional obligations connected with pity presented more and more as potential moments of confrontation? This chapter looks to the English Reformations for its answers, and begins with a consideration of how medieval charitable practice inserted itself into the emotional lives of its parishioners, and how changes to these emotional structures may have impacted English subjects.

Tracing the depiction of medieval charity in morality plays like *Hickscorner* (c.1513–1514), and *Everyman* (c.1518–1519), I discuss how this type of drama presents a formal vision of charity as a reliable way of expressing (or acting upon) compassionate instincts. This literature's emphasis on eternal salvation helps to package charity as an emotional practice that is both a vital instinct and a 'safe' one, something that strengthens rather than compromises the individual. Within the plays, the theological underpinnings of charity offer more than just an organisational framework for interpersonal relationships: the possibility of personal salvation gives earthly charity an added significance, and meaning. At the same time, these texts stress the relative instability of an emotion like secular pity, which is depicted as a flawed alternative to charity, precisely because of its secular grounding. I argue that these early literary formulations, which present a version of pity that is subject to

Introduction

the unreliable whims of human agents, are the origin of the later attitudes towards pity evident in early modern drama, where the human instinct to pity is typically inflected with a suspicious or 'dangerous' quality.

This chapter puts a range of dramatic texts in conversation with historical commentary from the period following the English Reformations. Although the issue of charity and poor relief was a Protestant priority – one of the expressed motivators for the Reformations, as evidenced by Poor Law legislation that developed between 1536 and 1601 – this chapter tracks published commentary from this period that suggests that people in fact felt freshly exposed to the plight of those around them: more aware of the suffering of others, less connected to a compassionate emotional community, and mourning the perceived loss of a support structure. This commentary, I contend, suggests that the official 'loss' of the Church as mediator in charitable exchange coincided with a widespread impression of a decrease in organised human compassion. As a result of this restructuring, I argue that men and women in the early modern period felt, simultaneously, more isolated from one another and more exposed on both an emotional and a social level. In this environment, the rhetoric of pity – arguing for the emotion's centrality to human identity, and its social value – increases significantly as a means of coping with an evolving emotional society that felt increasingly harsh and unfeeling.

In this context, I present *King Lear* (1606) as a formal expression of this altered emotional state. This reading presents Shakespeare's tragedy as a reworking of the morality play form, designed to portray a society languishing without the structure of a formal penitential community. In the world of *Lear*, I contend, characters are both reliant on the human capacity for pity, and vulnerable to the emotion's inherent instability. *Lear* imagines extreme consequences following the loss of a clearly delineated format for emotional exchange. This chapter therefore uses drama to track an uncomfortable evolution in the English emotional landscape between the medieval and early modern periods, and demonstrates how one's susceptibility to pity – and by extension, one's capacity to manage his/her emotional environment – became central concerns of early modern selfhood.

Chapter 2 reconsiders the call for pity as a type of emotional confrontation by examining the visual dynamics introduced when the compassionate subject has sustained obvious violence. Viewing this kind of subject, I argue, itself registers as another type of emotional violence. While the impact of this emotional violence has largely dominated the critical response to texts like Shakespeare's *Titus Andronicus* (1594), where the Lucrece-like Lavinia suffers graphically violent wounds, I suggest that plays like *Titus* emphasise the visuality of emotional stimuli precisely in order to suggest a more productive consequence of emotional confrontation. The power of the

Pity and Identity in the Age of Shakespeare

shared emotional gaze, evident both in *Titus* and in Shakespeare's *The Rape of Lucrece* (1593), harness the visuality of these famously violated women in order to capitalise on the community-building potential of shared emotional violence. This uniquely Shakespearean gloss on the Lucrece figure is made all the more evident when read alongside contemporary Lucrece narratives from the late sixteenth and early seventeenth centuries.

This chapter examines texts in which an imagined audience is asked (or forced) to respond to a visibly violated woman; through these texts I track the attitudes towards being 'forced' to respond emotionally. The chapter begins with John Day's 'Printer's Note', preceding the 1565 edition of *Gorboduc*, where Day describes an earlier (to his mind, poorly edited) version of the text as a raped woman, who herself is referred to as a type of Lucrece figure. Day expects that both the metaphorical 'woman' and the text have the capacity to cause emotional distress by their very presence. Although Day mobilises and exploits the concept of compassionate reflex in his description of the restorative action he has taken toward the text, what is more present in the note is a desire to 'correct' a source of visual and emotional distress for himself and for others: less interested in soothing the imagined 'woman' than redressing a public wound, Day's preface poses a number of questions about what really motivates emotional response, and if there is any capacity to control it. The note also suggests a current of discomfort that underpins compassionate response, indicating that while that discomfort might ultimately benefit someone, it is not always the violated person (or thing).

The premise of Day's note – that the sight of physical violation also represents an emotional provocation, and that that provocation is what motivates restorative action – is applied to a number of depictions of violated femininity significant to early modern audiences, ranging from early modern translations of the Livy and Ovid Lucrece (1600, 1640) to the revisions produced by Shakespeare (*The Rape of Lucrece* [1593], *Titus Andronicus* [1594]) and Thomas Heywood (*The Rape of Lucrece* [1608]). Focusing in particular on the ways in which the early modern period uses these texts to adapt classical versions of the Lucrece, Philomel, and Io tales, this chapter argues that these narratives emphasise the visual prompters of emotional response as a way of making clear the intensity and discomfort inherent in emotional provocation. This chapter, perhaps more than any other, scrutinises the apparent pain induced by the forceful elicitation of pity, showcasing the emotion as dangerously unsettling to the individuals who encounter it. Shakespeare's adaptations in particular work against the notion of pity evident in Day and others, where pity is framed as a type of compassionate revulsion. The Shakespearean accounts stress instead a more positive community-building element fostered by piteous visual spectacle

Introduction

and visual connection. I suggest that the repeated expression of anxiety over emotional penetration also indicates a growing understanding of pity as a fundamental, unavoidable component of human social experience – a central element of English early modern selfhood that was vital, even in spite of the associated challenges outlined in Chapter 1. A brief conclusion looks forward to Marina Abramović's 2010 piece, *The Artist is Present*, as a way of demonstrating both that this early modern English view of emotion, visuality, and confrontation has contemporary resonance, and that this type of 'emotional thinking' has a particular tie to the performative arts.

From the tragic intimacy of pitying communities in Chapter 2, Chapter 3 situates dramatic treatments in relation to the earlier and established use of pity in English lyric. This chapter tracks how one very specific kind of pity appeal, inherited from the poetic tradition, was transplanted and repurposed on the early modern stage. I argue that the comic reimaginings of the Petrarchan lover's appeal to pity represent a major contribution to drama's larger reworking of the emotion as a core feature of the early modern English emotional landscape. Practices of generic interplay figure prominently here, as the material I present reveals an instinct – both in poetry and in drama – to use emotion to frame and articulate distinct literary identities. Each genre reaches towards the other as a counterpoint and counterbalance in order to define itself.

The real-life exchange between George Rodney and Frances Howard (c.1600) frames the tensions that sit at the core of this chapter, neatly demonstrating the interplay between poetry, drama, and real life. Rodney's failed poetic attempt to garner Howard's pity is documented primarily in her own poetic response, an answer predicated on her reading of his appeal as part of a long poetic tradition. Rodney's eventual suicide (by knife, sword, or by some accounts, his own pen) moved the poet beyond his text to become a real-life, self-professed 'pyramis [monument] of pity'. His self-slaughter challenged the terms of Howard's rejection, but also revealed the poet as at odds with his chosen literary tradition. The contemporary response to the physical fact of Rodney's death emphasised both a scale of emotional intensity and a tragic physicality that set him at odds with the generic conventions of courtly love and lyric. In committing so wholly to poetic pity as a viable outlet for his emotion, it seems, Rodney was understood to have overstepped his generic bounds, stumbling towards the emotional registers of drama.

This chapter attends to pity's literary relationship with lyric, focusing on the familiar figure of English Petrarchism: the abject lover, appealing for pity from his mistress. The emotional potency of the poetic speaker's piteous appeal suffered from overuse, lost its popularity and was all but extinct from English lyric poetry by the late 1590s. Ultimately, the professed emotion was too consistently understood as mere poetic convention. Although the Rodney–Howard exchange shows, at the turn of the seventeenth century, a clear distaste for this kind of emotional posturing in poetry, the figure of the abject poetic lover became increasingly common on the early modern stage as a source of comedy: a character who either intentionally misuses pity as a means of sexual conquest, or otherwise misunderstands the emotional 'play' of courtly love. I argue that by staging these recognisably 'poetic' figures of pity as comic and easily dismissed characters, English dramatists were able to move beyond pity's poetic inheritance and its negative association as disingenuous. These figures appear in the work of a broad range of dramatists (including Thomas Dekker, Thomas Heywood and William Rowley, John Marston, and Shakespeare). These seemingly trivial 'piteous' moments onstage, I contend, help to facilitate the emotion's broader theatrical development as I outline it elsewhere in the book: as a core component of personal subjectivity on the early modern stage.

The range of dramatic material presented in this chapter demonstrates a typical way of staging these particular 'pitiful' exchanges as emotionally suspect: an obvious method of emotional manipulation. In this mode of generic usage, moreover, Shakespeare is in good company, sharing patterns of usage and representation with contemporary dramatists. I suggest that the dramatic reworkings of this appeal intentionally build upon a poetic heritage, in order to dismiss an already recognisable literary form of pity as something separate and easily distinguished from the other dramatic pity exchanges examined in the book. On the stage, these mis-users of pity, in their restricted and sexualised use of the emotion, intensify the impact of other characters using pity as a defining feature of humanity. This large-scale dramatic de-legitimisation of poetry's abject pitiful lover, I argue, created space for literary pity to be re-worked within the dramatic genre, and to imagine a meaningful reach beyond the context of courtly love.

The final chapter, Chapter 4, returns to dramatic depictions of pity that position the emotion as a vital component of early modern identity construction, situating it as a defining principle for socially embedded selfhood. This chapter traces a pervasive habit, in Shakespeare's dramatic work, of using emotion to theorise the boundaries of humanity. This method for constructing humanity positions the capacity for pity as an essentially human characteristic – something fundamentally tied to what it means to be human, a quality whose *absence* pushes characters into identity-otherness. Moments in *The Merchant of Venice*, *Titus Andronicus*, *Richard III*, and *Henry VI pt. 3* all assign piteous failures (the absence of pity or the failure to offer it) to other identity categories, such as animal, monster, or devil. This chapter suggests however that these category distinctions are only really interested in flagging the utility of non-humanity. These are not positive

Introduction

formulations of what it means to be animal, monster, or devil, but rather a way of framing lack. In this way pity is conceptually used to construct taxonomic categories of non-humanity that work in service of humankind. Humanity is in turn partially defined by the proximate failures of other categories, categories that are themselves characterised specifically to stabilise and consolidate the boundaries of humanity. This is a muddy discourse that relies on imagined systems of compassionate obligation, and places humans and non-humans within these systems. My particular emphasis in this chapter is on what I call Shakespeare's 'proximal' humans: the emotional subjects who challenge these delicate systems of distinction by existing in the unsettling interstitial spaces between human and non-human. These characters highlight a permeable and unstable emotional boundary between human and non-human populations, but they also make clear the fundamental instability of the human category, and the violence embedded in relational definition.

The majority of this chapter attends to the extensive probing of emotional subjectivity and relational definition in *The Tempest*, a play that explores a knotted relationship between pity, humanity, and social privilege. The emotional theorising that occurs throughout *The Tempest* clarifies the role of non-human or proximally human characters in defining humanity, by questioning conventional distinctions of kind-ness. Caliban, Ariel, and Miranda are all explicitly categorised according to their relationship to pity, and each of these characters, I contend, articulates emotional subjectivity from a position of proximal humanity, of 'nearly, but not-quite'-ness. As the play goes on, it also becomes clear that what these characters lack – the very shape of their own incompleteness – relationally clarifies Prospero's privileged humanity, making him look more stable, more complete, and by extension more powerful. Shakespeare's play therefore situates its meditation on human pity in what, for Prospero, is a self-serving system of power, privilege, and self-definition. As the play stresses the role of non-humanity in defining the human characters of early modern drama, it also problematises the profound emotional burden undertaken on behalf of humankind. *The Tempest* therefore clarifies humankind's tenuous privilege, revealing a subjectivity position that, however dominant, is also acutely aware of the precarity of being *self*-determined and *self*-narrated. In a final turn to Ben Jonson's *Bartholomew Fair*, I argue that the ideological work of *The Tempest* manifests in Jonson's play. Both plays test the boundaries of humanity, the definitional role of non-humans, and consider how principles of pity and compassion both clarify and confuse definitions of kind. Jonson's reframing of these issues in *Bartholomew Fair*, I suggest, helpfully clarifies the darkness of what is really at stake in *The Tempest*, and demonstrates how socially exploitative these modes of posturing can be.

Pity and Identity in the Age of Shakespeare

The dramatic material in this chapter represents a conversation about the concern with pity traced in the rest of the book: it illustrates the importance not just of managing one's emotional environment, but of managing it well. These texts also imagine pity as something vitally navigated by the self, an emotion about which, and for which, subjects necessarily had to form opinions and codes of practice. This tension, I suggest – in which pity became, simultaneously, something vital and positive *and* something potentially dangerous and corrosive – showcases the underpinning concerns about emotional selfhood that were created in the wake of the Reformations, and in the pages of early modern English drama.

Put together, these chapters not only illuminate the extent to which pity was woven into English early modern culture, but also more broadly highlight the value of using dramatic material in order to trace the relationship between interpersonal emotion and individual identity in this period. It is my contention that pity, even where it is not explicitly discussed, is always at work as a general principle in English early modern social interaction: people worry about it, negotiate it improperly, try – and fail – to evade it, or excise it from their lives, and still it presents itself as a recurring issue. Central to this are the English Reformations, the impact of which must be understood not just in religious, political, or social terms, but in affective terms as well. The Reformations drastically altered the emotional lives of people in early modern England, making them feel especially vulnerable to *feeling*; this book is an attempt to begin an affective history of the English Reformations by outlining its impact on the literary and textual output of the period that immediately followed it. Equally crucial to this book is the idea that people in the early modern period were convinced that there *was* such a thing as emotional obligation, even as they objected to it, and fought against it. What is most important here, however, is that this obvious discomfort surrounding early modern emotion should not be taken as evidence of unimportance: quite the contrary. The emotional vulnerability evident in early modern depictions of pity demonstrates just how challenging – and vital – it was, at this time, to feel for others.

Chapter 1

'MY NAME IS PITY':
MEDIATED EMOTION AND *KING LEAR*

It is the contention of this book that the drama of Shakespeare and his contemporaries testifies to a widespread cultural preoccupation with pity, and that this emotion specifically was felt to be something that challenged and defined the limits of early modern English identity. In what follows I will argue that early modern drama tracks the emergence and development of a very particular kind of pity (earthly, human, secular), and examines how that emotion (for better or worse) shapes the individual, and how it situates them in their community. The literary materials presented in this book confirm, above all else, an uneasy attitude towards pity; a sense that the emotion is unwieldy, not always fit for purpose, and yet still – somehow – understood as unavoidable and vital. This combination of resistance and dependence, I will suggest, is partly a condition of the early modern English emotional landscape, which itself was forever changed by the uncertainty ushered in by the English Reformations. The aim of this book is to show that cultural constructions of pity in early modern England felt newly relevant, and that Shakespeare and his contemporaries undertook much of this cultural 'work' on pity in their dramatic writing, as they attempted to reconcile the many conflicts and contradictions that emerged in the discourses surrounding pity. This chapter argues that Shakespeare's *King Lear* represents one such attempt, that queries pity's capacity to shape a stable emotional landscape, particularly in the absence of the structures of organised religion. This reading of *Lear* sees the play as saturated with a number of emotional and dramatic inheritances, a deeply nostalgic piece that draws on the structures and impulses of medieval morality drama to reflect the consequences of the emotional restructuring that happened in the wake of the English Reformations.

* * *

Pity and Identity in the Age of Shakespeare

In using the plural 'English Reformations' I am (partly) adopting the manner suggested by Christopher Haigh for approaching these events. As Haigh points out:

> The term "Reformation" is applied by historians to a set of historical events, often treated as if it was an inexorable process: a theological attack on Catholic doctrine, the abolition of papal authority, the reduction of priestly power, the suppression of monasteries and chantries, the abolition of the mass, the introduction of simplified Protestant worship, the enforcement of Protestant ideas, the conversion of people from Catholic to Protestant loyalties. In England, such events did not come in swift and orderly sequence, as consecutive steps of a pre-planned programme or a protest movement: they came (and went again) as the accidents of everyday politics and the consequences of power struggles.[1]

Haigh's insistence on the plural form here goes a long way towards capturing a sprawling, exhausting, precarious run of events: it highlights an important instability, but also a lack of containment, a series of revisions and reversions that kept coming, but also that seeped beyond their obvious religious and political contexts. Moreover, as Haigh notes, these Reformations are distinct in ways that cannot be overlooked: 'these *political* Reformations [Henrician, Edwardian, Elizabethan]' he notes, 'could not make England Protestant' but merely 'gave England Protestant laws and made popular Protestantism possible'.[2] These political events, for Haigh, only created the opportunities needed for 'the parallel evangelical Reformation': work that had to be done on a smaller and more personal level, through evangelicals and preachers, and which Haigh contends 'was never completed'.[3] 'England', he concludes, 'had blundering Reformations, which most did not understand, which few wanted, and which no one knew had come to stay'.[4] The term 'Reformations' is, to borrow Cathy Shrank's phrase, 'grammatically cumbersome'.[5] Nevertheless, I have preserved the plural here precisely because the term feels unwieldy in practice. 'Reformations'

---

[1]   Christopher Haigh, *English Reformations: Religion, Politics, and Society under the Tudors* (Oxford: Clarendon, 1993), p. 13; on the use of the plural 'Reformations', see also David Aers and Nigel Smith, 'English Reformations', *Journal of Medieval and Early Modern Studies*, 40.3 (2010), 425–438.

[2]   Haigh, p. 14, my emphasis.

[3]   Ibid., p. 14.

[4]   Ibid., p. 14.

[5]   Cathy Shrank, 'Disputing Purgatory in Henrician England: Dialogue and Religious Reform', in Andreas Höfele, Stefan Laqué, Enno Ruge, and Gabriela Schmidt (eds.), *Representing Religious Pluralization in Early Modern Europe* (Berlin: Lit Verlag, 2007), pp. 45–61 (p. 46, n. 8).

Mediated Emotion and King Lear

acts as an important reminder of what these events represented to those who lived through them: an expansive and shifting field that both unsettled and complicated the social, political, religious, emotional lives of everyone.

My specific interest in this chapter – and more broadly, in this book – is the emotional weight of these events, how they are addressed in contemporary literature, and how these literary portrayals can help us form a clearer picture of early modern emotional subjectivity. Even so, it is worth noting that the emotional stakes of the English Reformations shape more modern histories of them as well. Norman Jones gestures towards these emotional charges in the compelling and parodic opening of his own recent work:

> Once upon a time the people of England were happy Medieval Catholics, visiting their holy wells, attending frequent masses and deeply respectful of purgatory and afraid of Hell. Then lustful King Henry forced them to abandon their religion. England was never merry again. Alternatively, once upon a time the people of England were oppressed by corrupt churchman. They yearned for the liberty of the Gospel. Then, Good King Harry gave them the Protestant nation for which they longed.[6]

More than just detailing shifting religious frameworks, what Jones highlights is how consistently historical narratives of the Reformations have also, essentially, become accounts of the English emotional landscape, infused with claims of yearning and longing, of happiness lost and won. Although Reformation scholars increasingly question how usefully and widely such narratives can be applied, there is nevertheless a critical consensus that by the time Shakespeare reached his majority in the 1580s, 'very few people had clear memories of a time *without* religious confusion'.[7] The significance of those feelings, of being profoundly unsettled, and the permeating sense of confusion, cannot be overstated. For many people, these were the defining characteristics of the English emotional landscape, an enormous part of what gave the Reformations such a profound reach. As Steven Mullaney points out, the impact of the Reformations was felt in every aspect of early modern life, not just forcibly reworking understandings of faith, but also altering ideas about community, personal identity, and the social and emotional landscape in England:

> The religious crises of the Protestant Reformation fractured and transformed Western Christianity, but they also precipitated other, less well-documented crises – crises of social identity as well as religious belief, cultural cohesion as well as church doctrine, felt relations with

[6] Norman Jones, *The English Reformation: Religion and Cultural Adaptation* (Oxford: Blackwell, 2002), p. 1.
[7] Ibid., p. 3.

Pity and Identity in the Age of Shakespeare

the past and present as well as eschatologies of times to come. The Reformations of faith coincided with a great many other changes, and these included reformations of the heart.[8]

These 'forces of disintegration', Mullaney observes, 'served to make uncertain, at the least, what we might call the affective core of individual and collectives identities'.[9] Beyond any shift of doctrine, any redistribution of social and political power – historical views that might be captured on a much larger scale – there is also a story to be told about what was felt to be happening, on the more intimate scale of the individual and their immediate community. This is in many respects a much harder story to tell, of enormous change filtered through individual bodies and daily interactions. Nevertheless, as Susan Brigden points out, 'The Reformation was made by individuals, not by social forces'.[10] A turn to imaginative material can be immensely helpful here, if not in capturing precise microhistories of real individual experience, then in forming a composite image of how those emotional currents might have registered on individual subjects. Within this turn, drama's emphasis on mimesis – the genre's reliance on the bodies of actors to communicate meaning and to cultivate affective communities with audiences – is especially relevant. All of the dramatic material covered in this chapter, from medieval moral interludes to Shakespeare's *King Lear*, directs emotional language through individual speaking subjects to achieve a social end, whether it be to reinscribe the stability and comfort of religious practice, or to emphasise the profound cost of losing those structures.

Contemporary writing from early modern England confirms the picture that Mullaney presents, in recurring accounts of disintegration in all directions. As Janel Mueller notes, the literature from the period of the Reformations 'coalesces in angry laments over the dissolution of community, in which there is very little positive social vision or portrayal'.[11] These accounts claim not just that things were bad, but specifically that they were *worse*. For example, in a 'note to the christian Reader' preceding Philip Stubbes' *The second part of the anatomie of abuses* (1583), the writer 'I.F.' offers a detailed account of a grim picture:

---

[8] Steven Mullaney, *The Reformation of Emotions in the Age of Shakespeare* (Chicago, IL and London: University of Chicago Press, 2015), pp. 7–8.

[9] Ibid., p. 7.

[10] Susan Brigden, *London and the Reformation* (Oxford: Clarendon Press, 1989; repr. London: Faber & Faber Ltd., 2014), p. 4.

[11] Janel Mueller, 'Literature and the church', in David Loewenstein and Janel Mueller (eds.), *The Cambridge History of Early Modern English Literature: The Tudor Era from the Reformation to Elizabeth I* (Cambridge: Cambridge University Press, 2003), pp. 257–310 (p. 297).

Mediated Emotion and King Lear

There was never any age, or time (christian reader) since the beginning of the world how corrupt so ever, that was comparable to this our thrise unhappie age in all kind of corruption, wickednes, and sin, with greefe of conscience I speake it, with weeping eies I behold it, and with sorrowfull hart I lament it. And therefore seeing wickednesse doth so abound, the Lord (least his children frosen in the dregs of their sinne should perish with the wicked) raiseth up in his mercie good men (as we see he hath done our good brother the author hereof) to plucke off the visors of sinne from their faces, and to lay them open to the view of the whole world, to the end that everie one seeing the dung of his wicked waies, and the filthie dregs of sinne throwne in their faces, may blush at the same, be ashamed, repent, amend, and turne to the Lord Jesus, and so eternally be saved.[12]

Resonant in this account is the range and extent of a perceived social problem. There is a historical scale, of course, as the author draw on the fullest conception of time – 'since the beginning of the world', which adds to the hyperbolic language condemning the current moment: 'never … so ever … our thrise unhappie time'. There is also an emotional impact detailed here, a sadness that reaches the conscience, the eyes, and the heart: as if the pervasive 'corruption, wickednes, and sin' is so large-scale that it registers on the subject in the fullest sense, penetrating both mind and body. This movement, traced from the big-picture social view to the intimate spaces of the body, echoes a top-down sense of confusion and emotional turmoil concentrating in the individual. It is a reminder that the policies, conflict, and power struggles of England were felt on a far more intimate scale.

Descriptions detailing the moral illness of early modern England abound. While every era sees some version of this nostalgic complaint – every period has its misery merchants, who lament the loss of an older, better time – the emphasis of these critiques can say a lot about what the perceived issues really were. John Stow's *Survey of London*, for example, frames its historical nostalgia by praising the charity of London's 'ancient citizens':

[…] but now wee see the thing in worse case then ever […] as in other places of the Suburbes, some of them like Midsommer Pageants, with Towers, Turrets and Chimney tops, not so much for use, or profites, as for shew and pleasure, bewraying the vanitie of many mens mindes, *much unlike to ye disposition of the ancient Citizens, who delighted in the building of Hospitalles, and Almes houses for the poore* and therein both imployed their wits, and spent their wealthes in preferment of the common commoditie of this our Citie.[13]

[12] Philip Stubbes, *The second part of the anatomie of abuses* (London: 1583), sig. A2^v.
[13] John Stow, *A survay of London* (London: 1598), sig. Aa1^r, my emphasis.

Stow's investment in the superiority of the older ways is clear, as is his withering opinion of human behaviour in his own time. His account details more than just a schedule of charitable work; it also imagines that work underpinned by purer instincts, undertaken by people who 'delighted' in it. The loss, therefore, is not just a loss of the work itself, but apparently also a perceived loss of good will. Thomas Nashe's description of London in *Christ's Tears Over Jerusalem* is still more direct. Setting Jerusalem during the siege against modern London, Nashe positions the oration of Miriam – the starving mother who cannibalises her son to survive – at the heart of the text, as a lurid counterpoint to sixteenth-century heartlessness. Nashe also glosses the absence of charity as a more general loss of benevolent fellow-feeling. '*London*,' Nashe writes, 'thy heart is the hart of covetousnes, all charitie and compassion is cleane banished out of thee'.[14] Again, a broad geocultural landscape (London) is reworked, newly imagined as a single figure with a (now cold) heart. Taken together, these accounts give the flavour of a larger body of moralising complaint literature; in each one, the author places feelings of loss and nostalgia alongside obvious references to the concepts, people, and structures that previously helped to organise compassionate action. Nashe specifically notes that charity is banished; Stow references the construction of hospitals and almshouses. For Stow and Nashe especially, the deteriorated emotional landscape described is one that specifically emerges in the perceived absence of compassionate action. In each case, the emotional impact of huge social reorganisation lands on individual bodies, reinforcing a particular intimacy to the way such change was absorbed. Whereas as Nashe and the writer of the Stubbes note manage to be both comprehensive in their condemnations and vague in the supporting details, Stow's is a more precise account of what has been lost. Ian Archer describes Stow's *Survey* as 'suffused with nostalgia', arguing that as a whole the piece explicitly 'articulates the "catholic" interpretations of the medieval past as a time of "charity, hospitality, and plenty"'.[15] In this it is possible to point to something more specific that has been lost, beyond an inchoate sense of goodwill. If 'plenty', or the overarching perception of social and moral well-being are subjective and more difficult to define, charity is more easily captured. Medieval charitable practice was, moreover, a core target of the Protestant Reformations, an emotion-laden structure that was lost as a result of these religious crises.

[14] Thomas Nashe, *Christs Teares over Jerusalem* (London: 1613), sig. O3ᵛ.

[15] Ian W. Archer, 'The Nostalgia of John Stow', in D.M. Smith and R. Strier (eds.), *The Theatrical City: Culture, Theatre, and Politics in London, 1576–1649* (Cambridge: Cambridge University Press, 1995), pp. 18–34 (p. 21).

Mediated Emotion and King Lear

* * *

Above all else, medieval charitable practice emphasised the role of the church in mediating an individual's salvation, laying particular emphasis on the importance of 'good works'. As J.A.F. Thompson puts it, 'Behind all giving in the Middle Ages lay one basic motive, the good of the donor's soul'.[16] For this reason, Thompson suggests, 'it is often impossible to separate pious gifts from charitable ones, because no such differentiation existed in the mind of the donor'.[17] Each act contributed to a larger state of being 'in charity', and many forms of charitable giving carried the explicit expectation of heavenly intercession for the giver anyway, either via funeral attendance, endowed chantries, or other forms of prayer for the dead.[18] The significance of death in late medieval England can hardly be overstated: the preoccupation with 'dying well' has been called an 'obsession', and the preparation for death, some have argued, was 'the key to medieval religion'.[19] Charity and 'Good works' formed the foundation of that preparation. As Eamon Duffy suggests, on the level of the individual, it was the combination of faith and the inevitability of death that produced a unique interest in good works:

---

[16]   J.A.F. Thomson, 'Piety and Charity in Late Medieval London', *Journal of Ecclesiastical History*, 16.2 (1965), 178–195 (p. 194).

[17]   Ibid., p. 180.

[18]   There are some exceptions here, and this picture refers mostly to the kinds of giving that can be traced through historical record, such as wills. People were also encouraged to give regularly throughout their lives and would have had frequent opportunity to give either more anonymously or to act in more intimate ways in their communities: Judith Bennett has done excellent work, for example, on medieval and early modern 'charity ales' which channelled giving through sociability and, instead of being directed at the very poor, typically helped members of the community in unusual moments of hardship. See Judith M. Bennett, 'Conviviality and Charity in Medieval and Early Modern England', *Past & Present*, 134 (1992), 19–41. For a more detailed discussion of the problem of capturing the full picture of medieval charity (and some proposals for working around it) see Joel T. Rosenthal, *The Purchase of Paradise* (London: Routledge & Kegan Paul, 1972) and Miri Rubin, *Charity and Community in Medieval Cambridge* (Cambridge: Cambridge University Press, 1987). For more information on provision for the poor in medieval wills, see Michael M. Sheehan, *The Will in Medieval England* (Toronto: Pontifical Institute of Mediaeval Studies, 1963), esp. pp. 258–259; and Claire S. Schen, *Charity and Lay Piety in Reformation London, 1500–1620* (Farnham: Ashgate, 2002; repr. Abingdon: Routledge, 2016).

[19]   Susan Brigden, 'Religion and Social Obligation in Early Sixteenth-Century London', *Past & Present*, 103 (1984), 67–112 (p. 84); Christopher Daniel, *Death and Burial in Medieval England, 1066–1550* (London: Routledge, 1997), p. 1.

> It was the religious complex of these last things, death, judgement, Hell, and Heaven, that formed the essential focus of late medieval reflection on mortality, coupling anxiety over the brevity and uncertainty of life to *the practical need for good works*, to ensure a blissful hereafter.[20]

The financial burden of these 'good works' – including purchased prayers, almsgiving, bequests, indulgences, chantries, and participation in religious guilds – figures prominently in the medieval Christian identity, making that identity both material and social. But there was also a real sense in which this activity had a concrete emotional value, providing clearly delineated pathways for managing the anxiety and uncertainty that Duffy mentions.

As many modern critics have pointed out, there is ample room for concern about the consequences of this ideological framework. To begin with, a charitable doctrine that explicitly encouraged individuals to take earthly action on the premise (or promise) of divine reward at least hints, in Joel Rosenthal's words, at the possibility of 'the purchase of paradise'.[21] Many have argued that the golden carrot of eternal salvation introduces an obvious and problematic opportunity for self-interested calculation at the very core of medieval Christian identity. 'Charity', as Miri Rubin asserts, 'cannot be satisfactorily understood as a purely altruistic act since gift-giving is so rich in rewards to the giver'.[22] The spectre of self-interest, as Rubin has argued, also extends beyond the larger context of salvation and produces more immediate social benefits: 'the ability to contribute to the general welfare', she writes, 'became a test of status and prosperity as well as a reflection of moral health and virtue'.[23] The darker side of these virtuous activities becomes apparent when one turns to the difficult position that the poor occupied within this framework of activity.[24] As Rubin explains, 'The conservative view prevailed which valued the existence of poor people as an opportunity for the practice of soul-saving charity'.[25] Ian Forrest describes this exchange more explicitly in terms of transferring emotional burdens: 'the rich', he explains, 'could make reparations for their sin of avarice by giving to the poor, and the poor could, in return, offer prayers for their benefactors *or simply fulfil a useful function as a*

---

[20] Eamon Duffy, *The Stripping of the Altars: Traditional Religion in England, 1400–1580* (New Haven, CT: Yale University Press, 1992), p. 308.

[21] Rosenthal, pp. 11–30.

[22] Rubin, p. 1.

[23] Ibid., p. 289.

[24] A.L. Beier, *The Problem of the Poor in Tudor and Early Stuart England* (London: Routledge, 1983).

[25] Rubin, p. 85.

Mediated Emotion and King Lear

vehicle for the alleviation of guilt.[26] In these respects and in others, the superior Christian virtue also relied on structures of power and privilege, and if charitable donors had a marked advantage, then the Church itself, as an institution, was even better placed. The emotional stakes involved in thinking about death, judgement, and preparation open myriad opportunities for exploitation and abuse of power. But here again, anxiety and uncertainty loom large: the prospect of salvation means that charitable activity *might* not be straightforwardly altruistic, but it does not preclude the possibility of genuine action; the emotional vulnerability embedded in planning for death and judgement *might* provide opportunity for abuse and corruption, but those opportunities may not have been universally exploited. It is also obvious that this is a mottled picture, one that may well vary on a person-to-person basis, but simply cannot be captured on a comprehensive level. This is, moreover, an exploration of motivations and inner emotional states that would require impossible access into subject interiority. Taken together, these very real worries represent some of the core arguments against the structures of medieval charity, which were used by Protestant reformers and have also been a central concern, as Norman Jones highlights, of Reformation historians as well.

The programme of 'good works' that fell under medieval charity was inextricably linked to the concept of purgatory. Most reformers denied any scriptural basis for purgatory, arguing instead, as Simon Fish put it in 1529, that there was 'not one word spoken of hit in al holy scripture'.[27] Peter Marshall has acknowledged that 'Controversies over the doctrine of purgatory can seem a rather peripheral aspect of contemporary religious thought, a side issue in the Reformation's great debates about free will, grace, justification, and sacraments'.[28] And yet, he continues, 'it did not take long for both defenders and assailants of the old order to understand that if this thread were pulled upon vigorously enough, the entire fabric might start to unravel'.[29] The suggestion of a link between earthly action and divine reward – central to the conflicts over purgatory and intercessionary culture – was a (perhaps *the*) key issue of the Reformations, and certainly the conflict that most fully captures the social and emotional stakes. By denying the possibility of 'ensuring' salvation through charity, Protestant reformers also emphasised the threads of anxiety and fear

---

[26] Ian Forrest, *Trustworthy Men: How Inequality and Faith Made the Medieval Church* (Princeton, NJ: Princeton University Press, 2018), p. 235, my emphasis.

[27] Simon Fish, *A supplicaycon of beggers* (London: 1529), sig. A6ʳ.

[28] Peter Marshall, *Beliefs and the Dead in Reformation England* (Oxford: Oxford University Press, 2002), p. 47.

[29] Ibid., p. 47.

embedded in medieval doctrine. Reformers sought a 'fundamental redefinition' of charity and its purpose, proposing a 'new relationship between faith and works' that, as Marshall interprets it, 'was to restore society to a condition of feeling at ease with itself'.[30] The tight relationship between emotion and doctrine is a crucial factor in these disputes, and to accept the premise of reformations as *restorations* of the emotional landscape, Marshall points out, 'is to accept at face value a contingent aspect of their own propaganda'.[31] The Protestant denial of a link between earthly works and salvation effectively removed a motivation (or pressure) for undertaking charitable work, but it also challenged many of the ways of performing and cultivating one's Christian identity. This became a major pressure point, as Marjorie Keniston McIntosh has noted: 'The framers of an official Protestant ideology and church', she writes, 'were acutely aware of the need to demonstrate that their faith and social vision could be put into practice, creating a more truly Christian community'.[32] In this way, the Reformations depended in part on the ability to articulate emotional and rhetorical appeal: as Mueller acknowledges, 'a given religious tenet or disposition [...] became culturally transformative only to the degree and in the measure that psychological, ethical and rhetorical suasion operated to make it appealing, energising, even directive in people's thoughts and lives'.[33] Controlling the emotional narrative was a vital component of reworking religious frameworks.

* * *

---

[30] Felicity Heal, *Hospitality in Early Modern England* (London: Clarendon Press, 1990), p. 122. Peter Marshall, *Religious Identities in Henry VIII's England* (Aldershot: Ashgate, 2006), p. 59. For more on the transition between medieval and early modern thoughts on charity, see also John Bossy, *Christianity in the West, 1400–1700* (Oxford: Oxford University Press, 1985); Susan Bridgen, 'Religion and Social Obligation in Early Sixteenth-Century London'; W.K. Jordan, *The Charities of London, 1480–1660: The Aspirations and Achievements of the Urban Society* (London: George Allen & Unwin Ltd., 1960) and W.K. Jordan, *Philanthropy in England, 1480–1660: A Study of the Changing Pattern of English Social Aspirations* (Westport, CT: Greenwood Press, 1978).

[31] Marshall, *Religious Identities*, p. 59.

[32] Marjorie Keniston McIntosh, *Controlling Misbehavior in England, 1370–1600* (Cambridge: Cambridge University Press, 1998), p. 203. On the subject of the Protestant interest in creating an association between Protestantism and charity, see also Ian W. Archer, 'The Charity of Early Modern Londoners', *Transactions of the Royal Historical Society*, 6.12 (2002), 223–244.

[33] Mueller, p. 258.

Mediated Emotion and King Lear

An A.B.C. to the spiritualte.

Awake ye gostely persones / awake / awake
Bothe preste / pope / bisshoppe & Cardinall.
Considre wisely / what wayes that ye take
Daungerously beyngelyke to have a fall.
Every where / the mischefe of you all.
Ferre and nere / breaketh oute very fast
Godde will nedes be revenged at the last.
Howe longe have ye the worlde captyved
In sore bondage / of mennes tradiciones?
Kynges and Emperoures / ye have depryned
Lewedly usurpynge / their chefe possessions.
Muche misery ye make / in all regions [...]
Poore people to oppresse / ye haue no shame
Qwakynge for feare / of your doubble tyranny.[34]

The remarkable 'An A.B.C. to the spiritualte', the prefatory poem in William Barlow's *A Proper Dialogue Between a Gentleman and a Husbandman* (1530), rehearses some of the most familiar attacks on the medieval Catholic church, directing a threatening eye toward 'preste | pope | bisshope & Cardinall' and pointedly referring to 'the mischefe of you all'. The poet's speaker also claims and directs God's wrath, raising the stakes on the charge of corruption that follows. It is both a very specific account of privileged parties – the clergy 'lewedly' overstepping their bounds to deprive kings and emperors – and a much broader account of social impact: 'How long have ye *the world captive* | In sore bondage | of mennes tradiciones?' (my emphasis). The poem is typical of a larger body of reformer rhetoric that replaces scriptural debate with a more immediate and intimate form of conflict. This piece, as Cathy Shrank notes, is 'an outspoken assault on the Church's propagation of the belief in [purgatory]', and one which portrays Church doctrine as 'tyrannous, extortive, false, ruinous to the nation's economy, and punitive to the poor above all'.[35] The poem relies on the language of emotional and bodily intimacy to reinforce its sense of a pervasive social ill that spreads, at speed, both 'Ferre and nere' before registering in the individual body of one who quakes with fear. Reformists stressed the immediacy of their objections with images of clergy penetrating personal space with corrupted doctrine, infiltrating 'the hartes consciences & soules of men' with the 'cruell tyranny' that Hugh Latimer famously identified as

---

[34] William Barlow, *A proper dyaloge, betwene a gentillman and a husbandman[n] eche complaynynge to other their miserable calamite, through the ambicion of the clergye. An A.B.C. to the spiritualte* (Antwerp: 1530), sig. A1ʳ.

[35] Shrank, p. 48.

45

Pity and Identity in the Age of Shakespeare

'purgatory picke pourse, that was swaged and couled with a franciscans cowle'.[36] These are allegations of corruption that are specifically framed as emotional abuse, where the perceived misrepresentation of scripture was intentionally designed to make people vulnerable. John Frith outlines this malicious, corrupt streak in his own treatise against purgatory: 'their paynfull purgatorye was but a vayne imaginacion', he writes, 'it hath of longe tyme but deceaved the people and mi[lk]ed them from their monye'.[37]

The concept of purgatory figured prominently in the 'religious complex' at the heart of medieval charity doctrine, which also included beliefs about death, judgement, Hell, and Heaven.[38] Taken together, these concepts manifested as a profound emotional weight, and also necessitated particularly emotional forms of labour. As Duffy observes, anxiety and uncertainty were significant motivators that highlighted the practical need for 'good works'. Almsgiving is often seen as the 'most enduring definition' of charity and 'good works', but it is in fact only one part of a much larger picture that included many other opportunities for giving and expressing faith, at all stages of life.[39] Beyond this, there were also numerous church-moderated rituals that contributed to the *satisfactio operis* – the programme of activity that people undertook to avoid punishment after death. These were, as Miri Rubin explains, part of 'the process of penance along with fasts and prayers'.[40] Taken together, these activities form a policy of earthly action that looks beyond the mortal realm, towards death and judgement.

Many reformers emphasised the threads of anxiety and vulnerability embedded in charitable doctrine and directed their scriptural objections towards them, targeting what they saw as the problematic emotional landscape propagated by the medieval church. What was less frequently acknowledged, however, was how charitable structure may have also absorbed the uncomfortable daily emotions that might be produced in the confrontation of human suffering, in the interpersonal social exchanges embedded in charitable practice. A turn to the poor – who also figured prominently in Protestant attacks on the medieval church – further clarifies the emotional stakes. For Protestant reformers, the poor were often invoked as a provocative symbol of a corrupt and broken system of Catholic charity. Great emphasis was placed on the plight of the poor, the intensity and cause of their suffering, the ineffectuality of Church-sponsored charity

---

[36] William Tyndale, *The practyse of prelates* (London: 1548), sig. A3ᵛ; Hugh Latimer, *Fruitfull sermons* (London: 1562), sig. B1ᵛ.

[37] John Frith, *A disputacio[n] of purgatorye* (Antwerp: 1531), sig. A5ʳ.

[38] I borrow the term 'religious complex' from Duffy.

[39] Bennett, p. 21.

[40] Rubin, p. 64.

Mediated Emotion and King Lear

and the desperate need for new solutions: the suffering poor were crucial to communicating the urgency of the Protestant social vision. Protestant rhetoric stressed the proximity of that suffering, presenting it in visceral terms to increase the sense of looming crisis. Simon Fish offers a compelling example of this brand of polemical rhetoric in the opening passage of his 1529 work, *A Supplication for Beggars*:

> Most lamentably compleyneth theyre wofull mysery unto youre highnes youre poore daily [beadsmen] [...] sore people, nedy, impotent, blinde, lame, and sike, that live onely by almesse, howe that theyre nombre is daily so sore encreased that all the almesse of all the wel disposed people of this youre realme is not halfe ynough for to susteine theim, but that for verey constreint they die for hunger. And this most pestilent mischief is comen uppon youre saide poore [beadsmen] by the reason that there is yn the tymes of youre noble predecessours passed craftily crept ynto this your realme an other sort (not of impotent but) of strong puissaunt and counterfeit holy [...] These are (not the herdes, but the ravinous wolves going in herdes clothing devouring the flocke) the Bisshoppes, Abbottes, Priours, Deacons, Archedeacons, Suffraganes, Prestes, Monkes Chanons, Freres, Pardoners and Somners.[41]

The scale of this description is important, making the suffering more immediate and concrete through a swollen composite image of the alms-dependent: sore, needy, impotent, blind, lame, and sick. At the same time, this imagined mass expands and loses shape and definition through its rapid increase: 'Theyre nombre', Fish explains, 'is *daily* so sore encreased', that 'all the almesse [...] is not halfe ynough'. And yet, it is not so much the lack of resources that Fish targets but their misdirection, and a moral and spiritual pestilence: these 'counterfeit holy', clergy who are 'ravinous wolves going in herdes clothing devouring the flocke'. Institutional betrayal is made close and intimate in the conflation of bodily disease and ideological weakness: the failure of office is repackaged in the language of grievous bodily harm, brought close to the physical body that is imaged as devoured.

Aligning betrayal of office with the language of illness and disease was a common and enduring theme for reformers, seen also in Hugh Latimer's well-known 'Sermon on the Ploughers': 'soore word for them that are neglygent in dischargynge theyr offyce, or have dooen it fraudulentlye, for that is the thynge that maketh the people yll'.[42] In these ways, reformers

---

[41]   Simon Fish, *A supplicaycon of beggers*, sig. A1ᵛ.

[42]   Hugh Latimer, *A notable sermo[n] of ye reverende father Maister Hughe Latemer which he preached in ye Shrouds at paules church in Londo[n], on the xviii. daye of January. 1548.* (London: 1548), sig. A7ᵛ.

brought an ideological ill close, permeating (at least rhetorically) even the boundaries of the individual body. The recurring slippage between corrupted clergy, the spiritual 'illness' of the people, and the obvious physical suffering of the poor also emphasises the emotional stakes, the closeness and intimacy of the threat. 'London was never so yll as it is now', Latimer claimed, going on to suggest that 'In tymes past, men were full of pitie and compassyon, but nowe there is no pitie, for in London their brother shal dye in the streetes for colde, he shal lye sycke at their doore'.[43] This is a stunning, threatening vision of unassisted human suffering, in which Latimer peoples London's landscape with the sick and dying. Of course this is a call to action, and yet in stressing its urgency, Latimer also figures the poor as an emotional provocation brought too close, to the very doorsteps of peoples' homes; he redistributes a society's emotional labour to individuals and their intimate spaces. Latimer is also laying claim to very specific terminology, as he connects this broken, uncomfortable landscape explicitly to the absence of pity and compassion. There is 'no pitie'; the pity and compassion that existed once has now been lost. His rhetorical strategy is both a marker of nostalgia's appeal – all sides in the Reformations understood its power, and variously claimed to be working to *re*establish, *re*build, *re*prioritise something that had once existed – but in noting their absence Latimer also importantly distinguishes pity and compassion from the formal structures of Catholic charity. Pity and compassion are used instead to capture a more intimate, human-to-human connection, an instinctive reaction to the presentation of suffering Latimer offers. The most significant conflicts of the Reformations were not just scriptural, but social: conflicts of language, practice, and emotion.

These conflicts, though packaged in the language of large-scale social change and the promise of a system of being that might feel *better*, often seem to rely on small distinctions. The rich catalogue of complaint literature (from all sides) gives real shape to a confused social landscape, and emphasises above all the profound distance between ideologies and perceived realities. The language of Stow and others confirms that however pure the intention of Protestant reformers, their ascendance was not experienced as a wholesale improvement to England's emotional landscape. This is true even though there is in fact minimal evidence to support claims that Protestant teachings ushered in a period of greater vulnerability and suffering.[44] No large-scale reduction in charitable giving actually occurred in the wake of the Protestant Reformations, but the perception of this charitable deterioration was, nevertheless, repeatedly voiced. In her own account of early

[43] Latimer, *A notable sermon*, sigs. B1ᵛ–B2ʳ.
[44] For more on this, see: Archer, 'The Charity of Early Modern Londoners'.

Mediated Emotion and King Lear

modern London, Susan Brigden has noted the particular historiographical challenge posed by this extensive body of complaint literature:

> So many were the complaints, that the historian must look beyond any society's perennial pessimism that it is sliding into a pit of selfish profligacy, to discover whether charity really was declining and, if it was not, why it was that people thought the estate of poverty was so unrelieved. Was it true that Londoners were neglecting their Christian duty of charity and, if so, why more in the sixteenth century than formerly? They were not: there was, in fact, an increase in charitable giving.[45]

The more recent accounts of this charitable increase broadly support but also complicate W.K. Jordan's influential vision of a Protestant Reformation that also reshaped charitable ideologies to bring about a more centralised and efficient form of Christian charity.[46] The question of whether or not these alterations represented – or were understood as – actual improvements at the time is a separate question, and one that is far more difficult to answer. Attempts to chart a sharp change between the Catholic and Protestant approaches – in either direction – might be an 'unproductive question', particularly in a broader discussion of a culture that was frequently at the mercy of widespread disease as well as economic and religious crises.[47] Besides, as Brigden notes, the distinctions often seemed very minor indeed: 'the dichotomy between the charity animated by the old faith and the new', she observes, 'cannot have been so marked, nor the inspiration so different; certainly they often seemed the same'.[48] 'What the sixteenth century witnessed', according to Archer, 'was not a *collapse* of community, but *its articulation in different forms*'.[49] However minor these rearticulations may appear, the reach and depth of their emotional impact is clear.

Within the much broader conflicts of the English Reformations, in what follows I will focus more specifically on a few key disputes and their subsequent impact on the emotional landscape of early modern England, tracing their representation in a range of dramatic material as a way of adding shape and clarity to an otherwise muddled picture. The first dispute revolves around the presence, value, identity, and authority of a mediator in the redemptive process; the second is an issue of language, that charts the emergence of pity as a related but distinct term from 'charity'. This latter

---

[45] Brigden, 'Religion and Social Obligation', p. 104.

[46] See W.K. Jordan, *The Charities of London, 1480–1660* and *Philanthropy in England*.

[47] I borrow this phrase from Marjorie Keniston McIntosh, *Poor Relief in England, 1350–1600* (Cambridge: Cambridge University Press, 2012), p. 12.

[48] Brigden, p. 106.

[49] Archer, 'The Nostalgia of John Stow', p. 25, my emphasis.

Pity and Identity in the Age of Shakespeare

development, I argue, gives the concept of pity a growing and important secular association – shifting the emphasis onto human-to-human connections – but it also intensifies the perception of social and emotional instability, bringing it closer and making it more intimate. As several key pieces of medieval drama make clear, secular, humane pity cannot offer the same emotional structures as religious charity; this is something that Shakespeare's *King Lear* dwells upon as it explores the consequences of losing that structure.

* * *

The dispute over charity and its related concepts – compassionate action, good works, and their earthly and spiritual value – suggests above all else the emotional value that medieval religious institutions had for individuals: they provided a cultural framework through which (and with which) people thought and felt. The social activity typically associated with 'good works' formed only one part of what it meant to be 'in charity' in the medieval church: this was a much larger picture that included the expectation of confession, penance, and repentance, and in so doing prominently positioned the physical spaces and personnel of the Church into the lives of parishioners. These rituals, the significance of which also drew on the belief that their observance would guide people into heaven, crucially required direct involvement (and assurance) from a Church representative in a mediator role. Even the writer of the Stubbes note acknowledges the appeal of a structured process of redemption, giving his account a similar impression of procedural order: he imagines that each person 'seeing the dung of his wicked waies' will subsequently 'blush [...] be ashamed, repent, amend, and turne to the Lord Jesus, and so eternally be saved'. These absent instincts, behaviours, and processes, it is implied, could return – or could helpfully *be returned* – and thereby restore both the spiritual and the earthly wellbeing of individuals and their communities. In the Stubbes note, crucially, the process of this redemption is still initiated and overseen by a privileged figure, someone whom God 'raiseth up in his mercie [...] to plucke off the visors of sinne from their faces'. The recurrent presence of a mediating figure, and the apparent objection to the absence of these figures, overwhelmingly indicates a widespread expectation of support, of needing to channel both the fear of judgement and compassionate instincts through a broader community and purpose.

The play *Everyman*, a 1518–1519 English reworking of the Dutch play *Elckerlijc*, gives a very clear example of how the structures of charitable process also stand as a form of emotional support and stability. As a piece that tracks the progress of the eponymous character towards the grave (and judgement), *Everyman* supports and supplements medieval Church doctrine,

Mediated Emotion and King Lear

and from the beginning, the play makes clear the reliability of the redemptive process, both in terms of achieving the desired outcome and in providing a framework for action.[50] The inevitability of death and judgement define the space in which *Everyman* operates, as the play advertises in the *incipit*: 'Here beginneth a treatise how the High Father of heaven sendeth Death to summon *every creature* to come and *give account* of their lives in this world ...'[51] This marrying of inevitability (Death summons every creature) and procedure (and requires them to give an account) highlights a pressing emotional vulnerability, making obvious that this should be felt especially intensely in the absence of charitable action (the expected content of said account).

In a speech that neatly summarises the action of the first half of the play, Everyman details a cycle of abandonment that emphasises just how vulnerable and alone he really is, within his earthly company:

> EVERYMAN
> Oh, to whom shall I make my moan
> For to go with me in that heavy journey?
> First Fellowship said he would with me go –
> His words were very pleasant and gay –
> But afterward he left me alone.
> Then spake I to my kinsmen, all in despair,
> And also they gave me words fair.
> They lacked no fair speaking,
> But all forsook me in the ending.
> Then went I to my Goods, that I loved best,
> In hope to have comfort, but there had I least;
> For my Goods sharply did me tell
> That he bringeth many into hell. (ll. 463–475)

---

[50] The use of medieval drama as an extension of the pulpit is a popular critical theme: Eamon Duffy considers these plays 'a fundamental means of transmitting religious instruction and stirring devotion' (p. 67); this is essentially an echo of David Bevington's perspective in his influential volume on medieval drama. Even those critics who move away from this idea – Claire Sponsler's reading of medieval theatricality as a form of resistance to disciplining discourses is a good example – use the obvious representation of Church doctrine in the plays as a starting point. See: Sarah Beckwith, *Signifying God: Social Relation and Symbolic Act in the York Corpus Christi Cycles* (Chicago, IL: University of Chicago Press, 2001); David Bevington, *Medieval Drama* (Boston, MA: Houghton Mifflin, 1975); Eamon Duffy, *The Stripping of the Altars*; Claire Sponsler, *Drama and Resistance: Bodies, Goods and Theatricality in Late Medieval England* (Minneapolis, MN: University of Minnesota Press, 1997).

[51] *Everyman*, from *Everyman and Mankind*, ed. by Douglas Bruster and Eric Rasmussen (London: Arden Shakespeare, 2009), *Incipit*, my emphasis. All subsequent references to *Everyman* will be to this edition, and given parenthetically.

Pity and Identity in the Age of Shakespeare

Notable is the range of Everyman's emotional labour: he references his 'moan', the heaviness of the forthcoming journey, and his 'despair'. But there is also the weight of (misplaced) feeling in his report that he is abandoned by the Goods he 'loved best'. Rather than the comfort he expects there, he finds sharpness, and the spectre of Hell. These emotions have a social frame made clear by the language of desertion: 'he left me alone' – 'all forsook me in the ending'. Something has been lost along with these companions. Even in his comment that with Goods he had 'least' comfort, Everyman imagines an emotional community, and expects to draw emotional support from without. Systematic abandonment prompts his inward turn, where the emotional language is both intensified and condensed alongside the recurring use of the personal pronoun:

EVERYMAN
Then of myself *I* was ashamed,
And so *I* am worthy to be blamed.
Thus may *I* well myself hate. (ll. 476–478, my emphasis)

Again and again, *Everyman* uses emotion to emphasise the doctrinal point: the systematic social desertion that Everyman experiences forcibly directs his focus towards Good Deeds, and the redemptive capacity of charity. As Andrew Hadfield has noted, the English reworking of *Elckerlijc* significantly expands the dialogue between Everyman and Good Deeds, suggesting that 'the English author was eager to explore the relationship between good deeds and salvation'.[52] However the play also emphasises the emotional burden carried by Good Deeds. In a cast of characters who are impassive to Everyman's pleas for assistance, Good Deeds is the only to show willingness. Her inability to help – because of Everyman's neglect – further underscores the point that to turn away from charity is also to neglect one's own emotional security:

EVERYMAN
Of whom shall I now counsel take?
I think that I shall never speed
Till that I go to my Good Deed.
But, alas, she is so weak
That she can neither go ne speak. (ll. 479–483)

Through her name, the cause of her weakness, and her later role in Everyman's redemption, Good Deeds makes clear the personal value of attending the suffering of others. Moreover, the reference to her physical atrophy

---

[52] Andrew Hadfield, 'The Summoning of *Everyman*', in Thomas Betteridge and Greg Walker (eds.), *The Oxford Handbook of Tudor Drama* (Oxford: Oxford University Press, 2012), pp. 93–108 (p. 93).

Mediated Emotion and King Lear

importantly parallels the language of social deterioration and weakness marked in the absence of charitable activity: what Good Deeds lacks at the beginning of the play is actively corrosive, a visceral threat to Everyman's soul.

The corrective course of action prescribed to 'rebuild' Good Deeds (and in so doing, to redeem Everyman) centrally locates the Church and religious practice alike. Rather than going back to tend to the poor (for it is too late for that), Everyman is instead obliged to seek 'Knowledge', whom Good Deeds describes as 'a sister' (l. 519). Positioning Good Deeds and Knowledge as sisters clearly position earthly works alongside religious practice, and Knowledge's doctrinal role is further confirmed with the announcement that she will lead Everyman to 'Confession'. Confession, who oversees Everyman's penance, is an obvious priest figure, characterised by the observation that he is 'in good conceit with God almighty' (l. 544). Everyman's redemption follows the familiar model: hoping that Confession will 'Wash from me the spots and vices clean, | That on me no sin may be seen' (ll. 546–547), Everyman announces that he 'come[s] with Knowledge for [his] redemption, | [and] Repent[s] with heart and full contrition' (ll. 548–549). Although Everyman represents mankind collectively, he is also, vitally, each of us at our most *individual* moment: alone, vulnerable, and accountable. Everyman's interaction with Confession uses deeply personal rhetoric – 'Wash from *me* – That on *me*', that focuses on the health of his individual soul. Confession, in turn, and again fulfilling the role of priest, behaves as the earthly link to paradise, assuring that 'a precious jewel I will give thee, | Called penance, voider of adversity' (ll. 557–558). It is also only through the interaction with Confession and completion of the penance that Everyman finally restores Good Deeds, reiterating the point that one's 'good deeds' ultimately fall under the jurisdiction and supervision of the Church. Even the provisions that Everyman does finally make, in his will – 'In alms, half my good I will give with my hands twain | In the way of charity with good intent' (ll. 699–700) – falls in line with the expectations of the Church, calling to mind William Lyndwood's reminder in the *Provinciale* that 'Those who do not relieve the needy kill spiritually, *as do those who withhold [from the poor]*'.[53] *Everyman* clarifies a medieval emotional culture in which human interaction, particularly as it pertains to the relief of suffering, is imagined as being regulated by the Church under the name of charity.

Within this framework, *Everyman* only directly mentions pity five times, but nevertheless offers a powerful vision of pity's relevance to charity. The play takes pains to make clear that pity is a distinct concept, a particularly

---

[53] 'Spirtualiter enim occidunt qui non reficiunt indigentes' (compiled c. 1420), in William Lyndwood, *Provinciale seu constitutiones Angliae* (Oxford: 1679, repr., Farnborough: 1968), Lib I.tit.I I.c.I, pp. 57–58, my emphasis.

Pity and Identity in the Age of Shakespeare

human and earthly practice that lacks the divine structure underpinning charity. Instead, pity is a seductive trick of the earthly world, something that unsettles and threatens Everyman's emotional security. *Everyman's* articulation of that difference is central to the play's overarching affirmation of church doctrine. The idea of pity first appears in conjunction with the character Fellowship, who uses the emotion both to characterise the Everyman figure and to position himself in relation to him: 'Sir why lookest thou so piteously? If anything be amiss, I pray thee me say, that I may help to remedy' (ll. 206–209). This is a straightforward representation that places emphasis on interpersonal exchange: one character's recognition of another's suffering, followed by the desire to see (and contribute to) its relief. 'Sir, I *must* needs know your heaviness', Fellowship argues, claiming he has 'pity to see you in any distress' (ll. 216–217, my emphasis). The immediacy of response here is a comforting promise, as is the suggestion of an emotional bond swiftly formed. This exchange looks to be very intimate, motivated entirely by Fellowship's participation in Everyman's emotional state: he sees Everyman's distress, pleads to hear more about it, pledges his physical presence at Everyman's side, and in the interest of his friend's relief, vows to avenge him even in the face of violence, or death. In this moment, the bond between these characters looks strong and reassuring. In reality – and as it becomes apparent later – they are much farther apart than they seem. Fellowship is not mirroring Everyman's emotions, nor is he really aligned with what Everyman is feeling. The dissonance in pity and intensity between the characters is a striking expression of the distance between them: Fellowship is bold, buoyant, and performative in the face of Everyman's crisis. Fellowship is unencumbered by this plight, light in the way he offers his pity here, without understanding what is at stake.

This exchange is notably tunnel-visioned: Fellowship responds only to the visual cue of Everyman's distress, and even as he imagines future action on Everyman's behalf, he cannot look beyond immediate, earthly conflict. 'If any have you wronged', he claims, 'ye shall revenged be, | Though I on the ground be slain for thee. | Though that I know before that I should die'. (ll. 218–220). This seductive, ardent claim does not – seemingly cannot – look beyond the earthly realm, to the possibility of God and judgement. Fellowship has not considered a divine adversary, nor has he conceived of the scale of Everyman's situation: though Fellowship gestures towards the possibility of his own death, he does not consider (even for himself) what might follow it. And yet, Fellowship's inability to access Everyman's religious plight is, in fact, precisely the point. Compared to the overarching tone of the play – the importance of acknowledging God's impending judgement – this interaction is distinct in its sole focus on entirely earthly bonds, and their security.

54

Mediated Emotion and King Lear

Through Fellowship, *Everyman* takes pains to illustrate that this vision of secular pity – though attractive – emphasises the human vulnerability to weak or fleeting emotional bonds. For all that Fellowship dangles the possibility of comfort and salvation in human community, this promise remains unfulfilled, and quickly evaporates in the face of real trouble. Fellowship flees just as Everyman reveals the full scope of his plight:

FELLOWSHIP
That is matter indeed! Promise is duty,
But, an I should take such a voyage on me,
I know it well, it should be to my pain;
Also it maketh me afeard, certain. (ll. 248–251)

The cruelty of this exchange rests on the earlier offer of emotional support that seems somehow physical and tangible. Everyman's flourishing hope at the promise of an ally is quickly dashed when the companionship and commitment implied in Fellowship's pity evaporates. What is made equally clear is pity's position in a hierarchy of emotion: Fellowship's offer of pity is undercut by his own fear. While it is not obvious that Fellowship means to be cruel or deceitful – he may be lying to Everyman about his commitment, but he could, equally, be overestimating the strength and durability of his own emotion – this abandonment tarnishes the appeal of earthly Fellowship, even as the play has acknowledged it, and undermines the pity that accompanies it, making the emotion look unreliable and insubstantial. This model of pity offered and withdrawn is adopted by every other representative of human community that Everyman petitions, most notably 'Cousin' and 'Kindred', creating a relentless gauntlet of abandonment: 'My kinsmen promised me faithfully' Everyman reflects, 'For to abide with me steadfastly, | And now fast away do they flee' (ll. 381–384) As James Simpson has pointed out, this cycle is the source of the play's emotional impact: 'the dialogue gains its poignancy', he argues, 'from the way in which everyday affirmations of solidarity break in the presence of death'.[54] The insertion of Good Deeds into this broken space – as well as her agents of redemption – confirms the play's religious agenda, but also makes that agenda explicitly emotional.

Everyman's focus is on representing religious practice, and it is easy to understand why the play has been called 'a didactic work under a dramatic form', a play straightforwardly written to reinforce doctrine.[55] That said, in pursuing this agenda the play also highlights the social instincts that guide

---

[54] James Simpson, *Reform and Cultural Revolution: 1350-1547* (Oxford: Oxford University Press, 2004), p. 556.

[55] Lawrence V. Ryan, 'Doctrine and Dramatic Structure in *Everyman*', *Speculum*, 32.4 (1957), 722–735 (p. 722). See also: Rainier Pineas, 'The English Morality Play

Pity and Identity in the Age of Shakespeare

human behaviour, and in staging Everyman's repeated turn to the (antici-pated) comforts of human fellowship, the play articulates an important point about emotion, and emotional burdens. Though the play makes the point that pity is unreliable, *Everyman* also effectively demonstrates how freely the language of pity and compassion can enter the discourses of human fellowship, how often these emotions emerge in periods of great suffering and distress. *Everyman* sets out, clearly, what it sees as the correct path, but in demonstrating the 'correctness' of charity it also acknowledges how potentially messy and unwieldy the surrounding emotional landscape might be. The emotional frameworks of *Everyman* are ultimately secure, precisely because they are supported by complementary religious frameworks, and because the play is careful to distance itself from secular expressions of pity that cannot be institutionalised. The play is clear that the compassion of Fellowship, Cousin, and Kindred cannot be a comfort because it is so fleeting, and staging these moments of emotional abandonment reinforces the point. Even so, that element of repetition is also a powerful statement of how frequently this language emerges in social exchange, how easily it can bleed into, or obfuscate religious practice, and how thoroughly this unstable emotion might divert someone from their own salvation. While *Everyman* proposes religious practice as a reassuring, clearly delineated way of navi-gating these issues, the Tudor moral interlude *Hickscorner* creates more space for disorder while narrating some of the same tensions.

* * *

It would be needless to point out the absurdities in the plan and conduct of [*Hickscorner*]; they are evidently great. It is sufficient to observe that bating the moral and religious reflection of Pity, etc., the piece is of a comic cast, and contains a humorous display of some of the vices of the age. Indeed, the author has generally been so little attentive to the alle-gory, that we need only substitute other names to his personages, and we have real characters and living manners.

We see then that the writers of these moralities were upon the very threshold of real tragedy and comedy, and therefore we are not to wonder that tragedies and comedies in form soon after took place ...[56]

When, in the 1876 *Relics of Ancient English Poetry*, Thomas Percy dismissed the 'absurdities' of *Hickscorner*, he nevertheless imagined it as part of a

---

as a Weapon of Religious Controversy', *Studies in English Literature 1500-1900*, 2.2 (1962), 157–180.

[56] Thomas Percy, *Relics of Ancient English Poetry*, vol. I (London: Bickers, 1876–1877), p. 130.

Mediated Emotion and King Lear

dramatic moment 'upon the very threshold of *real* tragedy and comedy' (my emphasis). The tone and ideology of this teleological view of English drama is not one I wish to represent in these pages, and yet there is, I think, an opportunity in these lines to stress the influence of medieval drama. To ignore Percy's dismissal – to dwell instead on some of *Hickscorner's* myriad oddities – opens up some interesting possibilities for the present study and its interest in the dramatic material that follows in Shakespeare's era. *Hickscorner* stages pity as a named character who hopes, with others, to redeem the eponymous Hickscorner and his wayward companions 'Free Will' and 'Imagination'. Through its representation of pity, the piece produces many of the tensions that later motivate *King Lear,* and helps to clarify why Shakespeare may have seen pity as a problem to be untangled, and why the emotional value of religious structure silently looms over *King Lear.*[57]

Pity's opening line in *Hickscorner* is a bold claim of significance: 'My name is pity, that ever yet hath been man's friend'.[58] In a play that bears many of the structural and thematic characteristics of medieval allegorical drama, and was published roughly 50 years before the English theatrical Renaissance began, this statement looks like an inconveniently early account (to my purposes) of an intimate relationship between pity and humankind, with 'ever yet' giving the added impression of a long established link.[59] Nonetheless, the inconsistencies of this play highlight some of the core conflicts between pity and charity, highlighting the conditions that make *King Lear* possible. *Hickscorner's* Pity is figured in explicitly religious terms – making it something quite different to the focus of the present study – a

---

[57] *Hickscorner* was likely composed between 1513 and 1514, and was printed by the London publisher Wynkyn de Worde in 1515. For more on *Hickscorner's* possible origins, see Greg Walker, *Plays of Persuasion: Drama and Politics at the Court of Henry VIII* (Cambridge: Cambridge University Press, 1991), pp. 37–59, and Ian Lancashire's magisterial account of the play in *Two Tudor Interludes* (Manchester: Manchester University Press, 1980).

[58] *Hickscorner,* in *Two Tudor Interludes,* pp. 153–238, ll. 5–6. All further reference to *Hickscorner* will be to this edition, and given parenthetically.

[59] Although there has been some dispute over this play's generic classification (morality play or interlude), the commonplace is to call *Hickscorner* an interlude, or occasionally a 'moral interlude'. On the distinctions, see: Nicholas Davis, 'The Meaning of the Word "Interlude"', *Medieval English Theatre,* 6 (1984), 5–15; Alan C. Dessen, 'Homilies and Anomalies: The Legacy of the Morality Play to the Age of Shakespeare – Review Article', *Shakespeare Studies,* 11 (1978), 243–258; and *Shakespeare and the Late Moral Plays* (Lincoln, NE and London: University of Nebraska Press, 1986), pp. 10–16; and more recently Eleanor Rycroft, '*The Interlude of Youth* and *Hick Scorner*', in Thomas Betteridge and Greg Walker (eds.), *The Oxford Handbook of Tudor Drama* (Oxford: Oxford University Press, 2012), pp. 465–481.

Pity and Identity in the Age of Shakespeare

'friend' to humankind insofar as he imagines himself part of a salvation double-act, with Charity:

PITY
Charity and I of true love leads the double rein;
Whoso me loveth damned never shall be.
Of some virtuous company I would be fain;
For all that will to heaven needs must come by me,
Chief porter I am in that heavenly city. (ll. 25–29)

This divine companion, a sort of mediator between humankind and heaven (literally, the 'porter') swiftly introduces an element of confusion, undermining the stability of the 'double rein' structure with Charity with a prompt transition to singular pronouns – 'Whoso *me* loveth'; '*I* would be fain'; 'needs must come by *me*'; 'Chief porter *I* am' (my emphasis). This near-immediate move away from charity is easy to overlook, however, since 'Charity' never materialises as a physical character. This omission perhaps encourages further conflation between pity and charity as terms, but in another sense Pity is too weak a character to stand as a convincing replacement. Far from being the play's authority in instructing salvation or providing friendship, the majority of Pity's limited time onstage is spent being ignored or abused by those he seeks to save. Ultimately, Pity has to be rescued from the stocks before finally being sent offstage by his companions, Contemplation and Perseverance. Pity neither returns nor is acknowledged at the interlude's conclusion, much like the title character Hickscorner, who similarly disappears without comment and without being prepared for judgement.[60] It becomes difficult therefore to reconcile *Hickscorner's* varied vision of pity into a coherent stance. As a character, Pity has the slight dramatic advantage of being first on stage, and speaking first. In *word*, the emotion appears pre-eminent, though that opinion is only expressed by Pity himself. His subsequent disappearance undermines the strength of his own language, inviting us to re-evaluate the distance between the language of pity and practical utility. Still, Pity's precise identity – in spite of his explicit allegorical naming – remains unclear, as both the play itself and its critics move between reading Pity as a distinct character, and reading him as charity,

---

[60] David Bevington also comments on Pity's disappearance, noting that 'the play ends, rather lamely no doubt, lacking its title role and its hero [Pity]'. Bevington attributes this to staging limitations presented by actors doubling roles. Given the actual utility of Pity in the play, one might disagree with Bevington's classification of him as the play's 'hero'; the only evidence for this is the character's self-proclaimed significance. For more see David Bevington, *From Mankind to Marlowe* (Cambridge, MA: Harvard University Press, 1962), p. 139.

Mediated Emotion and King Lear

different in name only. The interlude *Youth* (1513–1514), likely a primary source text for *Hickscorner*, might suggest that this is simply a matter of linguistic imprecision: *Youth* also presents an ineffectual would-be saviour who is ignored by those he seeks to redeem and, like *Hickscorner*'s Pity, that character is also fettered. In *Youth*, the character is Charity.[61]

Hickscorner loudly fails to capture and redeem its only allegorical representative of humankind – the character Hickscorner, whose very name flags his 'scorn' for the religious instruction he escapes.[62] Still, through Contemplation and Perseverance the play manages to produce some familiar processes of mediated redemption.By the conclusion two other characters are saved from their own faithless morality, 'gradually worn down', as one critic put it, 'from cockiness to penitence'.[63] The rhetoric of death and judgement figure prominently in the redemptive efforts of Perseverance and Contemplation, but again these efforts only begin to work on Freewill after he is assured of divine reward. 'Sir', Freewill finally admits, 'if ye will undertake that I saved shall be, | I will do all the penance that you will set me' (ll. 863–864). Freewill's redemption is the longer of the two staged in *Hickscorner*, and even this procedure is heavily abbreviated, stripped down to a bare framework evoking the role of the medieval church: Freewill renounces sin and asks God 'To forgive all that I have offend' (l. 870); he is instructed 'hereafter [to] live devoutly' (l. 877). Imagination similarly asks for God's mercy, this time confirming the emotional burden of uncertainty: 'No thing *dread* I so sore as death' (l. 996, my emphasis). Even so, these concerns are secondary to a more earthly sense of lack. In their jocular resistance to penitence, both characters reference a type of social hardship, and both reference material relief as a vital part of their broader acceptance of faith. The discussion of souls prompts Freewill on a punning meditation on his need of a new pair of boots (soles); and Imagination, when asked if he will 'God's hests fulfil' (l. 988), speaks of more immediate need:

IMAGINATION
I will do, sir, even as you will.
But I pray you, let me have a new coat.
When I have need and in my purse a groat,
Then will I dwell with you still. (ll. 989–992).

---

[61] On the compositions of *Youth* and *Hickscorner* and their relationship, see Lancashire, pp. 41–44.

[62] This play seems to coin 'Hickscorner' as a way of describing impious characters of dubious morals, though the term subsequently gains some traction. For a selection of early modern allusions, see Lancashire, pp. 254–257.

[63] William Anthony Davenport, *Fifteenth-Century English Drama: The Early Moral Plays and their Literary Relations* (Cambridge: D.S. Brewer, 1970), p. 72.

Pity and Identity in the Age of Shakespeare

When Perseverance responds, positioning himself as the reassuring intermediary, the guarantor of smooth passage from death to eternal life, these material needs (shoes, a coat) are overlooked in favour of divine salvation: '[…] I beseech God Almighty | To bring [to heaven] your souls that here be present' (ll. 1023–1024). Even if for comedy, *Hickscorner* raises the spectre of material want alongside this series of lacklustre redemptions, highlighting the social embeddedness of these processes – what Marilyn Williams has called 'the desperate, ironic relation of the poor to their would-be saviours'.[64]

Hickscorner's allegorical saviours, and the redemptive structures they oversee, are given an important and recognisable humanity insofar as they are made to look explicitly like priests. Contemplation places himself directly within this community, the 'chief lantern of all holiness | Of prelates and priests – I am their patron' (ll. 48–49). He also *sounds* like a priest, recognisably borrowing their language in his Latin invocation of Job: '*qui est in inferno nulla est redemptio* [for him who is in hell there is no redemption]' (l. 787). In *Hickscorner* – as in so much of medieval drama – the penitential experience is framed as a process requiring assistance. That assistance reliably comes from a priest-like figure with doctrinal knowledge, someone made in some ways extra-human by the apparently direct connection to God, and the ability to anticipate the surety of another's salvation. In an otherwise messy play, these are the figures who give *Hickscorner* a recognisable structure: the stability they offer – tenuous as it may appear here – is what allows the piece to fulfil its promise of replicating religious and social practice.

Taken another way, we might therefore pull the confusion of *Hickscorner* together to form a more concerted, troubled vision of the play's emotional and theological climate: pity and charity are separate entities, but conflated; both ultimately are absent. Humankind ventures beyond the scope of the church and its agents, both ideologically and spatially. Expressions of faith are underpinned by expressions of earthly need, and redemption, when it comes, is rather underwhelming. This is a broken landscape, as Pity himself notes in a familiar catalogue of social and moral decay: 'virtue is vanished forever' (l. 552); 'charity many men loathes' (l. 556); 'Devotion is gone many days sin' (l. 583); 'Yet was there never so great poverty' (l. 593). More than this, Pity's constant refrain throughout this speech – 'Worse was it never!' (l. 553); 'Worse was it never!' (l. 557); 'Worse was it never!' (l. 561); 'Worse was it never!' (l. 597); 'Worse was it never!' (l. 601) – permeates the play with a hand-wringing nostalgia, a familiar sense of an alarming deterioration that is both

---

[64] Marilyn Williams, 'Moral Perspective and Dramatic Action in the Tudor Interlude', *NEMLA Newsletter*, 2.2 (1970), 29–37 (p. 31).

Mediated Emotion and King Lear

seen and felt.[65] These myriad confusions, moreover, are only easy to overlook because the salvations of Freewill and Imagination so strongly adhere to the conventions of religious practice, making the piece look more generically coherent than it actually is. Read alongside a more canonical example of morality drama, like *Everyman*, it becomes clear that these vital organising structures are more recognisably the domain of medieval charity doctrine, and that they perform crucial emotional labour, papering over the pressure points that emerge under sustained consideration. What *Everyman* and *Hickscorner* demonstrate, above all else, is that the dramatic depictions of religious practice situate medieval religion in a much larger cultural framework, demonstrating that doctrinal issues must also be read as social and emotional issues. Whereas the presence of religious practice in plays like *Everyman* and *Hickscorner* seems to confirm this interconnectivity, Shakespeare's *King Lear* pursues these intersections via absence or lack. Shakespeare removes the explicit religious framework of the morality tradition but, I will argue, he does this as a way of continuing the tradition. The social and emotional frameworks of *King Lear* are untenable, precisely because the religious frameworks are absent, and human pity is unable to bear the necessary load.

KING LEAR

The close relationship between early modern drama and the morality tradition is well established, and within this broader picture, *King Lear* represents an especially compelling example, particularly when considered alongside *Everyman*.[66] The basic structural elements are striking in their similarity: *King Lear* tracks its title character's progression towards his death, and like Everyman, Lear experiences the progressive loss of all of his earthly comforts, both emotional and material.[67] Over the course of the play, Lear

---

[65] Pity's repetition here also reflects the speech's debt to the 'now a dayes' ballad, which repeats the phrase twice in its final verses, and captures the spirit of Pity's social moralising: 'To the lord I make my mone | For you maist healpe us everich one | Alas the people is so wo begone | *Worse was it never*' ('The maner of the world now a dayes', Huntington Library Britwell HEH 18348, EBBA 32588. Accessed 30 April 2020, <http://ebba.english.ucsb.edu/ballad/32588/xml>).

[66] For more on this relationship, see Robert Potter, *The English Morality Play: Origins, History and Influence of a Dramatic Tradition* (London: Routledge & Kegan Paul, 1975); John Wasson, 'The Morality Play: Ancestor of Elizabethan Drama?', *Comparative Drama*, 13 (1979), 210–221; and John Watkins, 'Moralities, Interludes, and Protestant Drama', in David Wallace (ed.), *The Cambridge History of Medieval Literature* (Cambridge: Cambridge University Press, 1999), pp. 767–792.

[67] Curtis Perry and John Watkins write compellingly of a trajectory that runs from the character Everyman direct to Lear. See: 'Introduction', in *Shakespeare and the*

Pity and Identity in the Age of Shakespeare

must acknowledge that the love of two of his daughters – and any comfort he drew from it during his lifetime – was empty and false. The extent of his material fall is shocking, both to Lear himself and to those who witness his deterioration: he becomes 'A sight most pitiful in the meanest wretch, | Past speaking of in a king' (4.6.200–201). Abandoned by those who have been lavishly vocal in their support and affection, Lear's ultimate salvation comes from the characters whom he initially rejects. In setting Kent in the stocks, moreover, the play also reproduces one of the core images of the earlier dramatic tradition.[68] It is easy to see therefore why the play has been described as being 'as conscious of [the] morality tradition as *Hamlet* is of the contemporary theatre world'.[69] Nonetheless, it is obvious that by its conclusion, the feeling of *Lear* is markedly different to a play like *Everyman*: though Lear is reconciled with Cordelia by the end, there is nothing reassuring about their deaths, and no comfort to imagine beyond them. This is a stark contrast to the way *Everyman* frames the title character's death:

ANGEL
Now the soul is taken the body fro,
Thy reckoning is crystal clear.
Now shalt thou into the heavenly sphere,
Unto the which all ye shall come
That liveth well before the day of doom. (ll. 898–902)

Everyman confirms the reassuring value of religious structure as the play draws to a close, ending with the final crucial injunction: 'Amen, say ye, for saint Charity' (l. 922). *King Lear*, by contrast, takes away these religious structures entirely, presenting instead a world that emphasises the tragic

---

Middle Ages (Oxford: Oxford University Press, 2009), pp. 1–20 (p. 5). The structural similarities between *King Lear* and *Everyman* are outlined in more detail in Michael O'Connell, '*King Lear* and the Summons of Death', in Curtis Perry and John Watkins (eds.), *Shakespeare and the Middle Ages* (Oxford: Oxford University Press, 2009), pp. 199–216, especially at p. 210. *King Lear*'s connection to the morality plays is also thoroughly outlined in James Nohrnberg, 'About Suffering and On Dying: Shakespeare's Reinvention of a Theater of Eschatological Identity in King Lear', in Kathy Lavezzo and Roze Hentschell (eds.), *Essays in Memory of Richard Helgerson: Laureations* (Newark, DE: University of Delaware Press, 2011), pp. 107–129; Maynard Mack, *King Lear in Our Time* (Berkeley, CA: University of California Press, 1965), pp. 55–63; and Oscar J. Campbell, 'The Salvation of Lear', *English Literary History*, 15 (1948), 93–109.

[68] As Helen Cooper notes, the physical binding of a 'virtue' character was 'an episode already proverbial' by the time Shakespeare used it. Helen Cooper, *Shakespeare and the Medieval World* (London: Methuen, 2010), p. 123. On Shakespeare's use of the stocks as referencing a medieval tradition, see also T.W. Craik, *The Tudor Interlude* (Leicester: Leicester University Press, 1958), pp. 93–96.

[69] O'Connell, p. 203.

Mediated Emotion and King Lear

consequence of relying instead on a more secular view of pity. The resulting shift in the latter play's emotional landscape makes clear that the flawed structures of medieval charity also carried a vital affective load for individuals and their communities.

The unsettling of religious structure is, in *Lear*, complete: the play presents a muddy vision in which God (or the gods) are often referenced, but not obviously there. On the more intimate level of human interaction, the play's various compassionate misfirings testify to its missing religious framework. These are not characters who behave on the principle of living 'in charity', but equally it is not obvious that the vicious Regan, Goneril, and Edmund are flouting social convention. Rather, it seems these principles have no consistent hold in the world of *Lear*. In the reading of *King Lear* that follows, I trace how Shakespeare's tragedy recreates the anxious and uncertain emotional landscape that was inherited from the Protestant Reformations. In its efforts to navigate that landscape, I contend, the play engages not just with the content of pre-Reformation drama, but with the comfort of its structural elements as well.

* * *

GLOUCESTER
As flies to wanton boys are we to the gods,
They kill us for their sport.[70]

Certainly almost every possible point of view on the gods and cosmic justice is expressed [...] But the very multitude, concern, and contradictory character of these references do not cancel each other out, but rather show how precarious is the concept of cosmic justice.[71]

One of the central ways in which *King Lear* echoes the religious confusion of the Reformation era is through its own inability to adhere to a single eschatology, as Judah Stampfer noted in 1960: 'almost every possible view' he suggests, 'is expressed'. The muddiness of that thinking, Stampfer argued – the overwhelming number of possibilities here for organising a world view – only intensify the feelings of uncertainty and vulnerability that characterise the play. That precarity of position is further echoed in the critical history of *Lear* and religion, where scholars have argued passionately for the presence (or absence) of God, or the gods, and proposed various spiritual frameworks that render Lear's suffering

---

[70] William Shakespeare, *King Lear*, ed. by R.A. Foakes (London: Arden Shakespeare, 1997), 4.1.38–39. All references to *King Lear* are to this edition, unless otherwise noted.

[71] Judah Stampfer, 'The Catharsis of *King Lear*', *Shakespeare Survey*, 13 (1960), 1–10 (p. 5).

Pity and Identity in the Age of Shakespeare

either full of purpose or meaningless.[72] Gloucester's iconic lines above, of course, capture the cosmic scale of the play's brutality while simultaneously reinforcing its utter humanity. What it is also clear in Gloucester's theodicy is that he is grasping for any kind of comfort, even if that comfort is the reliability of cruelty. Transferring the play's human viciousness onto an unseen set of controlling divinities at least gives the minor comfort of minimising the play's intimate and fully human gamut of betrayal. As Séan Lawrence observes, Gloucester's is one of many references to the gods that 'only render their absence all the more conspicuous'.[73] The gesture towards the sporting cruelty of the unseen gods only reminds us that there are in fact no gods here, and there is no possibility of divine intervention. Edgar's offering to Edmund – 'Let's exchange charity' (5.3.164) – does not look like charity at all: it comes after a moment of violent confrontation. What he does offer is a theodicy: 'The gods are *just* and of our pleasant vices | Make instruments to plague us' (5.3.168–169, my emphasis). But of course, Cordelia's death will soon undercut any sense of divine justice.

David Loewenstein suggests that *King Lear* offers 'a brutal world in which neither a Christian God nor "the kind gods" (to borrow Gloucester's words, 3.7.35) respond to human savagery and suffering and offer any hope of consolation'.[74] This tragedy is human, and earthly: the play, in Jan Kott's influential reading, 'makes a tragic mockery of all eschatologies: of the heaven promised on earth, and the Heaven promised after death; in fact, of all Christian and secular theodicies'.[75] Alison Shell has recently suggested that the inscrutable messiness of the play's conflicting references to religion intentionally '[resist] a "totalizing explanation" of religious stance'.[76] For

---

[72] For more on the history of this debate, see Séan Lawrence, '"Gods That We Adore": The Divine in *King Lear*', *Renascence*, 56 (2004), 143–159. See also: Roland M. Frye, *Shakespeare and Christian Doctrine* (Princeton, NJ: Princeton University Press, 1963); William R. Elton, *King Lear and the Gods* (San Marino, CA: The Huntington Library, 1968); Rosalie L. Colie, 'The Energies of Endurance: Biblical Echo in *King Lear*', in Rosalie L. Colie and F.T. Flahiff (eds.), *Some Facets of* King Lear: *Essays in Prismatic Criticism* (Toronto: University of Toronto Press, 1974), pp. 117–144; René E. Fortin, 'Hermeneutical Circularity and Christian Interpretations of *King Lear*', *Shakespeare Studies*, 12 (1979), 113–125.

[73] Lawrence, p. 143.

[74] David Loewenstein, 'Agnostic Shakespeare?: The Godless World of *King Lear*', in David Loewenstein and Michael Witmore (eds.), *Shakespeare and Early Modern Religion* (Cambridge: Cambridge University Press, 2015), pp. 155–171 (p. 155).

[75] Jan Kott, *Shakespeare Our Contemporary*, trans. Boleslaw Taborski, 2nd ed. rev. (London: Methuen, 1967), p. 157.

[76] Alison Shell, *The Arden Critical Companion to Shakespeare and Religion* (London: Methuen, 2010), p. 186.

Mediated Emotion and King Lear

Shell, the determination to identify the play as either atheist or Christian misses the point, and introduces a worrying distraction that 'cheapens' the play's 'irresolvable sadness'.[77] This, I think, is exactly right: to attempt to impose a coherent system of belief on *Lear* is to miss the point of the play, to smooth out obstacles that should remain prominent and problematic to the characters. As Stephen Lynch explains, Shakespeare specifically alters his source material to make *Lear* a harsher, more unsettled landscape: 'anyone familiar with the old play [*The True Chronicle Historie of King Leir*], or with earlier versions of the story', he writes, 'would certainly be struck, if not horrified, by the apparent remoteness of the gods and the diminished sense of worldly justice in Shakespeare's tragedy'.[78] The ideological messiness of *Lear* is precisely what frames the play's sadness, providing, through its instability, the currents of emotional vulnerability that are core to its tragedy.

Even if the gods themselves are missing in *King Lear*, the trappings of religion (and more often, their absence) register at almost every level, and certainly in terms of content and form.[79] Beyond the grander scale of the gods, *Lear* also takes pains to weave the practices of early modern Christianity into the play's key moments. For example, Lear's emotional revelation on the heath:

LEAR
Poor naked wretches, wheresoe'er you are,
That bide the pelting of this pitiless storm,
How shall your houseless heads and unfed sides,
Your looped and windowed raggedness, defend you
From seasons such as these? O, I have ta'en
Too little care of this. Take physic, pomp,
Expose thyself to feel what wretches feel,
That thou mayst shake the superflux to them
And show the heavens more just. (3.4.28–36)

---

77 Ibid., p. 194.
78 Stephen J. Lynch, 'Sin, Suffering, and Redemption in *Leir* and *Lear*', *Shakespeare Studies*, 18 (1986), 161–174 (p. 161).
79 Cherrell Guilfoyle points out, 'in *King Lear* Shakespeare's characters are not Christians, but as the action of the play intensifies, they find themselves acting in scenic forms from the Christian story'. The symbolism of *Lear*, she concludes, reflects 'aspects of the pattern of Christian salvation as it had been shown in the "pantomime" of the cycle plays – the sacrifice of the Passion, the call to repentance leading to resurrection, the Judgment which will redeem the repentant and, of course, condemn the rest'. Cherrell Guilfoyle, 'The Redemption of King Lear', *Comparative Drama*, 23.1 (1989), 50–69 (p. 50, p. 68).

Pity and Identity in the Age of Shakespeare

'What is surprising', Michael Steffes has commented, 'is the ancient pagan king's being moved to something very much like Christian charity as urged by the theologians'.[80] For Debora Shugar, Lear's reference to the 'superflux' confirms this moment as an epiphany of Christian *caritas* for Lear, an expression of 'the social teachings of the medieval church'.[81] Lear's comments here do suggest a specifically medieval (pre-Reformations) understanding of charitable obligation, but absence looms large in Lear's reflections. In this moment, he only really articulates his own negligence of these practices, dwelling on his own experience and his newfound appreciation of an emotional burden he now recognises and registers. 'I have ta'en | Too little care of this' only confirms what the king has failed to do; it registers the absence of mindful activity. What makes the revelation feel promising is precisely the charitable progression he envisions coming next, the process of 'feel[ing] what wretches feel'; redistributing wealth to the 'houseless heads and unfed sides', and in this way showing 'the heavens more just'. But, it is an empty promise: something he now cannot do, though he has now found the will to do it. What is clear, however, is that this thinking has emotional value for Lear himself: if this is the pagan king's great Christian epiphany, it also points to the emotional burden that may be absorbed by these systems of belief. All of this activity – this great moment of charity – Lear imagines, will help him process the trauma of his daughters' cruelty by confirming much larger structures of justice. Put another way: framing justice on a more cosmic level crucially shifts the scale, resituating the intimate personal betrayals that Lear has suffered into a much bigger context that also affords an important emotional distance. This is not so much a vision that looks toward eternal salvation as it is a way of processing the more immediate compassionate failures of intimate human interaction.

Gloucester makes a comparable reference to charitable process in his later encounter with Edgar (acting as Poor Tom), where he speaks to the value of redistributing wealth:

GLOUCESTER
Here, take this purse, thou whom the heaven's plagues
Have humbled to all strokes. That I am wretched
Makes thee the happier. Heavens deal so still!
Let the superfluous and lust-dieted man

---

[80] Michael Steffes, 'Medieval Wildernesses and *King Lear*: Heath, Forest, Desert', *Exemplaria*, 28.3 (2016), 230–247 (p. 237).

[81] Debora K. Shugar, 'Subversive Fathers and Suffering Subjects: Shakespeare and Christianity', in Donna B. Hamilton and Richard Strier (eds.), *Religion, Literature, and Politics in Post-Reformation England, 1540–1688* (Cambridge: Cambridge University Press, 1996), pp. 46–69 (p. 53).

Mediated Emotion and King Lear

That slaves your ordinance, that will not see
Because he does not feel, feel your power quickly:
So distribution should undo excess
And each man have enough. (4.1.67–74).

As Poor Tom, of course, Edgar has intentionally styled himself after 'Bedlam beggars', invoking a representative image of the public poor: those who 'enforce […] charity' with their own spectacle (the 'horrible object'), and with a combination of 'roaring voices', 'lunatic bans', and 'prayers' (2.2.185–191). Gloucester's call for the dispersal of 'excess' shows him in a similar mind to Lear on the heath, and adds an important recognition of the value of the poor in a much larger cosmic calculation. Gloucester's reference to the poor man's 'power' has obvious ties to salvation and divine judgement; this is part of what Sears Jayne refers to as 'a gradual and painful indoctrination in sensitivity and charity', which Jayne suggests happens 'partly under the *loving* tutelage of Edgar'.[82] Even so, as it continues, the interaction between Edgar and Gloucester really only further emphasises the earthliness of this exchange, the absence of divine presence. In spite of Jayne's positive assessment of the love underpinning Edgar's 'tutelage', critics have long troubled over his behaviour in these scenes, particularly puzzling over an aside in which Edgar acknowledges the extent to which he is manipulating his despairing, blinded father: 'Why I do trifle thus with his despair | Is done to cure it' (4.6.33–34).[83] Edgar's efforts to pull his father from the depths of misery hinge on a turn to the divine, the orchestration of a complex scheme in which Gloucester is made to believe that he is saved from his own attempted suicide by divine intervention. As James Nohrnberg points out, through these manipulations Edgar effectively forces his father to 'rescript his history […] as a miracle play'.[84] At the conclusion of 'Edgar's theatrics', he encourages his father to 'Think that the clearest gods, who make them honours | Of men's impossibilities, have preserved thee (4.6.73–74).[85] Part of what makes this sequence of events so odd is that Edgar assumes a quasi-divine role, engineering an overly

---

[82] Sears Jayne, 'Charity in *King Lear'*, *Shakespeare Quarterly*, 15.2 (1964), 277–288 (p. 280). My emphasis.

[83] Bridget Gellert Lyons credits Edgar's grating didacticism with a dramatic inheritance that she traces to the morality play. See Bridget Gellert Lyons, 'The Subplot as Simplification in *King Lear'*, in Rosalie L. Colie and F.T. Flahiff (eds.), *Some Facets of* King Lear: *Essays in Prismatic Criticism* (Toronto: University of Toronto Press, 1974), pp. 23–38 (p. 25).

[84] Nohrnberg, p. 123.

[85] Huston Diehl, 'Religion and Shakespearean Tragedy', in Claire McEachern (ed.), *The Cambridge Companion to Shakespearean Tragedy* (Cambridge: Cambridge University Press, 2003), pp. 86–102 (p. 99).

complex intervention instead of engaging in the simpler human connection that Gloucester really needs: he is desperate for forgiveness from his son, but is forced instead to experience 'salvation' at the hands of a divine presence who is never really there. If this is a form of cruelty from Edgar, then that cruelty is produced when the divine is forcibly inserted into what should be a secular moment. These events suspect an emptiness in divine intervention – particularly when it comes through a human mediator – but equally they stress the impact of a pitiful misfiring. If this is character failure for Edgar, it is a failure of compassion, a missed opportunity to connect on a human level.

These moments – Lear's epiphany on the heath, Gloucester's orchestrated salvation – both position *Lear* as somewhat unsure of the stability and ultimate utility of the religious activity that might direct human behaviour on earth. However altruistic Edgar's intentions may be, Gloucester is still transparently manipulated into a system of belief; Lear's sudden turn to charity comes far too late, and only on the back of his own suffering. And of course, Lear is no longer even in a position to help himself, let alone others. As Jonathan Dollimore points out in his own influential reading of the play, Lear's revelation only confirms that 'where a king has to share the suffering of his subjects in order to "care", the majority will remain poor, naked and wretched'.[86] Pity is fundamental to *Lear*, 'precious yet ineffectual': desperately valued and longed for, but within the context of the play, devastatingly unregulated and unreliable.[87] If *King Lear* is, as one critic puts it, a play that takes as its premise 'the desperate need which human beings have for each other', then the play also uses pity to ensure that that need remains largely unfulfilled.[88] The understandings and deployments of pity in *Lear* stand as a kind of emotional superstructure in the play, a principle either denied or embraced that organises character behaviours. This way of organising interactions stands as an alternative to the faulty structures of charity that the play depicts elsewhere, a system that occupies the space created by the play's religious void. Even so, as the play moves through its tragedy, it also calls into question the very system it proposes, emphasising the instability of pity as an organising principle.

The move in *Lear* to situate pity in circumstances where one might otherwise expect to encounter charity is evident in Lear's iconic moment of clarity on the heath. His reference to charitable processes, however, are explicitly placed alongside pity: both its absence and, in another context, its failures.[89] The

---

[86] Jonathan Dollimore, *Radical Tragedy*, 2nd edn (London: Harvester Wheatsheaf, 1989), p. 191.

[87] Ibid., p. 193.

[88] Jayne, p. 277.

[89] Kent Lehnhof points out that many have taken this moment 'to express the overarching message of the play: namely, that compassion can cure us'. Kent R. Lehnhof,

Mediated Emotion and King Lear

storm is 'pitiless', as the Fool has already observed: 'here's a night pities neither wise men nor fools' (3.2.12–13). And yet this absence of pity is accepted and expected, easily explained according to its kind, as Lear acknowledges: 'I tax not you, you elements, with *unkindness*' (3.2.16, my emphasis). The storm is cruel, but cannot, as a non-human entity, be expected to recognise human vulnerability, or to offer pity in the face of it. What this moment makes clear is that Lear has a clear understanding of when pity ought to be expected, and according to what rules: the reference to 'unkindness' imagines pity as a specifically human comfort and function, one that should reliably be dispensed, and registers as a betrayal of *kind* when that dispensation fails. Further evidence of this system of emotional belief is apparent in Lear's method of disowning Cordelia at the start of the play:

> LEAR
> Here I disclaim all my paternal care,
> Propinquity and property of blood,
> And as a stranger to my heart and me
> Hold thee, from this, for ever. The barbarous Scythian,
> Or he that makes his generation messes
> To gorge his appetite, shall to my bosom
> Be as well neighbour'd, pitied, and relieved,
> As thou my sometime daughter. (1.1.114–121)

Lear's invocation of pity, alongside neighbourly behaviour and relief, hints at the doctrinal practice of almsgiving, of 'loving thy neighbour' as commanded by Matthew. At the same time, it makes a distinctly secular shift, placing a more explicit emphasis on the familial bond he shares with Cordelia, and severing that connection on the grounds that her actions align her with another, more 'barbarous' race. Lear understands his own emotional responsibilities as dependent on these structures of *kind*ness: Cordelia's actions reveal her as not of the same 'kind' as the rest of the family, not capable (or worthy) of participating in the family community, and in a more general sense, potentially not even human. In losing her status in the family, she also loses an important social protection afford by pity. Of course, the moment also confirms the instability of Lear's compassionate systems, as he alienates the very person who cares for him most.

From his initial rejection of Cordelia to the assessment of the pitiless storm, Lear's conception of pity importantly represents a turn away from the divine: his considerations of kind are informed by assumptions about what it means to be *human*kind, assumptions that are shared by Cordelia

---

'Relation and Responsibility: A Levinasian Reading of *King Lear*', *Modern Philology*, 111.3 (2014), 485–509 (p. 498).

even after she suffers the rejection of her father. Her speech to Lear at the moment of their reunion and reconciliation gives a comparable sense of a system of belief involving pity:

> CORDELIA
> Had you not been their father, these white flakes
> Did challenge pity of them.
> [...]
> Mine enemy's dog
> Though he had bit me should have stood that night
> Against my fire; and wast thou fain, poor father,
> To hovel thee with swine and rogues forlorn
> In short and must straw? Alack, alack! (4.7.30–40)

Cordelia will return repeatedly to the point of Lear's age, but here she also uses considerations of kind to emphasise what she sees as a gross failure to dispense pity. She references three kinds of human relationships in her outline of the pity connections, moving from strongest to weakest. Between the presumptively tender familial relationship (child to parent) and the more hostile one (with Cordelia's imagined 'enemy') is a more generic social relationship, in which Cordelia sketches the lines of emotional obligation between young and old. Her subsequent reference to her (imagined) enemy's dog, and the compassion that such an animal might reasonably expect in certain circumstances, again uses considerations of kind to outline a human system of emotional exchange predicated on the values of pity.

These assumptions about when and where pity can be expected will be repeatedly contradicted by Edmund, Regan, and Goneril, though they themselves show an awareness of pity and its influence over others. As Danielle St. Hilaire observes, 'Even Goneril and Regan, who never have a redemptive moment in the play, evince the power of pity in their fear of it'.[90] Regan's comment, after Gloucester's blinding and his subsequent escape, is a telling reflection on this troubled relationship with pity:

> REGAN
> It was great ignorance, Gloucester's eyes being out,
> To let him live. Where he arrives he moves
> All hearts against us. Edmund, I think, is gone
> In pity of his misery to dispatch
> His knighted life. (4.5.11–15)

---

[90] Danielle A. St. Hilaire, 'Pity and the Failures of Justice in Shakespeare's *King Lear*', *Modern Philology*, 113.4 (2016), 482–506 (p. 493).

Mediated Emotion and King Lear

What makes this comment so interesting is that Regan does reference pity as Lear, Cordelia, or Gloucester might understand it – a movement of the heart to tenderness and action, resulting from the visual stimulus of another's suffering – even as she expresses a desire to suppress those instincts in the unseen public. Her explicit reference to pity however – to Edmund's alleged plan to 'dispatch' his father and thus end his suffering – registers as further confirmation of how seriously she misses the mark: Edmund's plan to end his father's suffering (though it is not clear that such a plan actually exists) could hardly be seen as compassion given Edmund's primary role in manufacturing that suffering. Regan instead understands the strength and value of pity in the sense of it being an emotional current that might turn against her. Her fear of pity also stems from a worry about manipulation. At the climax of the dispute over his retinue, Lear's sarcastic prostrations – 'On my knees I beg | That you'll vouchsafe me raiment, bed and food' (2.2.344–345) – also make clear that Lear is now reliant on his daughters, and that there is nothing in place to ensure that charity. If this is an opportunity for pity, Regan rejects it, seeing instead an attempt to prey on emotional vulnerability: 'Good sir, no more. These are unsightly tricks' (2.2.346).

While Regan's aversion to pity also confirms her cruelty, *King Lear* still seems unable to endorse the emotion fully. Genuine acts of pity are consistently and brutally punished in the play, precisely because the instinct is shown *not* to be universally human: because some characters are able to steel themselves against pity, no one is truly safe to practice it. Geoffrey Aggeler suggests that while *King Lear* frames pity as 'an indispensable positive force', he also points out that:

> [Pity] does not make one who is moved by it invulnerable to evil. To feel is to suffer, and indeed the bitterest irony of the play is that the character who exhibits good pity in its purest form, Cordelia, is actually destroyed by it.[91]

Cordelia makes obvious her belief that Lear's is a situation to be pitied, and it is also clear that another's pity facilitates her return to England: 'great France', she notes, 'My mourning and important tears hath pitied' (4.4.25–26). Cordelia's eventual death is, for many, the play's great tragedy, the unforgivable emotional violation that Shakespeare adds in diverting from the earlier *The True Chronicle Historie of King Leir*.

The play's other shocking violation of course is Gloucester's, and that too results after a compassionate display:

---

[91] Geoffrey Aggeler, 'Good Pity in *King Lear*: The Progress of Edgar', *Neophilologus*, 77.2 (1993), 321–331 (p. 328).

> GLOUCESTER: Alack, alack, Edmund, I like not this unnatural dealing. When I desired their leave that I might pity him, they took from me the use of mine own house; charged me on pain of perpetual displeasure neither to speak of him, entreat for him, or any way sustain him. (3.3.1–6)

It is a moment that both emphasises Regan and Goneril's insistent suppression of pity for their father, and confirms pity's uncomfortable positioning as a replacement for charitable structures. As in *Hickscorner*, Gloucester's language reveals some slippage in its terminology. Almost in the same breath, Gloucester frames his instincts as charity, instructing Edmund to 'Go [...] and maintain talk with the Duke, that my *charity* be not of him perceived' (3.3.14–16, my emphasis). Gloucester finds that he has no institutional structures to sanction and direct his emotional instincts, and in fact, through Regan and Goneril, the play's power structures conspire to explicitly deny and contain these instincts: he tells Lear of his inability 'T'obey in all your daughters' hard commands' (3.4.145), to follow 'their injunction [...] to bar my doors' (3.4.146). With no one to guide or sanction Gloucester's compassionate impulses, he directs them himself, but the profound cost of this moment of emotional independence also reaffirms the point that pity cultivates personal vulnerability.

CONCLUSION

Shortly after Cordelia fails the love test, after Lear disowns her, and after Edmund begins his plot to alienate Edgar from their father, Gloucester reflects on the world of the play:

> Love cools, friendship falls off, brothers divide: in cities, mutinies; in countries, discord; in palaces, treason, and the bond cracked 'twixt son and father. This villain of mine comes under the prediction – there's son against father. The King falls from bias of nature – there's father against child. We have seen the best of our time. Machinations, hollowness, treachery and all ruinous disorders follow us disquietly to our graves' (1.2.106–114).

There is something of the early modern English moral complaint, and particularly Stow, in Gloucester's comments here, though they are offered long before the true horrors of *King Lear* unfold. This is the language of deterioration: love that existed but has now cooled, enmity taking the place of friendship, familial and social bonds broken. But it is also the language of nostalgia, a wistful fear that 'we have seen the best of our time', and that the weight of this new social era will extend beyond the mortal lifetime. Gloucester's reference to the 'Machinations, hollowness, treachery and all

Mediated Emotion and King Lear

ruinous disorders [that] follow us disquietly to our graves' could be yet another invocation of *Everyman*, a new way of considering the impossibility of making the 'Unburdened crawl toward death' (1.1.40).

In spite of the apparently pity-hostile environment in *Lear*, there is something important in the play's acknowledgement that the emotion remains somehow impervious to full suppression. These moments of piteous slippage from Edgar, Gloucester, and Cordelia both perpetuate the tragedy as their pitying instincts are punished and, for audiences, provide occasional respite from the play's otherwise relentless cruelty. In this, Shakespeare allows pity to function just well enough to demonstrate its continued appeal – if not in the world of the play itself, then in terms of dramatic impact. If these characters prove that pity does exist in the play, they also suggest that it floats around untethered. The resulting impression is that the emotion is ineffectual – even dangerous – without the accompanying support of an institutional power structure. In staging this tension between what we feel and the extent to which we are permitted to act on those feelings, the play also highlights a crucial difference between what pity *should* be – what we want to believe it can be – and what it might be in practice. *King Lear* juxtaposes the hope and impulse for pity with the emotion's capacity to fail (or the human capacity to mismanage it).

As Eric Langley argues, in *King Lear*, 'Shakespeare advocates pity as a poor but necessary human substitute for the divine compassion we lack'.[92] Shakespeare's play scrutinises a poorly functioning replacement for an earlier model of compassion that has been lost. Still there is, I think, more than just emotional scepticism at the heart of *Lear*. While the play demonstrates the essential fallibility of an emotion dependent on shared human goodness, it also acknowledges the persistent attractiveness of pity. The play laments something that has been lost, but it also acknowledges that there is perhaps no way of regaining it in its original form: in the face of that loss it accepts the instinct to seek some – or any – alternative. Ultimately, *Lear* offers an account of early modern humanity that is emotionally untethered. Edgar's professed hope, at the close of the play, that those remaining should 'Speak what we feel, not what we ought to say' (5.3.323) gestures towards an emotions-driven mode of being that sits at odds with the 'ought' of social expectation. However hopeful, this exhortation underscores the emotional failings of the characters who have been lost: an assembly of characters desperately in need of pity, often desperately wanting to offer it, but

---

[92] Eric Langley, 'Standing on a Beach: Shakespeare and the Sympathetic Imagination', in Kristine Steenbergh and Katherine Ibbett (eds.), *Compassion in Early Modern Literature and Culture* (Cambridge: Cambridge University Press, 2021), pp. 197–216 (p. 211).

Pity and Identity in the Age of Shakespeare

nevertheless wholly unsure how to manage it, how to make it efficacious, or what the consequences of offering it may be. By placing his characters in the familiar structures of medieval drama, Shakespeare highlights the challenge and the cost of being confronted by similar emotions in new, more intimate ways. Thomas Nashe's description of London in particular calls to mind the vision we are presented in *Lear*: a horrifying and extreme depiction of blood, death, and emotional suffering that is left unchecked, and remains both amplified and close. At the same time, the play reflects the sense of longing and regret implicit in Stow, a felt loss of emotional security that casts a different light on one of Cordelia's final comments, to Lear: 'We are not the first | Who with best meaning have incurred the worst' (5.3.3–4).

Chapter 2

VIOLENT SPECTACLE AND VIOLENT FEELING IN EARLY MODERN LUCRECE NARRATIVES

THE P[RINTER]. TO THE READER.

When publisher John Day released the second edition of Thomas Norton and Thomas Sackville's *Gorboduc* in 1570, he was releasing the material to a reading public that had already had printed access to the play for a full five years. In an oft-cited note preceding the text, Day conjures an anthropomorphic history of the 'exceedingly corrupted' first printing as his justification for the second edition:

> One W.G. getting a copie thereof at some yongmans hand that lacked a little money and much discretion, in the last great plage, an[no]. 1565, about five yeares past, while the said Lord[1] was out of England, and T. Norton farre out of London, and neither of them both made privie, put it forth excedingly corrupted: even as if by meanes of a broker for hire, he should have entised into his house a faire maide and done her villainie, and after all to bescratched her face, torne her apparell, berayed and disfigured her, and then thrust her out of dores dishonested.[2]

While the piece begins with a standard account of a corrupted copy accessed without the knowledge and permission of its authors, Day quickly escalates the emotional impact by recasting the first edition as an assaulted woman.[3] Lured in by a waiting tormentor, 'she' is physically attacked, then pushed

---

[1]   This 'said Lord' is most probably Thomas Sackville, who co-authored *Gorboduc* with Thomas Norton.

[2]   John Day, 'The P[rinter]. To the Reader', in Thomas Norton, *The Tragidie of Ferrex and Porrex* (London: 1570). sig. A2^r.

[3]   On Day's overlapping of 'scenes of writing and reading' and 'images of sexual violation and wantonness', see Wendy Wall, *The Imprint of Gender: Authorship and Publication in the English Renaissance* (Ithaca, NY and London: Cornell University Press, 1993), p. 182.

Fig. 1: Frontispiece to William Shakespeare, *The Rape of Lucrece* (London: 1655), 54018. The Huntington Library, San Marino, California.

Violent Spectacle and Violent Feeling

back out into the public bearing the signs of her torment. This shift places the earlier printing activity in the register of personal, moral, and physical violation, but in its editorial context, the stakes as Day lays them out are disproportionately dramatic. In truth, Day seems to have made relatively few content changes to the 1565 edition, a consideration which gives a distinct sense of the note – and its emotional strategies – as 'mischievous commercial special pleading'.[4] The distance Day seeks from the 'disfigured' and feminised 1565 text collapses further as his story continues, and he becomes entangled in increasingly problematic language:

> In such plight after long wandring she came at length home to the sight of her frendes, who scant knew her but by a few tokens and markes remayning. They, the authors I meane, though they were very much displeased that she so ranne abroad without leave, whereby she caught her shame, as many wantons do, yet seeing the case as it is remedilesse, have for common honestie and shamefastnesse new apparelled, trimmed, and attired her in such forme as she was before.

Day relies heavily on shame as a mobilising force, suggesting a number of ways in which the now-gendered text forcibly elicits action whenever it is encountered. The reader is led to believe that the physical damage comes dangerously close to erasing her identity altogether, as her friends are barely able to recognise her. And yet, as Helen Smith has argued, 'it is also the rags and shreds of her original dress', the very evidence of violation, that become the proof and foundation of the woman's identity.[5] She is re-constructed in violation.

Day's preoccupation with the physical markers of the woman/text's violation places the essence of this character in her visuality: she is created, destroyed, identified, and restored through her appearance. The authors undertake her revision and redress: the visual signs of her abuse are covered

---

4. Henry James and Greg Walker, 'The Politics of *Gorboduc*', *The English Historical Review*, 110.435 (1995), 109–121 (p. 120, n. 1). As both Sir Walter Greg and I.B. Cauthen observed, Day's most significant intervention was cutting an eight-line passage in Act 5. Otherwise, Cauthen noted that in spite of Day's effort to correct the corruption of the first quarto, 'Q2 retains at least five errors of Q1 and introduces some nine manifest errors of its own [...] despite Day's harsh judgment of Griffith's work, Q1 was not so dishonested that it could not be corrected to serve as copy-text for Q2' (p. 231). See: Sir Walter Greg, *A Bibliography of the English Printed Drama to the Restoration*, vol. 1 (London: Bibliographical Society, 1970), p. 115; and I.B. Cauthen Jr., '*Gorboduc, Ferrex and Porrex*: The First Two Quartos', *Studies in Bibliography*, XV (1962), 231–233.

5. Helen Smith, '"This one poore blacke gowne lined with white": The Clothing of the Sixteenth-Century English Book', in Catherine Richardson (ed.), *Clothing Culture 1350–1650* (London: Routledge, 2004), pp. 195–208 (p. 198).

Pity and Identity in the Age of Shakespeare

up as she is 'new apparelled, trimmed, and attired [...] in such forme as she was before'. But she is not made pure, only made to *look* pure.[6] Day's proclaimed motivations for the second edition suggest a focus on content and authenticity, the necessity of purging internal corruption. The language of the note, however, suggests that the *appearance* of these things has a higher emotional value. The outlined restoration of this character is tinged by an unsettling emotional current that prioritises the emotional state of the people *viewing* the woman, over the woman herself: this is perhaps the inevitable result of focusing on a victim's outward appearance. Emotion is frequently referenced in Day's account, but we are given little insight into the woman/text's feeling after the imagined attack: 'she' is framed as a human character when justifying the strong emotional response of the 'frendes' and authors, but her anthropomorphisation does not extend to allow her independent emotional expression. She remains an object in terms of her own perceived capacity for feeling.

In this and other ways, the emotional currents at work in this note are both confused and confusing. The authors' displeasure is directed not at the man who inflicted the violence but rather at the woman herself, for '[running] abroad without leave'. The active verb 'caught' of 'she caught her shame' assumes the possibility of physical autonomy and blame, even as it denies emotional agency: Day voices the woman's emotional consequence – shame – on her behalf. The remedial action taken, however, is not for the woman/text at all. The authors act though the case is 'remedilesse' – there is no hope for the woman herself, then – and they act out of their own 'shamefastnesse'. In spite of the compassionate, corrective tone Day uses here, his note perpetuates the feminised text's circumscription in a male-dominated narrative, both in terms of commercial enterprise and emotional community.

Only once the woman is reworked, and put in 'better forme' is 'she' passed on to Day:

> Since she hath come to me, I have harboured her for her frendes sake and her owne, and I do not dout her parentes the authors will not now be discontent that she goe abroad among you good readers, so it be in honest companie. For she is by my encouragement and others somewhat lesse ashamed of the dishonestie done to her because it was by fraude and force. (sig. A2ʳ)

---

[6] As Mark Breitenberg has argued, redress as Day formulates it 'can only be outward; her "form as it was before" is admitted to be nothing more than a disguised version of an "original" forever lost' (p. 206). Mark Breitenberg, 'Reading Elizabethan Iconicity: *Gorboduc* and the Semiotics of Reform', *English Literary Renaissance*, 18.2 (1988), 194–217.

Violent Spectacle and Violent Feeling

The only active reference to the woman's emotion, that 'she is […] somewhat less ashamed', comes after ameliorative action has been undertaken: she is only permitted to 'feel' once the visual evidence of her 'shame' has been erased, and even then it is once again Day who voices her emotional state. His comment that he has 'harboured her for her frendes sake and her owne' implies a certain sense of community, but the currents of guilt nevertheless remain directed at the imagined victim. This continues even as the passage shifts its emotional focus from the shame of the situation to the anticipated pity and compassion of the reading (and buying) public. The only emotional reference that appears situated within the woman rather than projected onto her ('she is … less ashamed', rather than 'she caught her shame') happens under strict guidance and permission: she feels this way, we are told, because Day has encouraged to her to. She is re-published, to be reconsidered in her new state. The male audience that has attributed shame here has now removed it, but both the attribution and removal are vital to the overall cultivation of a compassionate commercial audience. Even so, the warning that accompanies this publication suggests anything but a guaranteed compassionate reception:

> If she be welcome among you and gently entertained, in favour of the house from whense she is descended, and of her own nature courteously disposed to offend no man, her frendes will thanke you for it. If not, but that she shall be still reproached with her former missehap, or quarrelled at by envious persons, she poor gentlewoman will surely play Lucreces part, and of herself die for shame, and I shall wishe that she had taried still at home with me, where she was welcome […]. (sig. A2^r)

The imaginative capacity of this warning – the worry that she might be 'still reproached with her former missehap' – really only confirms Day's investment in the *appearance* of restoration. In re-presenting the text, Day claims to have removed the primary source of offence (the lack of textual integrity). Nevertheless, in reframing the text as a woman, in mobilising the visual provocation of violent attack, Day also exploits compassion's commercial promise, somehow positioning the text as a candidate for pity. In imagining a new audience, Day produces an important tonal shift: now, at the moment of distribution, the woman/text seems finally to be backed by the community that has restored her. It is made clear that this new woman/text is now in a sanctioned form, and therefore once again fit to 'goe abroad among you good readers'. She is ready for a compassionate reception, but more importantly she can now be viewed comfortably.

What is striking about Day's preface is not its use of emotion in depicting another's suffering, but how that emotion gets twisted, ultimately focusing more on the male audience than the assaulted woman/text. On the surface,

Pity and Identity in the Age of Shakespeare

the reception and restoration of the text is framed as an effort to help, a desire to see things put right. And yet the structure of the preface suggests that the 'pitying' reaction that Day is courting from a buying public is only possible because of the more worrying response from the authors and the publisher himself. Their first reaction to the female/text shares little with the connective or communal elements of an emotion like pity, but rather foregrounds displeasure. Day postpones his eventual pursuit of a compassionate audience in order to chastise the 'bescratched', 'berayed', 'disfigured', 'dishonested' woman/text, and emotionally position the men receiving her. She is blamed for '[running] abroad without leave', compared to other 'wantons', and accused of '[catching] her shame'. This behaviour, Day notes, cause the authors to be 'very much displeased' with her; their restorative efforts only come after they recognise 'the case as it is remedilesse', and even then – they repair her for their own benefit. Day's suggestion that the authors acted out of 'common honestie and shamefastnesse' implies a sense of responsibility to respond to the pitiable state of the text, but the reaction is preceded by blame rhetoric. They act because they must, but the response seems almost begrudging, as if they resent being compelled in this way.

Day goes on to envision an intimate, unsettling interaction between reader and text, in which the reader responds to and becomes involved with the text in complex ways: the errant 'W.G.' creates a victim whose presence causes discomfort, invites judgement, produces emotion in those who view it/her, and subsequently requires restorative attention and action. Day's final worry, that in the event of an unfavourable reception, this 'poor gentlewoman will surely play Lucreces part, and of herself die for shame', reminds the reader of a responsibility to respond with the appropriate emotion – and yet the 'appropriate' emotion is significantly different to the initial emotions expressed by the 'frendes' of this woman/text. This late reference to Lucrece is yet another signal of the passage's sharp emotional transition from shame to pity and compassion. Like Lucrece, Day assures us that the 'dishonestie' done to *this* violated woman 'was by fraude and force'; he notes that she is 'of her own nature courteously disposed to offend no man'. Day's reference to Lucrece gives his own violated woman a sense of legitimacy by aligning her with a more famous figure whose chastity is already confirmed.[7] It is

---

[7] Although Day employs Lucrece as a legitimising point of reference here, there is a long history of debate over Lucrece's complicity in her own rape. See for example Roy Battenhouse, *Shakespearean Tragedy: Its Art and Its Christian Premises* (Bloomington, IN: University of Indiana Press, 1969), pp. 3–41; another critic notes that Lucrece 'insists on killing herself because although her mind is innocent, *her body is guilty*' (p. 31, my emphasis), see Arthur L. Little, *Shakespeare Jungle Fever: National-Imperial Re-visions of Race, Rape, and Sacrifice* (Stanford, CA: Stanford University

a reminder to the reader to place the newly restored state of the text over the earlier, corrupted form, but the reference also reworks the source of emotional provocation: it is now not the state of the text to which readers must respond, but a larger history of violation and redemption. By pulling Lucrece into the preface, Day effectively grounds his edition of *Gorboduc* in a longer and more established narrative. As it is presented, this is a call for the reader to join a community of others who have responded with pity and compassion. The suggestion is that the Lucrece figure is made not just through violation, but also through the subsequent reception she endures: it is a cycle of emotional confrontation and response. The reader therefore becomes partly responsible for this 'woman's' fate.

Setting aside the emotional tensions at work here, Day's text also frames the violated woman as a place for men to meet. Beyond the more straightforward discussion of the violated text/woman as a figure that brings the friends, authors, publisher, and reading audience together, the woman of Day's text is repeatedly positioned in male-dominated space: Day speaks of the house of corruption, the home of her friends, the 'house from whense she is descended', and the printer's own 'home'. This restored text is also, of course, a product of the printing house. In each instance the violated woman becomes something to be worked on, within a specific communal and presumptively male space. While this reading positions the violated female as the central figure of its emotional community, Day's preface imagines her without agency: the woman/text is transferred to and from a number of spaces, she is repeatedly subjected to restorative work, and she is 'thrust out of doors' twice, both by her assailant and by Day, when she is re-presented to the public. Although the text is attributed human capabilities on a number of occasions – she 'runs' abroad, and 'catches' her shame – she never speaks. Always the subject of comment but never the speaker herself, Day's violated female *creates* an emotional community, but is not permitted to participate fully in it.

In many ways, Day's preface mobilises a number of themes common to early modern depictions of the Lucrece tale: the signs of female violation and its publication, the link between emotional provocation and looking, the solicitation of pity, and the more problematic emotions that might accompany or pre-empt that response. These elements combine to offer an insight into the formation of early modern community, and in particular

---

Press, 2000). Coppélia Kahn gives a survey of this type of critical interpretation in 'The Rape in Shakespeare's *Lucrece*', *Shakespeare Studies*, 9 (1976), 45–72 (p. 69). Catherine Belsey further explores notions of consent in Shakespeare's Lucrece story in 'Tarquin Dispossessed: Expropriation and Consent in *The Rape of Lucrece*', *Shakespeare Quarterly*, 53 (2001), 315–335.

Pity and Identity in the Age of Shakespeare

they shed light on the ways in which the violated woman participated in communities largely formed on the back of her violation and its publication. Through an examination of Shakespeare's early tragedy *Titus Andronicus* (written with George Peele), early modern translations of the Livy and Ovid Lucreces, Heywood's *The Rape of Lucrece* and finally, Shakespeare's *The Rape of Lucrece*, this chapter considers texts that work with the same emotional elements that Day outlines in his preface. Many of these examples, some of which are equally (if not more) disturbing in their depiction of violation, also imagine a greater capacity for female agency in these exchanges than is afforded by Day. Stressing the confrontation of visual distress and pity as tools for communication and community, in this chapter I argue that the Shakespearean Lucrece figures extend beyond the more traditional imaginings of violated female agency, to imagine something more positive, productive, and pointed in these moments of emotional confrontation. Responding to recent scholarship on Shakespeare's *The Rape of Lucrece* emphasising Lucrece's rhetorical strength, I contend that the invocation of pity in that poem in fact relies more on her visual agency, and feeds into an existing tradition of depicting non-verbal communication in Lucrece narratives.[8] Whereas in Day, the speechlessness of the Lucrece figure is negative – something that relegates her to mere topic, or object of speech – elsewhere the emphasis on visuality presents speechlessness something more positive, embodied, and unpredictable. Shakespeare's *The Rape of Lucrece* and *Titus Andronicus* scrutinise the notions of pity and community that Day and others exploit, while simultaneously creating new space for alternative channels of meaning and agency. Shakespeare explores a visuality that is more powerful than other early modern depictions of Lucrece imagine, and more positive than what is permitted by interpretations of Lucrece as a purely visual object.

AT THE BOUNDARIES OF EMOTIONAL EXTREMITY

The most extreme of the Shakespearean Lucrece figures, *Titus Andronicus'* Lavinia is a visual and an emotional provocation to those she encounters onstage. Through Lavinia, *Titus* explores the emotional impact of witnessing female bodily harm: we are confronted by the uncomfortable presence of the 'ruined' woman whose very image seems to demand pity. Through Lavinia, *Titus* highlights possible connections between visibly 'ruined' femininity, pity, and the creation of emotional subjects. These elements are further developed

---

[8]   See William Weaver, "'O, teach me how to make mine excuse": Forensic Performance in *Lucrece*', *Shakespeare Quarterly*, 59 (2008), 421–449, and Lorna Hutson, *Circumstantial Shakespeare* (Oxford: Oxford University Press, 2015).

Violent Spectacle and Violent Feeling

in *The Rape of Lucrece*, where the relationship between emotional vulnerability and interpersonal connection is more explicitly tested.

Titus is marked by its overwhelming violence, and its habit of leaving characters vulnerable to the cruelty to others. Opening with the eponymous character's 'cruel, irreligious piety' in denying pity to a suffering mother and claiming the sacrifice of Tamora's eldest son, the play promptly sees Titus kill one of his own.[9] Bassianus, Martius, and Quintus are quickly eliminated; Titus cuts off his own hand, and later he bakes Tamora's remaining sons into a pie and serves it to her.[10] The violence of these acts nevertheless pales in comparison to the aggression directed at Lavinia, who enters the stage during the second act, 'her hands cut off and her tongue cut out, and ravished' (SD 2.3).[11] This bloodlust, impossible to ignore, has been the subject of much critical scrutiny. Dover Wilson famously likened the play to 'some broken-down cart, laden with bleeding corpses', while another critic more recently commented that '*Titus Andronicus* stands out as especially histrionic in its virtuosic, almost gleeful depiction of bodily destruction'.[12] Coleridge believed that *Titus* was 'obviously intended to excite vulgar audiences by its scenes of blood and horror – to our ears shocking and disgusting'.[13] These observations all gesture towards the problematic distress the play causes. Eugene Waith argued that the play's violence, matched with its

---

[9]   William Shakespeare, *Titus Andronicus*, ed. by Jonathan Bate (London: Bloomsbury Arden, 1995), 1.1.133. All references to *Titus Andronicus* in this chapter will be to this edition and given parenthetically.

[10] S. Clark Hulse notes, that 'Even among revenge tragedies *Titus Andronicus* is especially brutal', and calculates that the play features, '14 killings, 9 of them on stage, 6 severed members, 1 rape (or two or three, depending on how you count), 1 live burial, 1 case of insanity, and 1 of cannibalism – an average of 5.2 atrocities per act, or one for every 97 lines' (p. 106). A.C. Hamilton famously praised the play for this precise reason, arguing that we should appreciate the play's excess as a test of 'how much reality a tragedy can contain' (p. 204). See S. Clark Hulse, 'Wresting the Alphabet: Oratory and Action in *Titus Andronicus*', *Criticism*, 21 (1979), 106–118; A.C. Hamilton, '*Titus Andronicus*: The Form of Shakespearian Tragedy', *Shakespeare Quarterly*, 14 (1963), 201–213.

[11] The stage direction appears in the first printed edition of the play in 1594, and is preserved in the second quarto (London, 1600), sig. E1ʳ; the third quarto (London, 1611), sig. E1ʳ; and of course, the First Folio (London, 1623), sig. Dd2ʳ.

[12] Dover Wilson, 'Introduction', in *Titus Andronicus* (Cambridge: Cambridge University Press, 1948), pp. i–lxxii, p. xii. William W. Weber, '"Worse Than Philomel": Violence, Revenge, and Meta-Allusion in *Titus Andronicus*', *Studies in Philology*, 112.4 (2015), 698–717 (p. 699).

[13] Samuel Coleridge, *Coleridge's Shakespearean Criticism*, ed. by T.M. Raysor (Cambridge, MA: Harvard University Press, 1930), II, p. 31, my emphasis.

Pity and Identity in the Age of Shakespeare

highly descriptive language, has 'served to damn the play utterly'.[14] Nonetheless, in Coleridge's comment in particular we might see something more: a suggestion that the violence of *Titus* equally defines the viewers, the audience themselves. What looks like slippage in Coleridge – the movement from visual ('scenes of blood and horror') to aural ('to our ears shocking and disgusting') – in fact gets to the heart of the critical response to this play. The central case against *Titus* is a combined issue of visual and aural excess: it seems that while staging extreme violence is itself problematic, it is simply unforgivable to force the audience to then experience the gore *again* by pairing the spectacle with a detailed description. One critic has argued this point specifically in the context of Marcus's first encounter with the ravished Lavinia at 2.4, commenting that his language in this scene 'forces us to see, detail by descriptive detail, the spectacle we are already beholding'.[15] Arguments objecting to *Titus* on the grounds of reasonable limits tend to focus on physical violence: these arguments are a response to the wounds the characters inflict on others, what they sustain themselves, and how much of this the audience can bear to witness.[16] However, the criticism surrounding the play also suggests a deeper-seated discomfort, something located beyond the physical display of severed hands and tongues. The critical discomfort around *Titus* suggests the play is equally invested in pushing emotional boundaries, a piece that relentlessly explores human limits and the consequences of exceeding them.

The bulk of scholarship on *Titus* has addressed what is perceived as gratuitous physical violence. Lavinia is really the central symbol of that violent tendency – both the most extreme representation of it, and the most

---

[14] Eugene Waith, 'The Metamorphosis of Violence in *Titus Andronicus*', *Shakespeare Survey*, 10 (1957), 39–49 (p. 39).

[15] Albert Tricomi, 'The Aesthetics of Mutilation in *Titus Andronicus*', *Shakespeare Survey*, 27 (1974), 11–19 (p. 17).

[16] The issue of the play's effect on an audience is a constant worry. Peter Brook's 1955 Stratford production – which has been credited as the first step in redeeming the play's reputation in popular opinion – made a number of revisions that Richard Findlater classified as 'formaliz[ing] the horror'. Richard Findlater, 'Shakespearean Atrocities', *The Twentieth Century* (October 1955), 364–372 (p. 369). One notable example of Brook's revisions was evident in Lavinia, whose wounds were not staged explicitly but instead were represented by scarlet ribbons. Even in performances where the violence is presented as written, it is unusual to find a production that makes no concession to the audience whatsoever: the 2006 production of *Titus* at Shakespeare's New Globe in London, for example, published a warning of the risk of fainting, and provided first-aid attendants as a precaution. Stephanie Condron, 'Not for the Fainthearted', *The Telegraph*, 03 June 2006 <http://www.telegraph.co.uk/news/uknews/1520196/Not-for-the-fainthearted.html> [10 December 2011].

Violent Spectacle and Violent Feeling

consistent. Her frequent appearance onstage is a recurring confrontation, and one that denies any instinct to achieve distance and respite from her gruesome violation. Just like the characters onstage, we have no choice but to react to Lavinia's presence. Suggesting anything but a sympathetic, victim-focused reaction to a character like Lavinia is problematic, especially as her torment is both extreme and unjustified. And yet the critical response to *Titus* – both generally, and when directed towards the mutilated Lavinia in particular – hints at an underlying, barely-expressed unwillingness to engage with the spectacle of horror. There are many critical attempts to present Lavinia as somehow something *other* than a raped and mutilated woman, and it is difficult to avoid understanding these as large-scale critical avoidance. Carolyn Williams has suggested that because of audience reaction to the 'uncomfortable spectacle' of Lavinia's death, 'critics and directors prefer to make her a symbol of "the destruction of the Roman political order", rather than contemplating Lavinia herself'.[17] This trend of recasting Lavinia into something more palatable appears elsewhere in the scholarship on *Titus*.[18] Douglas Green, for example, concedes that the 'utter victim' Lavinia occasionally 'threaten[s] to usurp Titus's centrality', but he then immediately retreats from this position, going on to argue that this 'notorious female' is in fact '*made to serve* the construction of Titus', that her suffering *is not her own*, but rather an 'articulat[ion] of Titus' own suffering and victimization'.[19] Transferring the power of Lavinia's ordeal to her father neatly avoids direct confrontation with Lavinia, locating the significance of her character beyond her actual self, and certainly beyond her own suffering.

This tendency to remove or relocate the provocative aspects of Lavinia is echoed by another critic who suggests the impossibility of properly reading a character of whom we are 'offer[ed] only glimpses […] except as dismembered and silent', as if Lavinia's completeness as a character is

---

[17] Carolyn D. Williams, '"Silence, like a Lucrece knife": Shakespeare and the Meanings of Rape', *The Yearbook of English Studies*, 23 (1993), 93–110 (p. 93).

[18] Lavinia is frequently figured (both by critics and in the play itself) as a *text* to be read: see for example Mary Laughlin Fawcett, 'Arms/Words/Tears: Language and the Body in *Titus Andronicus*', *English Literary History*, 50.2 (1983), 261–277. Cynthia Marshall comments that for many readers and viewers, Lavinia is so 'undone by this overexposure that [she] fails to acquire a sense of subjective identity altogether; for them, she remains merely a sketch, a cartoon, an unfortunate image'. See: Cynthia Marshall, *The Shattering of the Self: Violence, Subjectivity, & Early Modern Texts* (Baltimore, MD and London: The Johns Hopkins University Press, 2002), p. 127.

[19] Douglas E. Green, 'Interpreting "her martyr'd signs": Gender and Tragedy in *Titus Andronicus*', *Shakespeare Quarterly*, 40.3 (1989), 317–326 (p. 319 and p. 322), my emphasis.

Pity and Identity in the Age of Shakespeare

somehow reduced by the loss of her limbs and tongue.[20] Still another critic views Lavinia as the best example of a number of Shakespearean women 'under erasure [...] marginalized by their gender, by their putative or real madness, or by their violation'.[21] Others hint at their unwillingness to dwell on Lavinia by directing disapproval towards those who do linger on her, as in the case of Harold Bloom's extraordinarily graphic assessment: 'If sadomasochism is your preferred mode, then *Titus Andronicus* is your meat, and you can join Tamora in her cannibal feast with the same gusto that you experience in raping Lavinia, slicing out her tongue, and chopping off her hands'.[22] Even where critics are not openly dismissive of Lavinia and her ordeal, this way of reading is directed by the impulse to redefine the character in a more manageable, distanced, sanitised way, or to find a good reason to ignore her in favour of other concerns. In this way the violated, emotionally provocative woman becomes a symbol of something else or an object (a corrupted text, if we return to the Day example), rather than a bald, unavoidable depiction of a human agent demanding direct emotional engagement.

On this reading, the negative reaction to *Titus* has less to do with the play's physical violence than the emotional violence that accompanies it. Perhaps critics of the play have had – even if it is on an unacknowledged level – difficulty directly engaging (or interacting for too long a time) with a character so visually and emotionally provocative. As such, we might wonder if the forcible elicitation of pity in this play is just an extension of its violence, this time directed at those who *view* or encounter the physical evidence of brutality. Bloom's remarkable comment above hinges on the projection of a sadomasochistic response to *Titus*: for Bloom, Lavinia draws in audiences who relish violence, but the language of his comment suggests that the only pleasure to be derived here is masochistic. In this sense, Lavinia becomes an instrument by which Shakespeare explores spectacle as a type of emotional aggression. For all that *Titus* has suffered critically for a perceived over-reliance on violence, this depiction of emotion as itself a type of violence is more original and nuanced than has previously been acknowledged.

For those who share the stage, Lavinia's presence is impossible to ignore, but she herself has no way of controlling these confrontations: her visual signs cause obvious anguish, but she has no way of containing them. In many ways, this strong visual presence aligns Lavinia with Lucrece – and

---

[20] Katherine Rowe, 'Dismembering and Forgetting in *Titus Andronicus*', *Shakespeare Quarterly*, 45.3 (1994), 279–303 (p. 300).

[21] Marjorie Garber, *Shakespeare's Ghost Writers: Literature as Uncanny Causality* (New York and London: Methuen, 1987), p. 25.

[22] Harold Bloom, *Shakespeare: The Invention of the Human* (London: Fourth Estate, 1999), p. 79.

Violent Spectacle and Violent Feeling

indeed, she is repeatedly likened to Lucrece when Aaron notes that 'Lucrece was not more chaste | Than this Lavinia' (1.1.608–609). However, true to the overarching tenor of *Titus*, Lavinia is Lucrece pushed to the extreme: whereas Lucrece's *greatest* tool (as I shall argue) is her visuality, Lavinia's visuality is her *only* tool. While Titus's daughter, without hands, or a tongue, is far more restricted in her expression than is Lucrece, these stark restrictions produce in Lavinia a focused depiction of the relationship between female visuality and emotional provocation: her options are strictly limited to vision and violent spectacle.

Read in the context of the many comparisons the play makes between Lavinia and other figures or objects, she is a largely derivative character, an 'amalgamation' or 'anthology' of other meanings and narratives.[23] She is Lucrece; she is Philomel (2.2.43); she is even a physical part of Rome's landscape, its 'rich ornament' (1.1.55).[24] Rather than signalling a lack of a distinct identity, for Lavinia's character the persistent allusions to other women offer crucial points of reference. Like Lucrece, Lavinia is a chaste woman; like Philomel, 'some Tereus hath deflowered [her]' (2.3.26).[25] In a play in which the men are singularly incapable of reading the women, Lavinia's alignment with better-known (literarily-inscribed) women helpfully glosses her own identity: she is categorised with women whose histories are already familiar and established in the culture of the educated male. However, placing Lavinia in the company of these women does more than signal her status as a symbol of violated female chastity: it puts her in a tradition of violated women who go on to communicate their distress to an active community of emotional agents. Lavinia's negotiation of this task, and the resulting pity she elicits, finally produces a distinct character.

Lavinia's relationship between the visual spectacle she presents and the emotion she prompts sets her apart from the women that make up her literary ancestry. Lucrece, as I will go on to suggest, uses vision in a very particular and active way, directing her gaze in order to stimulate pity and bind people to her. Though heavily reliant on her visual presence, Lucrece

---

[23] Sonya L. Brockman, 'Trauma and Abandoned Testimony in *Titus Andronicus* and *Rape of Lucrece*', *College Literature*, 44.3 (2017), 344–378 (p. 350); John Wesley, 'Rhetorical Delivery for Renaissance English: Voice, Gesture, Emotion, and the Sixteenth-Century Vernacular Turn', *Renaissance Quarterly*, 68.4 (2015), 1265–1296 (p. 1285).

[24] On Lavinia as an extension of Rome, see David Willbern, 'Rape and Revenge in *Titus Andronicus*', *English Literary Renaissance*, 8 (1978), 159–182, esp. pp. 161–163.

[25] The influence of Philomel's story on Shakespeare is further explored by Jane Newman in 'And Let Mild Women to Him Lose Their Mildness: Philomela, Female Violence, and Shakespeare's *The Rape of Lucrece*', *Shakespeare Quarterly*, 45.3 (1994), 304–326.

Pity and Identity in the Age of Shakespeare

does not forfeit speech altogether, but instead uses herself as a spectacle in conjunction with her words. Philomel engages with vision in some sense too, inasmuch as she creates an image that communicates a message on her behalf. However, Philomel's preference for language is clear: she only forfeits it because she is forced to do so. Golding's Ovid sees Philomel lose her tongue precisely because she demonstrates rhetorical prowess, and reveals her intention to use it:

> Yea I my selfe rejecting shame thy doings will bewray.
> And if I may have power to come abrode, them blase I will
> In open face of all the world. Or if thou keepe me still
> As prisoner in these woods, my voyce the verie woods shall fill,
> And make the stones to understand. Let Heaven to this give eare
> And all the Gods and powers therein if any God be there.[26]

It is only at this point that Philomel loses her tongue, after asserting a 'voyce the verie woods shall fill', a voice capable of bringing inanimate objects to understanding. The description of Philomel's severed tongue further suggests a part with its own agency:

> The tip fell downe and quivering on the ground
> As though that it had murmured it made a certaine sound.
> [...]
> The tip of *Philomelas* tongue did wriggle to and fro,
> And nearer to hir mistresseward in dying still did go. (sig. L4ᵛ)[27]

---

[26] William Golding, *The xv bookes of P. Ovidius Naso, entytuled Metamorphosis* (London: 1567), sig. L4ᵛ. In the original Latin: 'ipsa pudore proiecto tua facta loquar: si copia detur, in populos veniam; si silvis clausa tenebor, inplebo silvas et conscia saxa movebo; audiet haec aether et si deus ullus in illo est! [I will myself cast shame aside and proclaim what you have done. If I should have the chance, I would go where people throng and tell it; if I am kept shut up in these woods, I will fill the woods with my story and move the very rocks to pity]' (Book VI, p. 327). All Latin quotations from Ovid's *Metamorphoses*, and modern translations, come from Ovid, *Metamorphoses*, trans. Frank Justus Miller (London: William Heinemann, 1977). According to Lynn Enterline, Philomela represents a 'violated bod[y]' that 'provide[s] Ovid with the occasion to reflect on the power and limitations of language'. Lynn Enterline, *The Rhetoric of the Body from Ovid to Shakespeare* (Cambridge: Cambridge University Press, 2000), p. 3.

[27] 'radix micat ultima linguae, ipsa iacet terraeque tremens inmurmurat atrae, utque salire solet mutilatae cauda colubrae, palpitat et moriens dominae vestigia quaerit [The mangled root quivers, while the severed tongue lies palpitating on the dark earth, faintly murmuring; and, as the severed tail of a mangled snake is wont to writhe, it twitches convulsively, and with its last dying movement it seeks its mistress's feet]' (Book VI, Miller p. 327).

Violent Spectacle and Violent Feeling

This account of the severed tongue references independent movement: it 'wriggle[s] to and fro', and appears to move toward reunion with its mistress. The articulation of the tongue and voice's strength – both before and after severing – shows a clear bias towards language and oral communication. Philomel only takes to the tapestry out of necessity; it is clear where her expressive preferences lie. This same principle of necessity could easily be applied to Lavinia: also stripped of most methods of communication, she is restricted to options so limited she has to be guided towards them by another character. The restriction Lavinia suffers is a violence that acknowledges a literary tradition by curtailing the methods of post-trauma communication used by both Lucrece and Philomel. That restriction also prompts a response that differentiates Lavinia from her literary predecessors: the intensification of Lavinia's violation also intensifies the emotional confrontation she represents. The articulated need, in the play, to understand and avenge her, importantly reflects an intensified emotional state in those who view her. In this way, *Titus* showcases, among its many violences, the violent cultivation of emotional agents.

Both Lucrece and Philomel are restricted in ways that strike at the cores of their identities: for Lucrece, Tarquin threatens to destroy her husband's honour, something with which she strongly identifies. Philomel is silenced after demonstrating her predilection for words. Lavinia, however, loses the power of speech and (it is assumed) the ability to write. The moment in which she reclaims that capacity, where she 'takes the staff in her mouth, and guides it with her stumps, and writes' (IV.i.76, stage direction) strongly evokes Io, who, having been transformed into a white heifer, uses her hoof to scratch out her name and to reveal her identity to her father. Lavinia's loss of her hands and tongue evokes the comparable loss that Io experiences, after being transformed into the cow:

> [She] did devise,
> To *Argus* for to lift hir handes in méeke and humble wise,
> She sawe she had no handes at all: and when she did assay
> To make complaint, she lowed out. (Golding, sig. C3^r)[28]

Visually the two characters are very different, but they are also fundamentally the same: both lose crucial capacities, and for both, communication is virtually impossible. Before she regains her ability to write, Lavinia's inability

---

[28] 'illa etiam supplex Argo cum bracchia vellet tendere, non habuit, quae bracchia tenderet Argo, et conata queri mugitus edidit ore pertimuitque sonos propriaque exterrita voce est [When she strove to stretch out suppliant arms to Argus, she had no arms to stretch; and when she attempted to voice her complaints, she only mooed]' (Book I, Miller, p. 47).

89

Pity and Identity in the Age of Shakespeare

to communicate is the play's glaring issue: while the audience understands her attempts to explain her situation, her family remains unable (in spite of Titus's claims to the contrary) to 'interpret all her martyred signs' (3.2.36).

By restricting her communicative powers, Lavinia's wounds reduce her to an entirely visual presence. Even her scrawled writing is a visual cue, a sign of someone else's guilt. However, Lavinia's writing is relatively unimportant to the reaction she elicits: the revelation of her tormentors moves the play along, but it is to the *sight* of Lavinia that the other characters really respond. Given that her visual appeal is established almost as soon as she appears onstage – she is, remember, 'Rome's rich ornament' (1.1.55) – this is an obvious miscalculation on the part of Chiron and Demetrius: they believe they have restricted her ability to communicate, but in reality they have only succeeded in bolstering her visual (and by extension, emotional) impact. As she faces her tormentors, Lavinia shows some recognition that Rome (particularly male Rome) has a habit of looking at her. Begging Tamora to 'keep me from their worse-than-killing lust | And tumble me into some loathsome pit', Lavinia hopes at least to end up in a place 'Where never man's eye may behold my body' (2.2.175–177). She asks to be spared from Chiron and Demetrius's lust, *and*, via the pit, to be spared from the male gaze to which she has been (and later will be) subjected.

This scene of rape and mutilation hinges on Lavinia's failure to elicit the pity of the Goths, in spite of her repeated, explicit calls for it. 'Do thou entreat [Tamora] to show a woman's pity', she begs of Chiron (2.2.147). When he refuses, she pleads again: 'O be to me, though thy hard heart say no, | Nothing so kind, but something pitiful' (2.2.155–156). Lavinia identifies pity as the one thing that can help her in this moment, and she is single-minded in her pursuit of it. Given the otherwise muddled communication of Act III, and that Lavinia is, at this moment, at the height of her clarity, Tamora's response is ironic: 'I know not what it means; away with her!' (2.2.157). Lavinia has all her faculties here, and there can be no doubt about her message. Still, she is unable to elicit the pity she requires, unable to cultivate and direct emotions in others. The play is consistent in denying female characters the opportunity to win pity through oratory: Lavinia's failure here echoes Tamora's earlier pleas for her son's life (also futile). For many critics these pitiful failures characterise the play's overarching emotional perspective: David Willbern has argued that this dearth of human pity is an integral part of *Titus*'s cultural landscape, that there simply is 'no natural sympathy in Rome'; Thomas Dixon recently commented that from start to finish, *Titus* is 'a drama about the failure

Violent Spectacle and Violent Feeling

of pity'.[29] For Lavinia however the emotional landscape appears to shift in the wake of her violation: a number of characters become emotional agents explicitly in response to her, becoming almost desperate in their desire to offer her their pity. This pity is tinged with violence, predicated on blood and brutality, and almost forced by the extremity of the damage, from the other characters onstage (and perhaps, indeed, from audiences and critics as well). Lavinia's mere presence becomes provocative to those around her, who respond with great emotional force even before they are able to understand her situation fully.

The scenes in which the characters respond to the violated Lavinia are, for critics, among the most problematic in the play: the drawn-out efforts of Lavinia's family to understand her suffering are almost as difficult to watch as the scenes of graphic violence. Perhaps the most controversial of these communication scenes is that in which Marcus discovers his mutilated niece: it takes him forty lines to come to grips with what he sees. Critics have tended to classify Marcus's meandering descriptions of Lavinia as a cold, distant, and inappropriate response to a clearly assaulted woman.[30] This, I think, is the wrong way to understand Marcus's reaction: these moments are fraught with emotion, moments in which the mere sight of Lavinia renders Marcus incapable of a cogent response. He begins almost unwilling to engage with the reality of the situation, wishing simultaneously to be woken from this terrible dream, and removed from this life altogether:

[29] Willbern, p. 173. Thomas Dixon, *Weeping Britannia: Portrait of a Nation in Tears* (Oxford: Oxford University Press, 2015), p. 49. On this see also: Danielle St. Hilaire, 'Allusion and Sacrifice in *Titus Andronicus*', *Studies in English Literature, 1500–1900*, 49.2 (2009), 311–331. Richard Meek has also identified 'the absence of pity or compassion' as 'a key feature of the play' in his excellent study of sympathy in *Titus*. See: Richard Meek, 'O, What a Sympathy of Woe is This': Passionate Sympathy in *Titus Andronicus*, 287–297 (p. 294).

[30] There are a few notable exceptions: Lorna Hutson, for example, calls Marcus's speech 'extraordinarily humane and humanizing'. 'Rethinking the "Spectacle of the Scaffold": Juridical Epistemologies and English Revenge Tragedy', *Representations*, 89 (2005), 30–58 (p. 48). See also Hutson in *The Invention of Suspicion: Law and Mimesis in Shakespeare and Renaissance Drama* (Oxford: Oxford University Press, 2007), esp. pp. 90–103; Karen Cunningham, '"Scars Can Witness": Trials by Ordeal and Lavinia's Body in *Titus Andronicus*', in Katherine Anne Ackley (ed.), *Women and Violence in Literature: An Essay Collection* (New York, NY: Garland, 1990), pp. 139–162; Heather James, 'Cultural Disintegration in *Titus Andronicus*: Mutilating Titus, Virgil, Rome', in James Redmond (ed.), *Violence in Drama* (Cambridge: Cambridge University Press, 1991), pp. 123–140; and Liz Oakley-Brown, '*Titus Andronicus* and the Cultural Politics of Translation in Early Modern England', *Renaissance Studies*, 19 (2005), 325–347.

Pity and Identity in the Age of Shakespeare

MARCUS

If I do dream, would all my wealth would wake me;
If I do wake, some planet strike me down
That I may slumber an eternal sleep. (2.3.13–15)

Unable to escape, he instead describes each of Lavinia's injuries in agonising detail:

Speak, gentle niece, what stern ungentle hands
Hath lopped and hewed and made thy body bare
Of her two branches
[…]
Alas, a crimson river of warm blood,
Like to a bubbling fountain stirred with wind,
Doth rise and fall between thy rosed lips
[…]
But sure some Tereus hath deflowered thee
And, lest thou shouldst detect him, cut thy tongue.
Ah, now thou turn'st away thy face for shame,
[…]
Fair Philomela, why she but lost her tongue,
And in a tedious sampler sewed her mind;
But, lovely niece, that mean is cut from thee.
A craftier Tereus, cousin, hast thou met,
And he hath cut those pretty fingers off. (2.3.16–42)

It may be the case that Marcus's speech lacks tact, but it certainly does not lack emotion: these are the words of someone too overwhelmed by what he sees to speak eloquently. Marcus's exhaustive cataloguing – outlining the details of Lavinia's violation – is an attempt to piece together the reality before him. The account itself is not unfeeling, though it is more focused on the trauma Marcus sustains in *viewing* Lavinia, and its emotional impact on *him*. As William W. Weber has argued, this speech is really a search for *relief* – and predominantly, Marcus's relief: 'Marcus's first reaction is one desiring the relief of disbelief … his next, one desiring relief in death'.[31] The problem of the speech seems also to be that Marcus feels before he understands; he identifies the source of that feeling, the vision that provokes it, before thinking of what needs to happen next for the person behind that vision. 'Do not draw back', he begs Lavinia, 'for we will mourn with thee; | O, could our mourning ease thy misery!' (2.3.56–57). Marcus is distraught, and – perhaps in an effort to make himself feel better – attempts to bind himself emotionally to Lavinia long before she

---

[31] Weber, p. 708.

Violent Spectacle and Violent Feeling

finds a way to communicate what has happened. The emotional response of others – 'our mourning' is certain, even if its utility is not yet clear.

For Lavinia, this scene with Marcus begins a pattern of display and response, and we see in each case how quickly the sight of this woman elicits distress and pity from those who confront the spectacle of her. Moreover, Marcus expects that this will be the case, telling Lavinia to 'Come, let us go and make thy father blind, | For such a sight will blind a father's eye' (2.3.52–53). Marcus is not wrong to expect that Lavinia's presence will force a strong reaction from her father, though in many ways Titus's is the most measured response. When Marcus introduces Lavinia with, 'This *was* thy daughter,' Titus quickly corrects him: 'Why, Marcus, so she *is*' (3.1.63–64, my emphasis). Unlike the other characters, Titus's insistence on retaining the present tense – 'so she *is*' – also denies any suggestion that Lavinia's mutilation has erased the wholeness of her character. Lucius gives the more predictable reaction, falling to his knees and proclaiming, in a move that neatly robs Lavinia of her personhood, 'Ay me, this *object* kills me' (3.1.65, my emphasis). Sonya L. Brockman argues that 'in his despair, Lucius emphasizes Lavinia's new position as an *object* of spectacle [...] now only *a thing* that provokes pity and sorrow'.[32] Titus's insistence on Lavinia's continued humanity, however, seems intent on establishing her now as a person, an agent capable of provoking pity. He is moreover insistent on the impact of her image, almost relishing the discomfort that Lavinia provokes; he dwells on it, forcing Lucius to do the same: 'Faint-hearted boy, arise and look upon her' (3.1.66). Later he reiterates the demand, crying, '*Look*, Marcus, ah son Lucius, *look on her!*' (3.1.111).

The common theme amongst the Andronicii is the force of emotional reaction when confronted with Lavinia: Marcus, Titus and Lucius are all eager to offer Lavinia their pity; they all react as if forced to respond; they are all resolved to act on her behalf even before they fully understand what has happened to her. This is without question the result of the visual spectacle she presents: here, the visual confrontation supercedes the explicit call for pity. As Titus notes, it is not so much the thought of Lavinia's situation that impacts, but the physical evidence of it. He comments:

Titus
Had I but seen thy picture in this plight
It would have matted me; what shall I do
Now I behold thy lively body so? (3.1.104–106)

The distinction between the 'picture' and 'thy lively body' places an emphasis on the emotional power of Lavinia's physical presence: it gives her a new, specifically confrontational impact on those who encounter her. Moreover,

---

[32] Brockman, p. 355, my emphasis.

Pity and Identity in the Age of Shakespeare

her presence carries an important intensification of emotion, an ability to transfer that intensity to others.

Perhaps what is most interesting about Lavinia's narrative, however, is its ending. For all that he consistently demands that other people look at his ruined daughter, Titus eventually kills her. Is this because he can no longer stand her presence, and the emotion it prompts? Consider Saturninus's response, when Titus asks for his opinion on Virginius: Saturninus suggests that he was right to have killed his daughter, Virginia, after she was 'enforced, stained and deflowered' (5.3.38), 'Because the girl should not survive her shame, | *And by her presence still renew* [her father's] *sorrows*' (5.3.40–41, my emphasis). The discussion openly addresses the possibility that the sight of a mutilated woman will create distress for those who view her, and the scene acknowledges the negative audience reaction to Lavinia's mutilated body. Titus reveals the formerly veiled Lavinia – publishing the work of Chiron and Demetrius – and decrees, 'Die, die Lavinia, and thy shame with thee, | *And with thy shame thy father's sorrow die*' (5.3.45–46). Titus can avenge his daughter, but he cannot repair her: by seeing her tongue cut out, and her hands chopped off, Shakespeare ensures that Lavinia can never be, as Day proposes, 'new apparelled, trimmed, and attired her in such form as she was before'. Even once her rape and mutilation is revenged, there is no way to assuage the emotional distress she causes. This is a discomfort that cannot be endured permanently, with no hope of restoration, and so, in a turn that is both shocking (and, problematically, perhaps a bit relieving), she dies.

Lavinia's death is noteworthy especially because it is necessitated more by emotion than the traditional Augustinian objections about shame and dishonour: although Marcus initially expresses the worry that Lavinia feels ashamed – 'Ah, now thou turn'st away thy face for shame!' (2.3.28) – the reference in 5.3 is the first time that Titus makes any suggestion of it. From the first moment of confrontation with the vision of his mutilated daughter, Titus insists on preserving her identity as an Andronicii: he corrects Lucius's identification of Lavinia as an 'object', in one sentence protecting her position as a woman and as his daughter with his insistent 'so she is'. Even so, as Lavinia's wounds compromise her physical and vocal agency, they also make ambiguous the circumstances of her death, particularly in regard to her father's role in it. While the Folio edition of the play attributes Lavinia's death entirely to Titus – 'He kils her' (sig. Ee2ʳ) – the 1594 quarto makes no explicit reference. Without further stage direction, it is impossible to read Lavinia's attitude towards her death, though one might imagine that Titus is merely helping to facilitate his daughter's death.

The conversation preceding Lavinia's death makes clear that discomfort and publication are essential elements of her character. Once presented in 2.3, Lavinia's violation is repeatedly made public, and the resulting

Violent Spectacle and Violent Feeling

discomfort touches everyone: the other characters onstage, the audience, and even, it seems, critics. Lavinia elicits a strong reaction, in particular facilitating an emotional connection with and between those who try desperately to parse out her messages. Nonetheless, the 'publication' of her ruin is left, again as in Day, to the men around her: she is discovered by a man, who then returns her to an entirely male family. And it is a man, Titus, who displays her ruin publicly and then 'resolves' the problem she represents. In this way, Lavinia is comparable to other early modern models of Lucrece. What makes Lavinia different is the redirected focus: unlike Lucrece, her suffering is not mobilised in support of a political narrative. Rather, she is a clear exploration of the pity that is prompted by the sight of another's distress. In emphasising the emotional impact of Lavinia's situation, the character stresses both the connections formed by pity, the problematic discomfort caused by that sort of emotional response, and the productive effect of engaging with that type of emotion.

THE SPECTRE OF LUCRECE

The unnamed woman of Day's note and *Titus Andronicus*'s Lavinia both depend, for their effect, upon the larger cultural significance of Lucrece. In each case the invocation of Lucrece, whose story was deeply familiar in the sixteenth century, immediately accesses a common set of emotions, exploiting the violence, the pity, and the discomfort of a more famous tale. Day's note, for example, uses the Lucrece reference to bolster the impact of his own imagined 'lady', whom he wishes to present as being just as visually arresting and unsettling. The ubiquity of the Lucrece story, which inspired a number of retellings in the sixteenth and seventeenth centuries, is particularly reliant on the Latinate Lucreces found in Ovid's *Fasti* and Livy's *Roman History*.[33] Both were translated into English during

---

[33] Beyond those covered in this chapter, notable period references to Lucrece included longer treatments, such as Thomas Middleton's *The Ghost of Lucrece* (London: 1600), and more passing mentions. She appears in three more of Shakespeare's plays: *As You Like It* ('Lucretia's sad modesty' forms a portion of 'Rosalind of many parts' [3.2.145–146]); *Twelfth Night* (Malvolio identifies the seal, 'the impressure her Lucrece' and reads of 'Silence, like a Lucrece knife' [2.5.92, 104]); and *The Taming of the Shrew*, where Petruchio imagines that 'For patience [Kate] will prove a second Grissel | And Roman Lucrece for her chastity' (2.1.289–290). Lucrece's chastity, which significantly is only confirmed by the conviction suggested by her suicide, forms a major part of her reputation. This is evident in Quintilian: 'Shall I mind you of the Story of Lucretia, who ran a Sword into her own bowels, and took Vengeance on her self, thô the Act was forc'd? That her chast Soul might soon be severed from her defiled Body, she slew her self, because she could not kill her Ravisher.' (sig.

Pity and Identity in the Age of Shakespeare

the early modern period, and the Latin texts themselves were a staple of English grammar school curricula.[34] Though it is common to preserve, in some fashion, the concept of female violation as a visual concern in these narratives, Lucrece's emotional value is not traditionally an explicit focus. Rather, it has been her objectification and her utility as a political tool that has tended to capture the literary imagination. My work here is to highlight the agency of emotion in these re-workings of Lucrece – in Day and Shakespeare, specifically – where the impact of visible violation is bound to the dispensation of pity, where one person's bodily violation prompts, in another, a kind of emotional violation, and where this cross-violation can be imagined as having a positive impact on community building.

F1ᵛ). Lucrece's chastity is a feature that John Webster binds to her political significance in the conclusion of *Appius and Virginia* (written with Middleton): 'Two fair, but Ladies most infortunate, | have in their ruins rais'd declining Rome, | Lucretia and Virginia, both renown'd | for chastity. Souldiers and noble Romans | to grace her death, whose life hath freed great Rome, | march with her Course to her sad Funeral Tomb' (sig. I3ʳ). The fascination with Lucrece is by no means restricted to the early modern period: she is discussed at length in Chaucer's *The Legend of Good Women*, Book VII of Gower's *Confessio Amantis*, John Lydgate's *Fall of Princes*, at II. 1058–1099, and Augustine's famous discussion of chastity and self-slaughter in *The City of God*. See also: Quintilian, *The Declamations of Quintilian*, trans. John Warr (London: 1686); John Webster, *Appius and Virginia* (London: 1654); Geoffrey Chaucer, *The Legend of Good Women*, ed. by the Rev. Walter W. Skeat (Oxford: Clarendon Press, 1889); John Gower, *Confessio Amantis*, ed. by Russell A. Peck, trans. Andrew Galloway (Kalamazoo, MI: Consortium for the Teaching of the Middle Ages, 2006–); John Lydgate, *Fall of Princes*, ed. by Henry Bergen, vol. 1 (London: Published for the Early English Text Society by Oxford University Press, 1924); and Augustine, *Of the Citie of God* (London: 1610). In early modern art, representations of Lucrece were rendered, for example, by Raphael (1483–1520); Titian (1488–1490); Botticelli (1496–1504); Dürer (1518); and Lucas Cranach the Elder (1532).

[34] In *Ovid Recalled*, L.P. Wilkinson outlines 'the grammar-school grounding in Ovid that we may expect an Elizabethan poet to have had': the *Fasti* figures prominently. It was among the texts Wolsey required for Ipswich School in 1529; Thomas Elyot included the text in the programme outlined in *The Governour* (1531); Sturm recommended it for class work in 1538. See L.P. Wilkinson, *Ovid Recalled* (Cambridge: Cambridge University Press, 1955), p. 407. See also T.W. Baldwin, *William Shakspere's Small Latine and Lesse Greeke* (Urbana, IL: University of Illinois Press, 1944), and also *On the Literary Genetics of Shakespeare's Poems and Sonnets* (Urbana, IL: University of Illinois Press, 1950), pp. 97–153. Andrew Hadfield notes that the Renaissance was marked by a 'keen interest in histories of the Roman republic and enthusiasm for Livy', which was especially facilitated by Philemon Holland's translation of *The Romaine Historie*, published in London in 1600. See Andrew Hadfield, *Shakespeare and Renaissance Politics* (London: Arden Shakespeare, 2004), p. 10.

Violent Spectacle and Violent Feeling

Day's juxtaposition of his own editorial interventions and the alarming, feminised spectacle that supposedly prompts them more closely follows Ovid's narrative as John Gower translates it, though Gower also amplifies Ovidian references to Lucrece's visual effect.[35] The Gower Ovid describes the unmolested Lucrece as living art: 'Her lilie skin, her gold-deluding tresses, | Her native splendour slight art him pleases'.[36] As Tarquin's 'mazing fansie on her *picture* roves', Lucrece's fate is sealed by her every movement and attribute (sig. E6ᵛ, my emphasis).[37] Gower's use of 'art' and 'picture' here presents Lucrece explicitly as an object to be viewed, designed for and causing clear visual pleasure: she is in this way an

[35] In spite of the liberties Gower takes with Ovid's text, Ovid remains the obvious source for classical interpretations of Lucrece as a visual figure. Livy, by comparison, avoids consideration of Lucrece's image until she is dead, at which point he simply describes her mutilated body as a source of wonder: it is '*so strange a sight*' (sig. E3ʳ, my emphasis). Livy, *The Romane Historie*, trans. Philemon Holland (London: 1600). Even this concession to visuality is perhaps more attributable to Holland's translation of Livy, which again makes a habit of overemphasising the visual elements beyond the original text. Compare this to the original, which offers no explicit mention of 'sight': 'Elatum domo Lucretiae corpus in forum deferunt concientque miraculo, ut fit, rei novae atque indignitate homines [They carried out Lucretia's corpse from the house and bore it to the market-place, where men crowded about them, attracted, as they were bound to be, by the amazing character of the strange event and its heinousness]' (Book I: LIX, 3). *Livy*, vol. I, trans. B.O. Foster (London: William Heinemann, 1919).

[36] *Ovid's Festivalls, or Romane Calendar*, trans. John Gower (Cambridge: 1640), sig. E6ʳ, my emphasis. I have used the English translation, though evidently as the translation was not published in his lifetime – Shakespeare would have worked from the Latin text. The original Latin (with modern translation) will be provided in footnotes: these reveal some liberties in Gower's text, all of which match the prevailing occupation about visuality in the other early modern Lucrece narratives considered in this chapter. For more on Shakespeare's familiarity with Ovid, see Jonathan Bate, *Shakespeare and Ovid* (Oxford: Clarendon Press, 1993), p. 13.

[37] These translations from Gower take some departure from the original Latin, with the ultimate effect of exaggerating the existing references to the visual. From the original: 'forma placet niveusque color flavique capilli, quique aderat nulla factus ab arte decor [Her figure pleased him, and that snowy hue, that yellow hair, and artless grace]' (*Fasti* II, ll. 763–764); '"sic sedit, sic culta fuit, sic stamina nevit, neglectae collo sic iacuere comae, hos habuit voltus haec facies, hic décor oris erat" ['Twas thus she sat, 'twas thus she dressed, 'twas thus she spun the yarn, 'twas thus her tresses careless lay upon her neck; that was her look, these were her words, that was her colour, that her form, and that her lovely face]' (II, ll. 771–774). Ovid, *Fasti*, trans. Sir James George Frazer (London: William Heinemann Ltd, 1931).

Pity and Identity in the Age of Shakespeare

equal embodiment of Freudian *scopophilia* and Mulveyan '*to-be-looked-at-ness*'.[38] Gower's presentation of Ovid's narrative also implies that the culpability for visual impact belongs to the female, as is explicitly clear in Day's note, and hinted at in the final moments of *Titus Andronicus*.[39] In Gower, Tarquin's description of the lady assigns her control over her projected image:

> His mazing fansie on her picture roves;
> The more he muses still the more he loves:
> Thus did she sit, thus drest, thus did she spin,
> Thus plaid her hair upon her necks white skin;
> These looks she had, these rosie words still'd from her;
> This eye, this cheek, these blushes did become her. (sig. E6ᵛ)

By this conception, Lucrece sits a certain way, conscientiously arranging her hair to great benefit: these are choices intentionally made (it is imagined) for optimal visual presentation. This pattern of action makes her visually provocative, a potential hazard to any who view her, and therefore vulnerable to blame after the rape. The language is both confused and deeply misogynistic. It simultaneously suggests that Lucrece is more object than human – a 'picture' – but also that she is responsible for presenting herself in an intentionally provocative way.[40] Tarquin is, after all, afflicted by 'the love *her person bred*' (sig. E6ᵛ, my emphasis).[41] Gower's handling of Ovid suggests that Day's note – though it does not detail the moments before the

---

[38] Laura Mulvey, 'Visual Pleasure and Narrative Cinema', *Screen*, 16 (1975), 6–18 (p. 11). For more on Freud's theories of *scopophilia* (pleasure in looking), and its associated practices of objectification and subjectification, see Sigmund Freud, *On Sexuality*, ed. by Angela Richards, trans. James Strachey (Harmondsworth: Penguin, 1977), esp. at pp. 69–70.

[39] This is notion of a harmful vision of femininity is strikingly present in the original Latin as well: 'carpitur adtonitos absentis imagine sensus ille [Meantime the image of his absent love preyed on his senses crazed]' (*Fasti* II, ll. 769–770).

[40] This type of thinking relates clearly to one critic's insistence that the more significant rape in *The Rape of Lucrece* happens to Tarquin, that 'the attack on Tarquin's soul comes from within [...] the attackers are his own passions'. The argument prioritises Tarquin's emotional torment – what the sight of Lucrece *drives him to* – over the more obvious crime. See Sam Hynes, 'The Rape of Tarquin', *Shakespeare Quarterly*, 10 (1959), 451–453 (p. 452).

[41] 'ut solet a magno fluctus languescere flatu, sed tamen a vento, qui fuit, unda tumet, sic, quamvis aberat placitae praesentia formae, quem dederat praesens forma, manebat amor ardet et iniusti stimulis agitatus amoris comparat indigno vimque dolumque toro [as after a great gale the surge subsides, and yet the billow heaves, lashed by the wind now fallen, so, though absent now that winsome form and far away, the love which by its presence it had struck into his heart remained. He

Violent Spectacle and Violent Feeling

imagined rape of the woman/text, or consider this Lucrece figure before her ruination – is a continuation, a more explicit articulation of the suggested blame that can be read in the source text.

In the context of visual presence and its potential emotional effect, what is emphasised only *before* the violation in Ovid is only considered *after* the fact in Day. However, it is not just that Ovid ignores the spectacle of the abused Lucrece: he explicitly restricts it. The *Fasti* sees Lucrece call for her husband and her father, after the rape, but upon their arrival,

> She veils her modest face, nor any thing
> would utter [...]
> Thrice she assay'd to speak, thrice stopt; yet tries
> once more, but shamed to lift up her eyes (sig. E7^r, my emphasis).[42]

It is possible to see Lucrece here as more of a spectacle, simply because she so conspicuously attempts to conceal herself, but the presence of the veil importantly adds a containing element, restricting the visual access that has recently caused such harm. Read this way, the Ovidian Lucrece anticipates and seeks to avoid the critical response to which Day's violated woman is subjected. The classical Lucrece however enjoys a far more sympathetic audience: there is no displeasure directed at the lady herself, and both Collatine and Lucretius immediately 'forgive her forc'd adultery' (sig. E7^r).[43] This Lucrece is her own most severe critic, stabbing herself as she cries, 'That pardon you give, I deny' (sig. E7^r).[44] Nonetheless, this new reference to veiling, and Lucrece's consistent unwillingness to lift her eyes to meet the gaze of her family, are important decisions that distance Lucrece from the community around her. As much as Gower's translation of the *Fasti* links Lucrece's rape to open visual access, it also seems to conclude that the rape creates something that ought not be viewed. In both versions of the *Fasti* narrative, Lucrece recognises her easy identification as a ruined woman:

---

    burned, and, goaded by the pricks of an unrighteous love, he plotted violence and guile against an innocent bed]' (*Fasti* II, ll. 775–780).

[42] 'ter conata loqui ter destitit, ausaque quarto non oculos ideo sustulit illa suos [Thrice she essayed to speak, and thrice gave o'er, and when the fourth time she summoned up courage she did not for that lift up her eyes]' (*Fasti* II, ll. 823–824). Her covering is mentioned earlier: 'illa diu reticet pudibundaque celat amictu ora [She was long silent, and for shame hid her face in her robe]' (ll. 819–820).

[43] 'dant veniam facto genitor coniunxque coacto [Her husband and her sire pardoned the deed enforced]' (*Fasti* II, l. 829).

[44] '"quam" dixit "veniam vos datis, ipsa nego" [She said, "The pardon that you give, I do refuse myself"]' (*Fasti* II, l. 830).

Shall we ow Tarquine this too? ah! shall I,
Shall I here publish my own infamie? (sig. E7r)

The notion of shame and corruption as things that are *published*, put out before an audience, is new; the Latin speaks only of *voicing* shame, "'hoc quoque Tarquinio debebimus? eloquar,' inquit, "eloquar infelix dedecus ipsa meum?" ["Must I owe this too to Tarquin? Must I utter," quoth she, "must I utter, woe's me, with my own lips my own disgrace?"]' (*Fasti* II, ll. 825–826). Gower preserves Lucrece's refusal to accept complete culpability, noting that she 'ow[es]' this further torment to Tarquin as well, but he emphasises the assumption that she would be viewed as the responsible agent – 'shall *I*, shall *I*' – if she did 'publish' her 'own infamie'. Read alongside Day, Gower's interpretation gives a clear impression of the cultural response to the visibly ruined woman, especially in terms of her responsibility for the reaction she produces in others.

In spite of the apparent tendency to blame the victim, and the underlying discomfort about Lucrece's visual effect, she is consistently praised for the high standard to which she holds herself: she is further redeemed by the political value of her ruination. Early modern England in particular praised Lucrece for her part in the formation of the Roman republic, and this position is only achieved through her self-sacrifice: it is Lucrece's mutilated body that creates the symbol that spurs the political overthrow of the Tarquins.[45] Her presentation to an audience is a crucial component of her story, sanctioned in part because she does not present herself, but rather is presented, and because her suicide 'solves', in many respects, the visual/emotional problem she represents. This political emphasis is particularly evident in William Painter's *The Palace of Pleasure*, where the focus, as in Livy, is the revolution that Lucrece's rape prompts.[46] More than half of Painter's telling deals with the events following Lucrece's death, the bringing

---

[45] Christopher W.T. Miller describes Lucrece's body as 'an instrument to enter the minds of others and stir them to violent deeds'. See: Christopher W.T. Miller, 'Confusion of Tears: The Deadened Oedipal Couple and Predatory Identifications in *The Rape of Lucrece*', *American Imago*, 75.4 (2018), 489–515 (p. 511). Andrew Hadfield and Stephanie Jed both speak of the early modern significance of Lucrece in conjunction with republican ideals; Annabel Patterson specifically attributes the popularity of the Lucrece tale to republican culture. See Hadfield, *Shakespeare and Renaissance Politics*; Jed, *Chaste Thinking: The Rape of Lucretia and the Birth of Humanism* (Bloomington, IN: Indiana University Press, 1989); and Annabel Patterson, *Reading Between the Lines* (London: Routledge, 1993), esp. at pp. 297–312.

[46] William Painter, 'The Rape of Lucrece', in *The Palace of Pleasure*, vol. 2 (London: 1566), sig. B1r–B3v. Painter was, of course, a major source for many of Shakespeare's plays – making his interpretation particularly noteworthy in the context of Shakespeare's own rendering of the Lucrece tale.

Violent Spectacle and Violent Feeling

of her body to the marketplace, and the response: 'the people wondered at the vilenesse of that facte, every man complaining uppon the mischiefe of that facinorous rape, committed by Tarquinius' (sig. B2ᵛ). However, by the time Brutus's mob reaches Rome, Lucrece's rape is reduced to just one item in a list of complaints, including 'the pride and insolent behaviour of the king', and 'the miserie and drudgerie of the people' (sig. B3ʳ).

* * *

Thomas Heywood's 1608 play, *The Rape of Lucrece*, offers a compelling example of the politicisation of Lucrece.[47] Aside from the slightly jarring musical intervals, Heywood's handling of the Lucrece story shows a return to the shared focus of Livy, Ovid, and Painter as Lucrece's importance once again derives from her political value and her role as a figure of reform.[48] The pitiable elements that emerge in other narratives are here de-emphasised. Heywood's note, 'To the Reader', which precedes the text, offers a ready example: sharing the corrective theme of the *Gorboduc* note, Heywood notes that 'some of my plaies have (unknown to me, and without any of my direction) accidentally come into the Printers handes, and therfore so corrupt and mangled [...] that I have be as unable to known them, as ashamde to chalenge them' (sig. A2ʳ). Heywood's allegation of inaccurate printing reflects the still-relevant concern over corrupted texts, and considering the dates and the widespread popularity of *Gorboduc*, it is not impossible to think that Heywood was familiar with Day's note. Given the possibility of familiarity, Heywood's description of his own text's corruption is even more noteworthy for its ungendered neutrality. There is no mention of the text as a ruined

---

[47] Paulina Kewes has described Heywood's *Lucrece* not as a history of its title character, but as a play that 'anatomizes the rise of royal tyranny and the people's resistance to it'. See Paulina Kewes, 'Roman History and Early Stuart Drama: Thomas Heywood's *The Rape of Lucrece*', *English Literary Renaissance*, 32 (2002), 239–267 (p. 242).

[48] The play's title page flags the uniquely musical tone of Heywood's offering: '*The Rape of Lucrece: A True Roman Tragedie with the Severall Songes in their apt places*'. Thomas Heywood, *The Rape of Lucrece* (London: 1608), sig. A1ʳ. Most scholars object to Heywood's use of song, see for example: Ian Donaldson, *The Rapes of Lucretia: A Myth and its Transformation* (Oxford: Clarendon Press, 1982), p. 86; Martin Butler, *Theatre and Crisis, 1632-1642* (Cambridge: Cambridge University Press, 1984), p. 184; Barbara Baines, *Thomas Heywood* (Boston: Twayne, 1984); and Mercedes Maroto Camino, *"The Stage am I": Raping Lucrece in Early Modern England* (Lewiston, NY: Edwin Mellen Press, 1995), pp. 90–104. Notable exceptions include: Katherine Duncan-Jones, 'Ravished and Revised: The 1616 *Lucrece*', *The Review of English Studies*, 52.208 (2001), 516–523; and Andrew Bretz, 'Sung Silence: Complicity, Dramaturgy, and Song in Heywood's *Rape of Lucrece*', *Early Theatre*, 19.2 (2016), 101–118.

woman (indeed, no suggestion of textual subjectivity at all), and there are no allegations against the individuals who brought forth the corrupted texts. The only possible allusion to provocative visuality is Heywood's (still plausibly gender-neutral) comment that he has agreed to publish a corrected copy of the work because the plays themselves 'have beene so wronged in beeing publisht in such savadge and ragged *ornaments*' (sig. A2ʳ, my emphasis). The plays have been wronged, but as objects rather than as people. There is, of course, no need to gender a book – or indeed to assign it personhood – but read alongside Heywood's play itself – specifically, its relative lack of interest in Lucrece as a character – the move could well be read as an attempt to shift attention away from the emotive power of the pitiable female. The play bears almost no reference to emotion at all, and only one relevant reference to pity, in which Lucrece begs her tormentor, before the rape, to 'pitie, oh pitie | The vertues of a woman' (sig. G2ᵛ). Heywood devotes far more dramatic energy to the events preceding and following the rape than he does to the act itself: the main focus is on the rise and fall of the Tarquins.[49] The discussion of Lucrece and the rape, by contrast, is comparatively restricted: this is something of a surprise given the play's title. Heywood's offering is, at its core, a play about politics: it opens with King Servius's daughter, Tullia (also Tarquin Superbus's wife), who, in a series of moves highly evocative of Lady Macbeth, bullies her husband into killing her father and seizing the throne.[50] From there, after a lengthy discussion of what to do with the former king's body, there is a trip to the Oracle, to determine the political fate of Rome. The play continues in this fashion, offering meandering dialogues about the value of justice, and the necessity of providing an heir to the throne.

Lucrece, for her part, does not appear onstage until the second half of the play. Nonetheless, this appearance is noteworthy as it deviates from the source texts in order to show the lady's character and her manner of relating to others. The emphasis on the gaze is prominent in this moment, as Lucrece chastises her clown and her gentlewoman for 'looking' in specific ways:

> LUCRECE
> Sirra, I ha seene you oft familiar
> With this my Maid and waiting gentlewoman.
> As casting *amorous glances, wanton lookes,*
> And pretty beckes favouring incontinence.
> I let you know you are not for my service
> Unlesse you grow more civill. (sig. D4ʳ, my emphasis)

[49] In this respect, Heywood remains truer to the source texts, particularly Livy's *History of Rome*. For more on Livy's influence on Heywood, see Peter Culhane, 'Livy in Early Jacobean Drama', *Translation and Literature*, 14 (2005), 21–44.

[50] See Kewes, p. 241.

Violent Spectacle and Violent Feeling

With this, Lucrece recognises the existence of a loaded, sexualised sight, but she also suggests the possibility of forming emotional bonds through looking. Here, sight fosters emotion, and Lucrece aims to prevent the action that that emotion might prompt. Lucrece confirms her own moral stance while chastising her maid:

> Nay mistres I ha seene you answere him
> With gracious lookes and some uncivill smiles
> Retorting eies, and giving his demeanure
> Such welcoming as becomes not modesty. (sig. D4ᵛ)

Lucrece refuses to associate with those who *look* in this fashion, because she is one who is *looked upon*:

> [...] my reputation
> Which is held pretious in the eies of Rome,
> Shall be no shelter to the least intent
> Of loosenes (sig. D4ᵛ).

The passage indicates that the act of looking is significant to Heywood and to his Lucrece, but looking here is directed specifically towards the creation (or destruction) of reputation: Lucrece's description of how 'the eies of Rome' look at her is evaluative but not emotional like the 'amorous glances, and wanton lookes' exchanged between her maid and her clown. Rather, the act of looking for Lucrece is less concerned with emotion than with the construction of a respectable identity. Establishing Lucrece's unimpeachable character, this moment is a nod to Lucrece's wider significance to Rome – something that later bolsters her political utility in death. Lucrece regards the unsanctioned, familiar gaze shared by two servants, and worries that this will forge the reputation of her female servant. The concerns expressed here are intimately bound to Lucrece's awareness that her own identity is crafted by what 'Rome' sees of her. However, the exchange with the servant is never developed to its full potential, as the clown's denial of the allegation is interrupted by more political news – this time of a military victory won by Sextus Tarquin (hereafter Tarquin). Female subjectivity is therefore subsumed by more pressing political concerns, a tendency that continues throughout the play. Lucrece exits the stage shortly after this news is delivered, allowing for a more concentrated focus on the political developments; she returns after a considerable absence, and only when Collatine encourages Tarquin to evaluate her merits in a contest of the wives.

For all that Heywood seems to value Lucrece's rape only as a conduit to the more interesting subject of Rome's political development, he still appears to acknowledge hers as a primarily visual existence: there are a number of instances in which his Lucrece is affiliated with the vision she

Pity and Identity in the Age of Shakespeare

presents to others. However, the capacity for emotion is largely ignored, and Lucrece offers a hollow presence: she is written to be more spectacle than substance. This is most clearly illustrated by the events leading up to the rape, beginning with the wife competition initiated between Brutus, Collatine, and the other men. In every Lucrece tale, Collatine encourages the spontaneous viewing of the wives as part of the wager. Heywood, however, makes this point more explicit, having his Collatine specifically ask Tarquin to assess his wife: 'I commit my Lucrece wholly to the censure of Sextus [Tarquin]' (sig. F2^v). It is Collatine who authorises Tarquin's 'judging eies' (sig. F2^v). Tarquin 'cannot feed, but on [Lucrece's] face' (sig. H3^v) and as a result she becomes, for him, 'That bright enchantresse that hath daz'd my eies' (sig. G1^v). As in other Lucrece narratives, it is through another character's sight that Lucrece's importance is determined, and her fate sealed. Heywood's characters respond to the sight of Lucrece, but Lucrece has no real ownership over the image she projects: she is constructed by 'the eies of Rome'; she is a spectacle that her husband controls and places before the male gaze. For Heywood, Lucrece's inability to take control of her own visuality continues after the rape. Following the Ovidian model, Lucrece covers herself, causing Collatine's immediate objection:

COLLATINE
Why doost thou hide thy face? & with thy hand
Darken those eies that were my Sunnes of joy. (sig. H2^r)

Collatine's comment suggests ownership over the vision of his wife; he expects unfettered visual access. After a brief explanation she kills herself, leaving her father, husband, and the other men once again responsible for controlling public visual access to her. From there, she is instantly transformed into a political tool, as they decide to

[…] beare that chaste body
Into the market place, [where] that horrid *object*
Shall kindle them with a most just revenge. (sig. H3^v, my emphasis)

The display of Lucrece's body here is only really significant to the play insofar as it justifies the last quarter of the action: Lucrece, though referenced several times during the systematic destruction of the Tarquins, becomes little more than an object cast aside in the wake of political change. Read as it came, after Shakespeare's *The Rape of Lucrece*, Heywood's removal of any visual agency for Lucrece looks like a deliberate reaction to that earlier poem's more exploratory efforts. Pity gains no real purchase in Heywood's account, perhaps because for him, Lucrece cannot distance herself from her own political utility; her visuality contributes to her objectification, and as such she fails to achieve the humanity required to subsist as an emotional presence.

Violent Spectacle and Violent Feeling

SHAKESPEARE'S LUCRECE

As in Day's note, as in Heywood's *Lucrece*, and as in the classical origins of the tale, most representations of Lucrece give the prevailing sense of the violated female as someone (and more often, something) to be *looked at*. Shakespeare's *The Rape of Lucrece* makes a clear departure from this tradition, turning it on its head to explore the possibilities of a Lucrece who *looks*: the poem relies on a gaze that is distinctively and pointedly female. Shakespeare's emphasis on the capacity of the female gaze to foster emotional, pity-based connections gives Lucrece a significance beyond the political. As a result the poem is unique in the way it pursues the potential of Lucrece's spectacle, identifying her vision as something active, and something she herself directs. With this shift, Shakespeare harnesses the emotional unrest that writers like Day suggest, probing the possibilities of compromised visuality, and reclaiming the personal agency that is overwritten by blame rhetoric in other portrayals of Lucrece. This exploration of the emotional culture surrounding Lucrece's gaze represents a significant progression beyond the inherent misogyny of other versions of the story, one which opens new possibilities for interaction, over which the violated female has a new degree of control and a higher level of participation.

The critical interest in Shakespeare's *Lucrece* has tended to focus on the aggressive, sexualised male eye represented in Tarquin, and also related to the men who present the self-slaughtered Lucrece to a male viewing public.[51] Shakespeare preserves some of the visual emphasis from other sources, particularly in his inclusion of aggressive, consuming male vision. His Tarquin offers the best example, characterised by his 'greedy eyeballs'.[52]

---

[51] I have already mentioned Laura Mulvey, whose work defined the concept of an aggressive, consuming male vision, and developed the notion of 'the male gaze' as inherently predatory and damaging to women. Mulvey identifies male and female roles in viewing as active and passive (respectively), arguing that 'In their traditional exhibitionist role women are simultaneously looked at and displayed, with their appearance coded for strong visual and erotic impact so they can be said to connote *to-be-looked-at-ness*' (p. 11). This tradition of looking at women (particularly with pleasure) strips the female of any meaningful significance or agency. On the male gaze, see also Jean-Paul Sartre, *Being and Nothingness*, trans. Hazel E. Barnes (London: Routledge, 1989), pp. 252–302, and Jacques Lacan, *The Four Fundamental Concepts of Psycho-Analysis*, ed. by Jacques-Alain Miller, trans. Alan Sheridan (New York, NY: Norton, 1978).

[52] William Shakespeare, *The Rape of Lucrece*, in *Shakespeare's Poems*, ed. by Katherine Duncan-Jones and H.R. Woudhuysen (London: Bloomsbury Arden, 2007), l. 368. All further references to *Lucrece* will be to this edition, unless otherwise noted.

Pity and Identity in the Age of Shakespeare

Shakespeare later uses *anadiplosis* and *anaphora* to emphasise the inevitability of Tarquin's hungry and 'wanton sight' (l. 104):

> What could he *see* but mightily he noted?
> What did he note but strongly he desired?
> What he beheld, on that he firmly doted,
> And in his will his wilful eye he tired. (ll. 414–417)

Tarquin's vision leads him down this path towards its physical, violent conclusion; his 'lustful eye' somehow attacks Lucrece before the physical assault occurs (l. 179). And although Tarquin later accuses Lucrece of complicity ('The fault is thine | For those eyes betray thee unto mine'), the visual engagement leading up to the rape is only significant, and only sexualised, for him (ll. 482–483). Much is made of Lucrece's visual effect here, but really her participation is minimal: she is either unable to interpret his glance – 'she that never coped with stranger eyes | Could pick no meaning from their parling looks' – or asleep (ll. 99–100). While the description of Tarquin's individual experience plays on the contemporary cultural willingness (particularly evident in Day) to see a woman as culpable in her own rape, and responsible for whatever aggression her looks prompt, Tarquin's comments also rely on an already-established literary model of erotic, extramissive vision that uses the shared gaze as a method of binding characters together.[53] Nonetheless, the explicit outlining of Lucrece's non-participation challenges the idea of her complicity: in this instance, vision fails to produce a consensual connection. Instead, it is insular, predatory, violent, and destructive.

Shakespeare's emphasis on Lucrece's innocence during Tarquin's visual assault – her lack of awareness – challenges the contemporary literary conventions surrounding extramissive vision by denying this as a shared visual moment. With this in mind her later development into an explicit

---

[53] The Galenic model of vision – or extramission – understands sight as probing, or speculative: it imagined that sight was produced by the meeting of eyebeams emitted both by the viewer and the person or object viewed. In the scientific world, this notion was replaced by Kepler's model of intramissive (receptive) vision around 1604, but Eric Langley compellingly argues that seventeenth-century literature reveals 'some slippage, where the supposedly discredited theory remains in circulation' (p. 55). According to Langley, extramissive vision retains a certain literary appeal precisely because it allows for 'a kind of mutual accord between viewer and viewed, who both, through eye contact, participate in the emission and merging in an act of "sympathetic" ocular coupling' (p. 60). For Langley's exploration of the literary significance of extramissive vision, see Eric Langley, *Narcissism and Suicide in Shakespeare and His Contemporaries* (Oxford: Oxford University Press, 2009), pp. 53–107. See also Marcus Nordlund, *The Dark Lantern: A Historical Study of Sight in Shakespeare, Webster, and Middleton* (Goteburg: Acta Universitatis Gothoburgensis, 2006).

Violent Spectacle and Violent Feeling

viewing agent, able to cultivate pity and foster connection, is even more notable. This capacity for visual connection is moreover linked clearly to her violation: before the attack, she is far more reliant on rhetoric.[54] This is perhaps best demonstrated in her lengthy and varied plea to Tarquin just before the rape:

> She conjures him by high almighty Jove,
> By knighthood, gentry and sweet friendship's oath,
> By her untimely tears, her husband's love
> By holy human law and common troth,
> By heaven and earth, and all the power of both,
> That to his borrowed bed he make retire,
> And stoop to honour, not to foul desire. (ll. 568–574)

Lucrece is described as having both 'eloquence' and 'grace' as an orator, and the arguments against the rape are sound and wide-ranging (ll. 563–564). Nevertheless, her rhetorical appeal (which continues) fails to save her, as

> His ear her prayers admits, but his heart granteth
> No penetrable entrance to her plaining (ll. 559–560)

Her language *reaches* Tarquin, but fails to have any impact. As Nancy Vickers has pointed out, rhetoric has an enormous role in the poem, and Vickers' argument – that it is Collatine's *description* of his wife, rather than her actual image, that prompts Tarquin to rape her – works from this premise of dominant rhetoric.[55] The impact of rhetoric however seems problematically gendered: Collatine can prompt action with his descriptive language, but Lucrece cannot halt it with hers. Nonetheless, it would be a mistake to focus wholly on these characters as orators, to ignore the frequency with which the language of the poem emphasises *visual* experience, and to overlook the

---

[54] For more on the significance of Lucrece's rhetoric, see Enterline, *The Rhetoric of the Body from Ovid to Shakespeare*; Katharine Eisaman Maus, 'Taking Tropes Seriously: Language and Violence in Shakespeare's *Rape of Lucrece*', *Shakespeare Quarterly*, 37.1 (1986), 66–82; Heather Dubrow, *Captive Victors: Shakespeare's Narrative Poems and Sonnets* (Ithaca, NY: Cornell University Press, 1987); Joel Fineman, 'Shakespeare's Will: The Temporality of Rape', *Representations*, 20 (1987), 25–76; and Philippa Berry, 'Women, Language, and History in *The Rape of Lucrece*', *Shakespeare Studies*, 44 (1992), 33–39. For an exploration of the reciprocal relationship between vision and rhetoric in *Lucrece*, see Catherine Belsey, 'Invocation of the Visual Image: Ekphrasis in *Lucrece* and Beyond', *Shakespeare Quarterly*, 63.2 (2012), 175–198, and Richard Meek, *Narrating the Visual in Shakespeare* (Surrey: Ashgate, 2009), pp. 55–80.

[55] Nancy Vickers, 'This Heraldry in Lucrece's Face', *Poetics Today*, 6 (1985), 171–184, and 'The Blazon of Sweet Beauty's Best: Shakespeare's *Lucrece*', in Patricia Parker and Geoffrey Hartman (eds.), *Shakespeare and the Question of Theory* (New York, NY: Methuen, 1985), pp. 95–116.

Pity and Identity in the Age of Shakespeare

contribution that the visual makes to the emotional landscape of the play. Consider, for example, Collatine's language, when describing Lucrece:

> Collatine unwisely did not let
> To praise the clear unmatched red and white
> Which triumphed in that sky of his delight,
> Where mortal stars as bright as heaven's beauties
> With pure aspects did him peculiar duties. (ll. 10–14)

'Clear'; 'red and white'; 'bright'; 'beauties'; and 'aspects' (here referring to looks or glances): this is the rhetoric of sight. Later, Collatine refers to Lucrece as 'his beauteous mate' (l. 18). The brief description is wholly concerned with her visual properties. Language, here and elsewhere, primarily facilitates the characters' discussions about what they see, and how it affects them: the poem's descriptions, its observations, are constantly grounded in highly visual, ekphrastic terms. Tarquin may be inspired by Collatine's language, but he never, in the course of a considerable meditation on his motivation and justification to act against Lucrece, attributes his actions to Collatine's words. Instead, he stresses her visual impact, informing Lucrece that

> Thy beauty hath ensnared thee to this night
> Where thou with patience must my will abide (ll. 485–486).

In other moments, the poem seems explicitly to set image and language at odds, as when Tarquin tells himself that 'All orators are dumb when beauty pleadeth' (l. 268), and vows that 'My heart shall never countermand mine eye' (l. 276). This is, of course, a poem – a work of rhetoric, and visual language is still *language*. Nonetheless, the significance of the visual is undeniable: crucial, as the poem itself makes clear in the context of the cultivation of emotion.

To return briefly to Lucrece's exchange with Tarquin, in which she relies on rhetoric to elicit pity from her tormentor, we might wonder why she demonstrates such a preference for language when so much of what precedes this moment focuses on her visual impact. Her purpose, after all, is to have an effect on Tarquin: she wishes to secure her own safety through his pity. If the later interactions with Collatine are an indication of her visual agency, we might expect her to rely on that capacity here. That she does not is some indication that she is unaware of her own gaze, that Tarquin is unwilling to engage with it, or that her gaze is not yet so impactful. Lucrece seems sceptical that Tarquin's vision is functioning properly: 'wipe the dim mist from thy doting eyne,' she pleads, confident that if he does, he 'shalt see thy state, and pity mine' (ll. 643–644). Her language is the same visually loaded rhetoric that pervades the rest of the poem, and in many respects she is more heavy-handed with it than any of the male characters. With

Violent Spectacle and Violent Feeling

'pity-pleading eyes [...] sadly fixed | In the remorseless wrinkles of his face'
(ll. 561–562), she begs:

> My sighs like whirlwinds labour hence to heave thee.
> If ever man were moved with woman's moans,
> Be moved with my tears, my sighs, my groans:
> All which together, like a troubled ocean,
> Beat at thy rocky and wrack-threat-ning heart,
> To soften it with their continual motion;
> For stones dissolved to water do convert.
> O, if no harder than a stone thou art,
> Melt at my tears, and be compassionate!
> Soft pity enters at an iron gate. (ll. 586–595)

Lucrece has endured some critical scrutiny for the fervour with which she
expresses her suffering here. Critics such as F.T. Prince have suggested that
she exceeds the reasonable rhetorical limits of expressed abjection, and in
so doing alienates her audience and loses the pity she might reasonably
expect to elicit. Prince argues that Tarquin is the poem's more compelling
character, because Lucrece 'is forced to express herself in a way which
dissipates the real pathos of her situation [...] Lucrece loses our sympathy
exactly in proportion as she gives tongue'.[56] This reads very much like a
modern expression of Day's 1570 stance, insomuch as it interprets Lucrece's
appeal for pity as confirmation of her culpability, something that reduces
her significance as a victim rather than enhancing her impact. Here again,
the violated female is eclipsed by the feelings of those around her: for
Prince, most notably Lucrece is eclipsed by the very man responsible for her
violation. What Prince identifies as lack – something missing in Lucrece's
vast amount of speech – might in fact underscore the poem's emphasis on
the emotional impact of spectacle. The poem repeatedly hints that Lucrece's
complaint will be – must be – bolstered by her accompanying physical presence, but the poem's generic constraints ensure that this is an image that the
reader can only assume or imagine. Lucrece's 'tears' feature prominently –
'be moved at my tears', 'melt at my tears' – but description cannot match the
pitiful force of actually watching someone weep. In effect, the poem forces
us to confront the emotional limits of description.

The latter half of Shakespeare's poem, after the rape, deals almost exclusively with Lucrece's gaze: what she sees, how she uses her gaze to connect

---

[56]   F.T. Prince, 'Introduction', in *The Poems* (London: Methuen, 1960), pp. xi–xlvi (p.
xxxvi). William Weaver compellingly redeems Lucrece's lengthy appeal by relabe-
ling her 'complaint' as a defense that anticipates the accusations against her chastity.
Weaver, 'Forensic Performance in Lucrece' (2008).

Pity and Identity in the Age of Shakespeare

to others, and the emotional bond (facilitated by pity) between those who look at one another. This notion of the pitiable female's gaze is new, distinct from the passive visual properties of other early modern Lucreces, and a far cry from the clearly aggressive, insular way of seeing that Tarquin practices. This new type of sight is also indefinite, evolving constantly as the poem progresses. With varying degrees of success, Lucrece's manipulation of vision is about forming bonds and prompting emotional response from those around her. Perhaps the strongest example of this – the one in which Lucrece looks and is looked at with the greatest effect – comes at the moment when Lucrece reveals her torment to her husband and father. At this point, she understands the crucial role of spectacle, and actively manipulates the image she represents. Moreover, her actions prior to this scene suggest a growing view of sight as an integral sense for the cultivation of emotion. She calls her family to her side, rather than immediately sending a written account of her rape, because

> To see sad sights moves more than hear them told,
> For then the eye interprets to the ear
> The heavy motion that it doth behold,
> When every part a part of woe doth bear.
> 'Tis but a part of sorrow that we hear:
> Deep sounds make lesser noise than shallow fords,
> And sorrow ebbs, being blown with wind of words (ll. 1324–1330).

Beyond confirming Lucrece's own awareness of the image of torment she represents, her insistence that her family physically witness her suffering suggests a rhetorical belief that emotional appeals are augmented by an accompanying visual component.

For Lucrece, the critical moment for her gaze comes when Collatine and Lucretius arrive home. In this moment, Lucrece uses her now-active gaze to facilitate emotional communication and interpersonal connection. Unlike her Ovidian predecessor, Shakespeare's Lucrece embraces fully her visual markers: she is 'clad in mourning black' (l. 1585), and openly displays her face, rather than veiling it:

> And round her tear-distained eye
> blue circles streamed, like rainbows in the sky (ll. 1586–1587).

Moreover, her connection with Collatine is, at least initially, entirely based on their shared looks:

> […] when her sad-beholding husband saw,
> Amazedly in her sad face he stares:
> Her eyes, though sod in tears, looked red and raw,
> Her lively colour killed with deadly cares.
> He hath no power to ask her how she fares.

Violent Spectacle and Violent Feeling

Both stood like old acquaintance in a *trance*,
Met far from home, wond'ring each other's chance. (ll. 1590–1596, my
emphasis)

In this compelling moment, husband and wife are bound together by what she offers and he receives. It is little wonder that though Lucrece has her tongue, she barely uses it, claiming that

Few words […] shall fit the trespass best
[…]
In me moe woes than words are now depending
And my laments would be drawn out too long
To tell them all with one poor tired tongue. (ll. 1613–1617)

This notion of grief defeating the powers of speech is also echoed in the frontispiece of the 1644 edition of the poem, which references Lucrece's contemplation of Hecuba in its notation: 'The Fates decree that it is mighty wrong | To Women kinde to have more Griefe than Tongue' (see Fig. 1). The implication, both in the text and the accompanying image, is that the strength of Lucrece's emotion surpasses mere description. This imbalance represents yet another violation of boundaries, offering the sense that inexpressible grief is something separate and noteworthy, a 'mighty wrong'. The image necessarily confirms Lucrece's reliance on visual communication, and further emphasises an interest in *viewing*: Collatine regards Lucrece; she returns the gaze directly; both remain under the silent, watchful eye of their author. The poem's description of this moment is equally visual. Even before Lucrece speaks, Collatine receives the bulk of the information – including, significantly, the appropriate emotional reaction – by parsing the visual cues: 'What uncouth event,' he asks, 'Hath thee befall'n, that thou dost trembling stand? | Sweet love, what spite hath thy fair colour spent? | Why art thou *thus attired in discontent*?' (ll. 1598–1601, my emphasis). The reference to Lucrece as 'attired' in her discontent gives emotion a physicality: it makes it easily identifiable, related but also somehow separable from Lucrece herself, and vitally – transferable. Lucrece does eventually describe the assault, but the emotional response of her audience has already been determined by the visual cues she gives: she has, and keeps, their will to pity from the moment they lay eyes on her.

Lucrece's is a gaze that sidesteps some of the problems with pity that emerge in Day's note, without compromising the affective content of the scene. The power of this connection, though obviously formidable, still remains ambiguous. We are secure only in the knowledge that whatever the quality of this exchange, it is enough to put those involved in a 'trance': the connection occurs beyond the grasp of the reader. In this way, Shakespeare's

Pity and Identity in the Age of Shakespeare

depiction intensifies Livy's singular comment about Lucrece's visual presence. The assembly of revolutionaries, Livy notes, stems from the '*wondring* (as the manner is) at *so strange a sight*' (sig. A3ʳ). Here, it is the visual connection that holds them all together – including Lucrece herself.

Though this moment is unquestionably about gaze and spectacle, it is important to note that all this ultimately, and crucially, defines Lucrece's presence: an already visually striking female, someone accustomed to being regarded, she is transformed from something pleasing to an unsettling and demanding presence. In this way, Shakespeare's formal expression of Lucrece in this poem echoes other traditional responses, and certainly mirrors the crucial elements of *Titus*'s Lavinia. However, like so many of Shakespeare's works, it is not so much the subject matter of *Lucrece*, but the way it is handled that makes the contribution unique. What distinguishes Shakespeare's *Lucrece* is the particular interest in the sight of the ruined woman, and its utility: he not only emphasises Lucrece as a viewing agent, but also depicts both her gaze and her appearance as productive, crucial to her ability to elicit compassionate emotional response. Moreover, she is not only a visually and emotionally striking presence: she is, as a character, fully present in the poem as an active agent. Although we have seen in Day's reference, for example, hints of a more pervasive early modern understanding of the raped female as a distressing object to be viewed (rather than a viewing agent), Shakespeare's portrayal attributes far more agency to Lucrece, emphasising in particular a certain productivity in her pitiability. This tendency of characterising Lucrece as an image (rather than a person capable of directing a gaze herself) is consistent with the source texts, especially in terms of the lack of interest in Lucrece's own vision and the heightened focus on Lucrece's political utility after her suicide. Shakespeare however shows little interest in continuing the story beyond Lucrece's death. Indeed, for a poem that has been criticised for being indulgently long, Shakespeare sees Lucrece displayed to the Roman people and the Tarquins overthrown in only seven lines:

> When they had sworn to this advised doom
> They did conclude to bear dead Lucrece thence,
> To show her bleeding body through Rome,
> And so to publish Tarquin's foul offence;
> Which being done, with speedy diligence,
> The Romans plausibly did give consent
> To Tarquins' everlasting banishment. (ll. 1849–1855)

Speedy diligence, indeed. For Shakespeare, the banishment of the Tarquins is little more than 'a narrative afterthought', and the haste only confirms Lucrece's place as the undeniable star of the poem: she has the most

Violent Spectacle and Violent Feeling

development, and the greatest consideration.[57] As readers, we are most familiar with her feelings and her experiences. Moreover, the poem seems unable to survive without her: she appears within 50 lines of the poem's opening (and is referenced much earlier, in line 7); the poem only continues 125 lines after her suicide. This is a clear revision of the earlier source texts, which prefer instead to present the story as an historical-political narrative, an event whose significance is dependent on its relationship to the founding of the Roman republic. Shakespeare, however, seems less interested in Lucrece as an historical symbol, and more intrigued by the possibilities she offers as a woman and a pitiable subject; his is a far more intimate portrayal of the events, made more personal by the emotional connections in which Lucrece participates, and those she fosters along the lines of pity. Additionally, Lucrece's visual value is, for Shakespeare, inherently bound to emotion: she is able to connect and to provoke response in a way that other visual characters (such as Tarquin, with his penetrating male gaze) cannot. Lucrece's ability to create, in the members of her family, a trance-like state of emotional intimacy, suggests that Shakespeare acknowledges the commonplace image of the unsettling, provocatively pitiable violated woman, but then moves beyond it to explore the potential of embodying that image and purposefully directing its pitiability. Shakespeare's Lucrece therefore becomes more than a political symbol or tool, more than just an object to be fixed, and therefore, something different from other early modern Lucreces.

VISION, EMOTION, PRESENCE

To finish, I want first to fast-forward to a more contemporary exploration of the relationship between the female gaze and emotional response. In 2010, as part of the New York Museum of Modern Art's major retrospective on her work, Marina Abramović performed a piece called 'The Artist is Present'. Over two and a half months, during the 736 hours and 30 minutes that the museum was open, Abramović sat in silence opposite a simple wooden chair. Any visitor to the museum – anyone willing to remain silent and motionless – was invited to sit with Abramović and share her gaze for as long as they wished, or as long as they were able. The implication, of course, was that the experience might be so moving, so emotionally overwhelming, that prolonged exposure would be difficult to sustain. Response to the piece was massive, with visitors queuing for hours, often only to be ushered out at closing time without having locked eyes with the artist. Perhaps what

---

[57] Donaldson, p. 43.

Pity and Identity in the Age of Shakespeare

is most striking about the phenomenon of the piece, certainly the most important consideration in the context of this chapter, was the emotional response that Abramović so consistently elicited using only visual connection and her presence. The majority of participants wept – some almost immediately after sitting down. Not long after the exhibit opened and the performance began, unaffiliated artists began passing out buttons to those who succumbed to Abramović's gaze. They read simply, 'Marina Abramović Made Me Cry'.

Beyond the sheer endurance required of the piece, 'The Artist is Present' is noteworthy for its demonstration of the emotional power of vision; this is a clear case in which emotion is prompted by visual connection, and the charged presence of a shared gaze. Abramović emphasises the gaze as a tool used to communicate emotion, to transfer emotion, and to receive emotion. When interviewed about the piece, Abramović commented that during the experience: 'I gazed into the eyes of many people who were carrying such pain inside that I could immediately see it and feel it. I [became] a mirror for them in their own emotions'.[58] This idea of sight as a conduit of emotion is an important one, particularly for Shakespeare's Lucrece, who renders herself a spectacle of suffering in order to convey properly the depth of her despair. Nonetheless, each of the Lucrece figures I have examined here is associated with sight and spectacle in some way: these characters become distinguishable either by their ability to harness that visuality (as in the case of Shakespeare), or the way in which that visuality is used against them. Pity's role in these scenes becomes a marker of the positivity or negativity of the portrayal. In Shakespeare's *The Rape of Lucrece*, the visibly ruined female actively forms and shares emotional bonds on the basis of her pitiable spectacle, and pity draws people towards the violated woman, binding them to her. Elsewhere, the cultivation of pity separates the woman from those who view her. She becomes an object or a tool herself, something which creates a community of men that is provoked by her presence but separate from her. She remains isolated from that group until (or unless) she can be restored to a previous, more acceptable state.

While Abramović's piece focuses primarily on the effect of the gaze itself as emotionally penetrative, the title of the piece, 'The Artist is Present', reminds us of what makes these Lucrece figures so compelling: it is their presence that we find so jarring, their proximity that elicits emotional response, even against our will. These figures demonstrate the confrontational, yet binding component of pity, creating either inclusive communities that incorporate

---

[58] Sean O'Hagan, 'Interview: Marina Abramović' *The Observer*, 3 October 2010 <http://www.guardian.co.uk/artanddesign/2010/oct/03/interview-marina-abramovic-performance-artist> [28 September 2011].

Violent Spectacle and Violent Feeling

the woman (as in Shakespeare) or communities that form against her and the visual challenge she represents. In particular, the Lucrece figure reveals the more invasive nature of pity: there are some sights that force us to respond, and the forceful elicitation of emotion – as we can see in the critical history surrounding Lavinia – can produce discomfort and resentment alongside compassion. With both Lucrece and Lavinia, Shakespeare offers a physically assaulted woman whose presence feels, to others, like an assault itself, and in this respect these characters correspond to an established lineage of Lucrece figures. Although both of Shakespeare's creations retain the clear political value of the others – his Lucrece remains the catalyst to the overthrow of the Tarquins, Lavinia's violation eventually leads to the assassination of Saturninus – there is something more active and emotional about these characters, related to the severity of the image they present. The focus on grisly spectacle affords the opportunity to explore the full emotional effect of these women, an effect primarily shaped by the flow of pity. In the case of Lucrece, Shakespeare's emphasis on the agency of violated female characters is a deliberate attempt to move beyond the notion of the ruined woman as only a tool for prompting action, an object that would have to be repackaged for reinsertion into an already-established male community, even if such a thing were possible. Both Lucrece and Lavinia rely on the emotion of their situation, their pitiability and their presence, to form new bonds. In their violation, they find new ways to exploit their visuality and connect with those around them. In this way, they signal a new capacity to form interpersonal, emotional connections – through pity.

Chapter 3

DRAMATIC REWORKINGS OF POETIC PITY

'COMMEND THAT PITY I COULD NEVER FIND'

The real-life exchange between Sir George Rodney and Frances Howard is a rich and multi-faceted story that ends, tragically, with a rejected love suit and Rodney's death by suicide. There is much to discover in this history – about social power, gender politics, and the early modern marriage economy – but it is also a story about the English lyric tradition, poetic cliché, generic boundaries, and the seemingly impossible distance between *feeling* overwhelming emotion and adequately expressing it. Rodney had courted Frances Howard in the period between her first and second marriage, between 1599 and 1601. In 1601, after she had married another man, the Earl of Hertford, the bereft Rodney followed the newlyweds to Wiltshire, and ended up in a very brief poetic exchange with the Countess. The first and longer of the two poems he wrote to her, called the 'Elegia', closes with these thoughts:

> Fair, do not fret, nor yet at all be moved,
> That I have thus unfortunately loved,
> [...]
> Yet, if you have a thought to cast away,
> Cast it on me, and so you shall repay
> My service with some ease; and I, in mind,
> Commend that pity I could never find.
> Thus ever be as you were ever fair.
> Rest you in much content, I in despair.[1]

---

[1] Rodney's *Elegia* no longer exists in its original manuscript form: the strongest copy comes from Tobias Alston's 1639 commonplace book, held at the Beinecke Library (MS Osborn b197); it is also available at the Bodleian Library (MS Rawlinson poetry 160), which also contains a fragment of Howard's *The Answer* (where Alston omits it). The remainder of *The Answer* can also be found at the Bodleian (MS Ashmole 38). My references to Rodney or Howard come from the complete copytext compiled

Pity and Identity in the Age of Shakespeare

Nothing that Rodney says here or elsewhere in the 'Elegia' is particularly inventive or surprising, and in fact it is precisely this lack of originality that has driven the critical response to his work. As Eric Langley puts it, the 'Elegia' reads simply as 'one hundred and forty-two lines of stock Petrarchan verse'.[2] Situated comfortably within the conventional bounds of the complaint lyric and the love sonnet, Rodney's work has, Langley observes, 'not a thought in it unique, not a turn of phrase that may not be found frequently' amongst the better-known examples of these genres.[3] Like its language patterns, the emotional strategy of the 'Elegia' is equally recognisable for its adherence to generic convention. In its emphasis on pity sought and not obtained, on the consequences of an unfulfilled pity appeal, the passage quoted above aligns Rodney squarely with the *'poets Elegiack'* described, for example, by George Puttenham in *The arte of English poesie* (1589), one of the 'sort who sought the favor of faire Ladies, and coveted to bemone their estates at large, & the perplexities of love in certain *pitious* verse'.[4] In his *Observations in the Arte of English Poesie*, Thomas Campion similarly signals the tradition's linguistic patterns and its emphasis on pity, in his own showcase example of the elegy:

> Constant to none, but ever false to me,
> Traiter still to love through thy faint desires,
> Not hope of pittie now nor vaine redresse
> Turns my griefs to steares, and renu'd laments
> Too well thy empty vowes, and hollow thoughts
> Witnes both thy wrongs, and remorseles hart.[5]

Read together, these accounts of elegy make clear that Rodney's efforts neither innovate nor challenge a set of familiar poetic conventions: on the page, he is notable only in conformity. At the same time, the particulars of the Rodney–Howard exchange helpfully frame the core tensions of this chapter, not least because on one reading, Rodney so straightforwardly absorbs the language and emotion of his chosen genre. His use of pity in the 'Elegia' rehearses a lopsided emotional power structure that defined much of late sixteenth-century lyric. In this sense his work is part of a larger body

---

by Donald Foster, in '"Against the perjured falsehood of your tongues": Frances Howard on the Course of Love', *English Literary Renaissance*, 24 (1994), 72–103, here at 'Elegia' ll. 133–142.

[2] Eric Langley, *Narcissism and Suicide in Shakespeare and his Contemporaries* (Oxford: Oxford University Press, 2009), p. 9.

[3] Ibid., p. 14.

[4] George Puttenham, *The Arte of English Poesie* (London: 1589), sig. E2ᵛ, my emphasis.

[5] Thomas Campion, *Observations in the Art of English Poesie* (London: 1602), sigs. C1ʳ–C1ᵛ.

Dramatic Reworkings of Poetic Pity

of material that raises questions about the performance of early modern masculinity, especially as it is enacted against the subjectivity of real or imagined women. At the same time, Rodney's tragic conclusion complicates contemporary critical debates about the authenticity of professed emotion in early modern lyric.

On the most fundamental level, Rodney's story is desperately sad, an account of a tragically collapsed boundary between poetic speaker and emotional subject. The size and scale of Rodney's emotion is impossible to ignore, and has inspired a range of commentators. This begins – rather unusually – with Frances Howard herself. Howard's reaction is notable in part because she ignores the Petrarchan assumption of a silent female beloved and speaks – and not just for herself, but for all women entrapped in lyric poetry. On the whole however, both the seventeenth-century and the modern critical reactions focus more on the emotional register of Rodney's work, rather than the problematic gender dynamics that facilitate it: they articulate a more pressing discomfort about what Rodney represents in socio-literary terms. These responses imply that he is somehow unseemly, or *too much*: too much in his emotion, and therefore too much for his chosen genre. These reactions to the gentleman-knight also inspire the core question of this chapter: does early modern pity have specific generic identities? Is lyric pity a different prospect to dramatic pity? I believe it is, and that the Rodney case helps to clarify a genre-based attempt to distinguish different forms of literary pity.

The pity appeal in this kind of lyric poetry appears so frequently that it effectively identifies as Petrarchan the work in which it appears, signalling that work's sympathetic membership. The pity wielded by late sixteenth-century English Petrarchans has been read by critics as a disingenuous rhetorical strategy, a means of acquiring sex or social status. It has also been interpreted as a kind of violence or aggression, directed outward towards the (typically female) subject. Both these readings position lyric's emotional language as the key to understanding the aims and ambitions of the work more broadly. If we can determine how the emotion is being used, these readings imply, then we can better understand what the poet hoped to achieve through the work. This mode of thinking frames emotion as a tool, something deployed in service of a different goal. Rodney's tragic end, however, presents a striking counternarrative to this kind of critical discourse, reminding us of the possibility that the reference to emotion in lyric might just actually be a reference to emotion experienced. That this is one of the least common critical glosses on this kind of work suggests an interesting critical unwillingness to face masculine abjection, a phenomenon

Pity and Identity in the Age of Shakespeare

that Catherine Bates has tracked extensively and persuasively.[6] The reaction to George Rodney's case seems to confirm a similar discomfort with intense masculine abjection, but it also hints at something more. Descriptions of the hyper-Petrarchan Rodney as dramatic or theatrical suggest that he was understood as the victim of a serious navigational failure, one that was not just social and emotional, but also *generic*.

When Frances Howard responded to Rodney's 'Elegia', she did so in kind, with 'The Answer': a superior poem not just about Rodney's emotion but about the English lyric tradition itself. 'Poorly, methinks, you strive to play the poet', she writes, noting that true poets 'Hold flattery and lying the best grace' (ll. 122–124). Reflecting on Rodney's position she offers this stern counsel:

> No, no, I never yet could hear one prove
> That there was ever any died for love.
> Nor would I have you be the man begin
> The earnest dare to such a sportive sin –
> For that would prove a laughter for an age,
> *Stuff for a play, fit matter for a stage.* (ll. 119–144, my emphasis)

This might be a sincere effort to temper Rodney by reminding him that society was a kind of ever-present audience for people like them. At the same time, Howard's 'Answer' equally cements her position in this dynamic as the more commanding and competent literary figure. This is a person who understood and was able to articulate the underlying principles of lyric. She is also voicing serious claims about genre, particularly in suggesting that drama and poetry navigate differently the relationship between emotion, expression, and action. When Howard notes that Rodney '*Poorly* [...] strive[s] to play the poet', she implies a set of generic standards that her suitor fails to observe. For Howard, Rodney's claim that his emotional distress will manifest as a real-life physical threat is a move that pushes him away from poetry and into drama. Literally to die for love, she claims, would not only 'prove a laughter for an age', but would also make Rodney himself 'stuff for a play, fit matter for a stage'. If this is a strategy for containing his emotion, a manner of diffusing his threat of physical violence, it is also a claim that seeks to situate certain kinds of emotion generically. This is a suggestion that certain forms of literature may be better placed to express and accommodate certain scales of feeling.

Put another way, the Rodney–Howard exchange opens up questions about how emotional narratives fit within generic cultures, and how the framework of a given genre might help (or hinder) the expression

---

[6] Catherine Bates, *Masculinity, Gender and Identity in the English Renaissance Lyric* (Cambridge: Cambridge University Press, 2007).

Dramatic Reworkings of Poetic Pity

of emotion. In this chapter, I trace the central significance of pity in late sixteenth-century English lyric poetry, arguing that attending to pity illuminates the ways in which poetry understood and managed circuits of emotional overrun and interpersonal obligation. From there I return to drama, considering how (and why) the dramatic genre reproduced and revised these poetic frameworks for emotional exchange. I contend that the dramatic engagement with poetic pity represents a large-scale re-working of pity's emotional register, a constructive dismantling that creates space for a theatrical reimagining of pity's social significance.

By the time Rodney replicated the basic pattern of emotional exchange made famous by the key figures of English lyric – a pattern in which the male speaker confesses pure abjection and begs for the comfort of the beloved's pity – it was a recognisable poetic cliché, made impotent by repetition. Rodney's emotion, therefore, could no longer be effectively expressed within the literary framework he selected. On one reading of this situation, it is easy to see why Howard suggests a certain theatricality in Rodney's response: one of the near-contemporary reports of Rodney, for example, claims that he wrote his verses to the Countess 'in his own blood'.[7] But does this kind of exchange, which may effectively be distilled as a rejected romantic appeal for pity, truly resonate with contemporary dramatic style? This kind of moment – the abject lover's appeal for pity – appears regularly enough on the early modern stage, but the framing of these appearances is significant: they are more typically re-cast as comic. Presented this way, these references to pity resonate as a knowing wink to the clichéd modes that once dominated another form. These are therefore better understood as moments of generic posturing: direct references to poetic convention that, taken together, allow one very recognisable deployment of pity to be contained and framed as purely poetic. This is a move, I contend, that creates space for the more expansive vision of dramatic pity that I trace throughout this book – not a proposed solution for romantic agony, as Rodney would have it, or a rhetorical tool for social and/or sexual posturing, but rather something that more broadly situates the individual within their community, and structures systems of feeling and obligation.

PITY AND ENGLISH PETRARCHISM

It is easy enough to identify that Petrarchism was a defining literary phenomenon in early modern England, but the prospect of pinning Petrarchism down to more precise coordinates is a far more daunting task. As William

---

[7]   Arthur Wilson, *The History of Great Britain* (London, 1653), sig. Ll^v.

Pity and Identity in the Age of Shakespeare

Kennedy describes them, the various critical accounts of Petrarchism are successful only in 'construct[ing] a narrative of *multiple* Petrarchs'.[8] 'By the time the sonnet was in vogue in England', Heather Dubrow notes, 'poets who wished to write within or react against that tradition confronted not one but several traditions – and not one but several Petrarchs'.[9] This multiplicity is apparent in the very many components of Rodney's poetic outpouring that resonate as Petrarchan, and that are, like so many other examples of the genre, 'seemingly conventional enough to exemplify Petrarchism, [and] seemingly unremarkable enough to invite [only] the briefest summary of how it does so'.[10] Rodney's patterns of description are all easily located in the work of earlier poets, and the gentleman-knight owes a particularly striking debt to Philip Sidney's genre-defining *Astrophil and Stella*.[11] When Rodney remarks 'my heart shall bleed as fast as thine shall weep' (l. 8), it is hard not to think of Astrophil: 'I cry thy sighs, my deere, thy teares I bleede'.[12] Rodney's description of Howard as 'Sweet poison, precious woe, infectious jewel' (l. 33) remembers the account of Stella in Song 5: 'I said thou wert most sweet, sweet poison to my heart' (Song 5, l. 8). Rodney's closing reference in the 'Elegia' to 'that pity I could never find' evokes *Astrophil and Stella*'s Sonnet 44, which deals entirely with Astrophil's failed efforts to elicit Stella's pity:

> My words I know do well set forth my mind;
> My mind bemoans his sense of inward smart;
> Such smart may pity claim of any heart;
> Her heart, sweet heart, is of no tiger's kind:
> And yet she hears, yet I no pity find;
> But more I cry, less grace she doth impart. (ll. 1–6)

---

[8] William Kennedy, 'Petrarchan Poetics', in Glyn P. Norton (ed.), *The Cambridge History of Literary Criticism*, vol. 3 (Cambridge: Cambridge University Press, 1999), pp. 119–126 (p. 119, my emphasis).

[9] Heather Dubrow, *Echoes of Desire: English Petrarchism and its Counterdiscourses* (Ithaca, NY: Cornell University Press, 1995), p. 5.

[10] Ibid., p. 3.

[11] Using Sidney as a primary influence is, it must be said, further evidence of Rodney's lack of originality. As one critic memorably put it, *Astrophil and Stella* was so popular and influential that it became 'a quarry for pickpockets of others' wits'. See: Thomas P. Roche, *Petrarch and the English Sonnet Sequences* (New York, NY: AMS Press, Inc., 1989), p. 193.

[12] Sir Philip Sidney, *Astrophil and Stella* in Katherine Duncan-Jones (ed.), *The Oxford Authors: Sir Philip Sidney* (Oxford: Oxford University Press, 1989), pp. 153–211, Sonnet 93, l. 14. All other references to *Astrophil and Stella* will be to this edition, and given parenthetically.

Dramatic Reworkings of Poetic Pity

In part, what Sidney presents here is an account of a more intimate scale of reactive failure. It takes a general theory of how pity functions, and then directs it to an exchange between two people: 'And yet *she* hears, yet *I* no pity find' (my emphasis). A sense of thwarted process underpins this sonnet, as the speaker confirms both a conviction of method, and the beloved's rejection of it: the 'more I cry', Astrophil observes, the 'less grace she doth impart'. Astrophil's apparent faith in his own strategy – 'such smart may pity claim of *any* heart' – signals an understanding of pity as a universal function, something that can be relied upon to function given the correct combination of emotion and expression. This goes some way to explaining the broader prevalence of the poetic attempts to seek pity. A cursory glance at English lyric yields numerous overtures from other poets, each of whom apparently see pity as a means of attaining emotional release. This belief is evident in Thomas Wyatt, for example, where pity is imagined to dispel cruelty:

> Pass forth, my wonted cries,
> Those cruel ears to pierce,
> Which in most hateful wise
> Doth still my plaints reverse.
> Do you, my tears, also
> So wet her barren heart,
> That pity there may grow,
> And cruelty depart.[13]

For Wyatt, the efforts to communicate abjection are also an attempt to cultivate pity, and thereby overcome the obstacle of the beloved's perceived 'cruelty'. A similar desire for pity is also articulated early in Samuel Daniel's *Delia*: 'My humble accents crave the olive bough | Of her mild pity and relenting will'.[14] Each of these examples positions pity as a means of gaining access, but also as the key to restructuring the emotional landscape in favour of the poetic speaker's subjective position. By fostering – through poetry – this specific emotion in another, the speaker produces a space in which he can thrive.

Barnabe Barnes's *Parthenophil and Parthenophe* signals a similar desire for the beloved's pity with Parthenophil reminding his lady that his torment will persist 'Unlesse her pittie make my greefe asswage' (XXXV:8, sig. D1ᵛ).[15] He continues:

---

[13]   Joost Daalder (ed.), *Sir Thomas Wyatt: Collected Poems* (London: Oxford University Press, 1975), CXLVIII, ll. 1–8.

[14]   Samuel Daniel, *Delia*, in Gordon Braden (ed.), *Sixteenth-Century Poetry* (Oxford: Blackwell Publishing, 2005), pp. 464–483, Sonnet 4, ll. 11–12.

[15]   Barnabe Barnes, *Parthenophil and Parthenophe, Sonnettes, Madrigals, Elegies and Odes* (London: 1593). This sequence contains madrigals, sonnets, elegies, odes, and sestines. Sonnet citations are listed by sonnet number (in Roman numeral), line,

Pity and Identity in the Age of Shakespeare

> My sences never shall in quiet rest
> Till though be pitifull, and love alike:
> And if thou never pitie my distresses
> Thy crueltie with endlesse force shall strike
> Upon my witts, to ceaselesse writs addrest. (XVIII:9–13, sig. C1ʳ)

Like Wyatt, Sidney, and Daniel, Barnes's speaker frames pity as something desperately needed, and cruelly withheld. This is an emotional turn that repackages noncompliance either as a kind of emotional short-circuit – a failure or misfiring on the part of the beloved – or as a kind of pointed violence committed against the speaker. On any reading, this is a turn that asserts and defines the beloved's own agency, narrating and dictating both her engagement and her intentions. Both a literary and an emotional posture, this also facilitates a striking displacement of responsibility, as the speaker forcibly positions the 'unfeeling' beloved into the role of managing and maintaining the speaker's emotional distress. Somehow, she is expected to do this from a position of silence, without a voice in the narrative.

That pity is something to be sought – some sort of prize for the speaker, or a route for his emotional release – is one of the opening premises of *Astrophil and Stella*, where Astrophil identifies pity as a vital component in a broader process of achieving his aim:

> Loving in truth, and fain in verse my love to show,
> That she (deare she) might take some pleasure of my pain;
> Pleasure might cause her read, reading might make her know;
> Knowledge might *pity* win, and *pity grace obtain*,
> I sought fit words to paint the blackest face of woe. (Sonnet 1, ll. 1–5, my
>   emphasis.)

This description frames courtship and poetic appeal explicitly as a process to undertake. The speaker feels love and writes the agony of it in verse; the beloved reads, understands, and pities; that pity carries the 'grace' (the emotional and sexual release) needed to provide the desired relief. In one sense this is a formula for conquest, and one that hinges on pity. It is also true that the presentation here suggests a kind of subversive control: though Astrophil narrates the struggle of expression, in another sense he makes clear that he has both the knowledge of what to do, and the means to do it. As Alex Davis observes, Sidney's opening poem is 'on some level at least, thoroughly—wittily—disingenuous' in its performance of authorial

---

and signature (e.g. X:1–2, sig. D3ᵛ); madrigal citations follow the same format, but are numbered traditionally (e.g. 1:9–10, sig. D2ʳ). Elegy, ode, and sestine citations are distinguished by prefixes *Ele.*, *Ode*, and *Sest.*, respectively.

Dramatic Reworkings of Poetic Pity

inadequacy.[16] This performance of helplessness is both a core feature of the Petrarchan mode and, some suggest, a defining component of its deceit: 'to fall apart in a masterfully crafted sonnet', as Nancy Vickers puts it, 'is, in a sense, not to fall apart at all'.[17]

For many critics, the emotional posturing of English lyric presents a troubling paradox that demands resolution, not least because these literary narratives are predominantly and problematically controlled by men. Roland Greene has argued that lyric sequences 'posit and name selves', but of course it is always, and only, the subjectivity of the speaker articulated, and even this is fractured.[18] This sense of fracture is evident in one critic's observation that Elizabethan sonnet sequences 'manifest a desire to utter the truth of the self again and again in diverse combinations'.[19] It is also the case that the kinds of selfhood being named here – gendered, social, literary – are themselves in conflict, especially when these constructions of selfhood hinge on the expression and direction of emotion. As Heather Dubrow puts it: 'If storytelling is an assertion of male power, what happens when a man tells stories about his own defeat?'[20] In spite of the worrying power dynamics on display in these works, which routinely see the female subject narrated and defined without consent or control, it can be difficult to read any coherence in English lyric's emotional messiness. There are simply too many contradictions and complications. In the male-authored texts that represent the bulk of this material, the speakers repeatedly frame themselves both as men and as poets, though these subjective positions often seem fundamentally incompatible. Both the male speaker's professed powerlessness and his reports of bounded autonomy are undercut by the utter control he wields as poet. The male speaker complains that he receives no relief, no intercession from the beloved, but the poet also does not allow anyone else to speak.

In his language and literary debts, Rodney is a self-consciously poetic figure, closely following the approach to pity I have pointed to in other, earlier poets. Nevertheless, it is worth noting that he also makes an effort

---

[16] Alex Davis, 'Revolution by Degrees: Philip Sidney and *Gradatio*', *Modern Philology*, 108.4 (2011), 488–506 (p. 489). On this as an explicitly Petrarchan mode, see also: Germaine Warkentin, 'Sidney and the Supple Muse: Compositional Procedures in Some Sonnets of *Astrophil and Stella*', in *Sir Philip Sidney: An Anthology of Modern Criticism*, ed. Dennis Kay (Oxford: Clarendon, 1987), pp. 171–184.

[17] Nancy J. Vickers, 'Vital Signs: Petrarch and Popular Culture', *Romantic Review*, 77 (1988), 184–195 (p. 193).

[18] Roland Greene, *Post-Petrarchism: Origins and Innovations of the Western Lyric Sequence* (Princeton, NJ: Princeton University Press, 1991), p. 14.

[19] Scott Wilson, 'Racked on the Tyrant's Bed': The Politics of Pleasure and Pain and the Elizabethan Sonnet Sequences', *Textual Practice* 3 (1989), 234–249 (p. 235).

[20] Dubrow, p. 3.

Pity and Identity in the Age of Shakespeare

to evade the inherent conflict of subjective positions in the 'Elegia' by repeatedly identifying himself explicitly as a man (rather than a poet). He is the poem's 'forsaken man' (l. 45), and offers a sex-dependent classification when he acknowledges that 'The times may say (by what is done) | My father had one lost, degenerate son' (ll. 21–22). These references are vital positioning moments, but they also suggest an attempt to avoid the spectre of artifice associated with both form and tradition. Rodney's language here positions him clearly in relation to his assertion that 'The wisest clerks in learning best approve | In women, pity, and in men, true love' (ll. 37–38). His gendered self-reference importantly frames his identity in a way that consolidates his emotional agenda: he is a man, and his love is true. At the same time, it is precisely at this kind of posturing that Howard takes aim in her own response. By virtue of its very existence, Howard's 'Answer' is a denial of the traditional, one-sided accounts of English lyric, and her efforts to explicate both the futility of Rodney's suit, and the social context of their exchange begins with a refusal to let Rodney sidestep or downplay his poetic identity. In that memorable and cutting line, Howard forcibly reorients Rodney with his authorial, *generic* identifier: 'Poorly, methinks, you strive to play the *poet*'. The generic classification is a way of contextualising Rodney's professed emotion; it resituates him, clearly, in his chosen tradition. On a broader scale however, this interaction between Rodney and Howard helpfully glosses how the lyric tradition was understood and navigated in its own time, and specifically highlights the intersections between genre and emotion. What Howard is suggesting is that the form Rodney selects also frames the emotion he professes, and limits its scale.

Even so, these are incompatibilities that Rodney seems intent on denying. Pity takes a central role in one of Rodney's clearest expressions of the link between lyric, selfhood, and emotion, where he uses pity both to frame the stakes of their (at this moment, still one-sided) exchange, and to redefine his own subjectivity:

> Thus to thine angry beauty, precious dear,
> A pyramis of pity will I rear,
> A sacrifice of peace to end all strife –
> As true a heart as ever harboured life. (ll. 115–118)

As he recasts himself as a monument to his own feeling – 'a *pyramis* of pity' – Rodney's use of the word 'pyramis' here is particularly impactful, a word that brings together physical violence and emotion by evoking the self-slaughtering lovers Pyramus and Thisbe. In yet another sense however, this is an explicitly poetic reference as well: a 'piramis' is one of the shapes

Dramatic Reworkings of Poetic Pity

outlined in George Puttenham's *The Arte of Poesie* (1589), a poem laid out to visually evoke a pyramid.[21]

Rodney's description of himself as a monument to his own feeling was prescient, as the social commentary that emerged from these events offers an image of a man made socially pitiful through his ineffectual attempts to garner the lyric pity he sought. John Chamberlain, in two letters to Dudley Carlton (one before and one after Rodney's death) speculated that Rodney went 'out of his witts' for [Howard], '(whom he woed and could not obtaine)', and that 'his braines were not able to bear the burthen, but have plaide banckrout and left him raving'.[22] Chamberlain reads Rodney's turn to physical violence as a last testament to emotional veracity, commenting that he 'cut his owne throat as an earnest of his love'.[23] The image is one of emotional overrun and broken subjectivity, and it fits into a broader response to Rodney that seems intent on repositioning him at a social and emotional distance, as an aberrant figure. When Arthur Wilson gives an account of Rodney and Howard in *The History of Great Britain* (1653), it is again an account of Rodney's weaknesses, his failures, and his 'scattered Spirits'. Wilson writes:

> Rodney having drunk in too much affection, and not being able with his Reason to digest it, summoned up his scattered Spirits to a most desperate attempt; and coming to Amesbury in Wiltshire (where the Earl and his Lady were then Resident) to act it, he retired to an Inn in the Town, shut himself up in a Chamber, and wrote a large paper of well-composed Verses, to the Countess in his own blood (strange kind of Composedness) wherein he bewailes and laments his own unhappiness; and when he had sent them to her, as a sad Catastrophe to all his Miseries, he ran himself upon his Sword, and so ended that life which he thought death to injoy; leaving the Countess to a strict remembrance of her inconstancy, and himself *a desperate and sad Spectacle of Frailty*.[24]

---

[21] As Puttenham writes, the visual arrangement of a poem contributes to its overall success and beauty, insomuch as it 'yelds an ocular representation, your meeters being by good symmetrie reduced into certaine Geometricall figures, whereby the maker is restrained to keepe him within his bounds, and sheweth not onely more art, but serveth also much better for briefenesse and subtiltie of device' (sig. M4ᵛ). As the 'Elegia' only exists in commonplace transcriptions, it is not clear if the original piece was actually arranged in this way.

[22] John Chamberlain, *Letters of John Chamberlain*, ed. by Norman Egbert McClure, vol. I (Philadelphia, PA: The American Philosophical Society, 1939), p. 126; p. 116.

[23] Chamberlain, *Letters*, p. 126.

[24] Wilson, sig. Ll1ᵛ, my emphasis. The edits made in the course of Wilson's report obscure what to my mind is the most important detail: that this was a literary exchange between two active participants, rather than a solitary poetic testimony of one man's grief in

Pity and Identity in the Age of Shakespeare

In part, Wilson's is an account of the collapsed boundary between Rodney's literary and real-life existence. Describing Rodney's demise as a sort of literary event, Wilson references the 'large paper of well-composed Verses' that the gentleman-knight produces, their manner of production, and the resulting 'strange kind of composedness' that conflates Rodney's literary output with his own mental and emotional state. There is, in this account, no separation between the poet and the person: Rodney's verses are just one part of the 'strict remembrance' of his suit, and it is he 'himself' that becomes the 'desperate and sad Spectacle of Frailty'. Rodney's appearances in Chamberlain's letters (of 1601) and in Wilson's 1653 *History* both demonstrate a desire to set Rodney at a remove. Both these accounts suggest that Rodney made himself an enduring topic of (somewhat withering) social commentary. These accounts also reinforce the warning that Howard issues in the 'Answer': that in his response to a rejected personal and poetic appeal, Rodney might 'prove a laughter for an age'.

Read in these ways, the story of George Rodney produces a stark counternarrative to the critical habit of reading the recurring figures of pitiable masculinity in English lyric as figures of strength and empowerment, figures who might ultimately be read in terms of dominance and masculine prowess.[25] This view sees 'strategic' professions of abjection serving a higher purpose, either productively preying upon the sentimentality of the female, or serving to cement an advantageous social position. Critics have referred to 'the abject

---

love. Wilson's description here forms only one part of a longer sexist indictment of Frances Howard, a woman who achieved unprecedented social elevation through a series of increasingly advantageous marriages. For Wilson, Rodney's death becomes a testament to the lady's 'inconstancy'. With her part edited down, and compared against Rodney's obvious emotional distress, Howard is cast as the kind of cruel mistress who might 'easily' pass such a tragedy over. In terms of action, emotion, and literary output, Rodney is cast as markedly active, set distinctly against Howard's passivity. As Wilson tells it, the verses are *sent to* Howard, and Rodney's tragic action is a response to her silence, the conclusion of a conversation that was only ever one-sided. Howard is thus twice-defined by the literary descriptions of other men, the very thing she resists so stridently in her own verse. She is shaped by Wilson's retelling of events, just as she is shaped by Rodney's proximate emotional labour, and his physical actions. Cast as the point around which Rodney moves, Howard stands as the emotional absence that amplifies his own affective identity. In reality however, Howard's poetic input (and output) actually slightly surpassed Rodney's, line-for-line.

25 One of the earliest articulations of this stance is C.S. Lewis's analysis of medieval courtly love in *The Allegory of Love*: though Lewis notes that the men of this tradition 'seem to be always weeping and always on their knees before ladies of inflexible cruelty' (p. 1), he reads in these texts an exploration of 'worlds of new, subtle, and noble feeling, *under the guidance of clear and masculine thought*' (p. 255, my emphasis). C.S. Lewis, *The Allegory of Love* (Oxford: Clarendon Press, 1936).

Dramatic Reworkings of Poetic Pity

position of the lover' as a 'fiction', while others contend that the expressed vulnerability of the male subject is negated by the 'mastery of the poet'.[26] 'The beloved is never his whole concern', Carol Thomas Neely observes, noting that the 'focus is on the poetry itself – its function, its power, its limitations.[27] 'The poems', she contends, 'are intended for an audience other than the beloved'.[28] As Nancy Vickers explains, 'the speaker's investment in his song reveals itself to be not only – if at all – in winning the lost lady [...] but rather in winning a lost, or as yet unwon glory [...] through the exercise of an overpowering stylistic mastery'.[29] Interpretations like these have a profound impact on our understanding of the emotion underpinning this work: placing the poems squarely in the context of social gain and stylistic mastery importantly repositions emotion as just another of the poet's tools. Put another way: the notion of authentic emotion sits uncomfortably alongside social manoeuvring. This sense of disingenuous emotion must be at least partly due to the repetition embedded in this poetic tradition, what Natasha Diller describes as 'the formulaic nature of much of the Petrarchism of the 1590s, which became the *hollow repetition* of a recognisable stance for the sake of rehearsing a posture'.[30] Calling to mind the culture of textual circulation that is also so important in the Rodney–Howard exchange, Diller's reference to 'rehearsal' here acknowledges that lyric poetry represents a form of social posturing; it imagines a framework for emotion that is similarly embedded in self-conscious performance.

More than anything, this reaction to lyric poetry's emotional register suggests a driving need to account for and contain unwieldy feeling. As Cynthia Marshall observes, 'In the view of most modern readers, the Petrarchan code that shapes the sequences – suffering lover, scornful beloved, oxymoronic passions, obsessive complaint – registers their distance from actual emotional experience.[31] The drive in readers to identify

---

[26] Mary Villeponteaux, '*Semper Eadem*: Belphoebe's Denial of Desire', in Claude J. Summers and Ted-Larry Pebworth (eds.), *Renaissance Discourses of Desire* (Columbia, MO: University of Missouri Press, 1993), pp. 29–45 (p. 38); Patricia Parker, *Literary Fat Ladies: Rhetoric, Gender, Property* (London: Methuen, 1987), p. 62. See also: Lauro Martines, 'The Politics of Love Poetry in Renaissance Italy', in Janet Levarie Smarr (ed.), *Historical Criticism and the Challenge of Theory* (Urbana, IL: University of Illinois Press, 1993), pp. 129–144.

[27] Carol Thomas Neely, 'The Structure of English Renaissance Sonnet Sequences', *English Literary History*, 45.3 (1978), 359–389, p. 364.

[28] Ibid., p. 364.

[29] Vickers, 'Vital Signs', p. 186.

[30] Natasha Distiller, *Desire and Gender in the Sonnet Tradition* (Houndmills: Palgrave Macmillan, 2008), p. 63, my emphasis.

[31] Cynthia Marshall, *The Shattering of the Self*, p. 57.

Pity and Identity in the Age of Shakespeare

(or imagine) a secure distance between the speaker and his emotions seems part of a larger instinct to rebrand literary expression that might become threatening if brought too close to a real-life social dynamic. In his influential account of Petrarchism, for example, Leonard Forster establishes a clear divide between poetic and social realities. Forster describes a tradition in which 'we are introduced to a world in which women dominate', but this, he explains, is simply 'a literary *fiction* to compensate for a *real state of affairs* in which it was a man's world and a violent one at that'.[32] Forster's in particular is an early example of what has become a long tradition of 'recuperative narratives', Catherine Bates's term for the many critical accounts that insist on reading these poetic expressions of emotional weakness as a masculine, socially-embedded articulation of strength, power, and status.[33] While this way of reading the material does highlight the gender power imbalance that sits at the heart of this poetry – identifying the tools of female disempowerment that are embedded in this work down to a structural level – it also worryingly overlooks the possibility (and probability) of lyric poetry as an outlet for genuine sadness. According to Bates, these reading instincts ignore what might be a willing and masochistic embrace of abjection. 'The problem here', she suggests, 'is a refusal to contemplate what might be considered to be the most "perverse" position of all – namely, a truly disempowered position'.[34]

CONSEQUENCES OF EMOTIONAL OVERRUN

While Bates and others seek to reclaim lyric poetry as a body of work that might dismantle a long-cherished vision of stable and powerful early modern masculine subjectivity, this is also a literary tradition that illustrates the overwhelming power of emotion on individual subjects. Some have read the poetry itself as sufficient consolation for desolation, calling it the 'one thing the Petrarchan poet has, in compensation for his anguish', but at the same time the darker undertones present in this poetry also make clear that literary solace is not enough.[35] Masculine disempowerment, bound up as it is in the fruitless appeal for pity, manifests clearly in the threads of violence embedded in this literature.[36] That violence is, moreover, a testament to the threat and

---

[32] Leonard Forster, *The Icy Fire: Five Studies in European Petrarchism* (Cambridge: Cambridge University Press, 1969), p. 2.

[33] Bates, p. 6.

[34] Ibid., p. 5.

[35] William Kerrigan and Gordon Braden, *The Idea of the Renaissance* (Baltimore, MD: Johns Hopkins University Press, 1989), p. 172.

[36] See also Anne Ferry, *The "Inward" Language: Sonnets of Wyatt, Sidney, Shakespeare, Donne* (Chicago, IL: University of Chicago Press, 1983), where Ferry argues that

Dramatic Reworkings of Poetic Pity

consequences of the tradition's emotional structure. In Rodney's case, of course, this violence is especially hard to ignore, and tragically turned inward. Nevertheless, Rodney's case also sits in a broader narrative of violence that was more typically directed at a feminine beloved. These threads of violence offer another important way of scrutinising the central critical question over the sincerity and gravity of the poetic speaker's professed abjection. Close attention to this aggression confirms that the stakes of these emotional overtures are extremely high, while also making obvious that these appeals registered as a kind of subjective scattering. Thomas Lodge's *Phillis*, for example, acknowledges this when the speaker makes reference to 'the *Chaos* of my ceaselesse care'.[37] That chaos, moreover, is directly linked to the absence of pity, the beloved's failure to dispense it: the speaker's care 'Is by hir eies *unpitied* and unseene | In whom all giftes but *pity* planted are'.[38]

What many of these sequences make obvious is that left unanswered, the 'chaos of care' that Lodge references escalates in disturbing ways. The violent undertones (in some cases, overtones) often stem explicitly from these open bids for pity, and might also indicate a frantic resistance to the kind of subjective dismantling that eventually finds George Rodney. In the Barnes sequence, for example, the bitterness and aggression that emerges is explicitly tied to absent pity. This is made clear in the moments that lead to Parthenophe's rape, as Parthenophil wonders:

Why should I weepe in vayne, poore and remedilesse?
Why should I make complainte, to the deafe wildernesse?
Why should I sigh for ease, *sighes they breede maladie*?
Why should I grone in hart, *grones they bring miserie*?
Why should teares, plaintes, & sighes mingled with heavy
Practise their crueltie, whiles I complaine to stones?
[...]
Oh but Parthenophe turne and be pittifull!

---

early modern lyric poets reclaim the clichéd rhetoric of courtship by infusing it with genuine feeling; Marguerite Waller, 'The Empire's New Clothes: Refashioning the Renaissance', in Sheila Fisher and Janet E. Halley (eds.), *Seeking the Women in Late Medieval and Renaissance Writings* (Knoxville, TN: University of Tennessee Press, 1989), pp. 160–183; and Jonathan Crewe, *Trials of Authorship: Anterior Forms and Poetic Reconstruction from Wyatt to Shakespeare* (Berkeley, CA: University of California Press, 1990), in which Crewe calls into question the idea that any 'palpably crafted/crafty simulation of weakness, emasculation, or abjection must "logically" imply its opposite' (p. 28).

[37] Thomas Lodge, *Phillis* (London: 1593), sonnet 3, l. 2, sig. B3ʳ.

[38] Ibid., ll. 3–4, sig. B3ʳ.

Pity and Identity in the Age of Shakespeare

In the midst of Parthenophil's palpable resentment there is also a mounting aggression present, one that seeks to protect and advance the speaker's selfhood even (or especially) at the cost of the beloved. Why bother with emotional appeals, Parthenophil wonders, when 'sighes they breed maladie' and 'grones they bring miseries'? In the absence of the desired outcome, his emotion seeks alternative outlets, other methods of dissipation. It turns to violence.

The concluding episode of the sequence imagines Parthenophil using black magic – reaching beyond his earthly capabilities in a fantasy of control – to summon the nude Parthenophe, whose 'hardned hart [...] pittied not my teares' (*Sest.* 5:55, sig. T4ᵛ). Offering a justification that rehearses a familiar displacement of emotional responsibility onto the beloved – 'Her cruell loves in me such heate have kindled' (*Sest.* 5: 11, sig. T4ʳ) – he then rapes her, apparently in an effort to resolve an emotional gap by forcing the connection he has been denied:

> *Joyne joyne* Parthenophe thy selfe unbare,
> None can perceive us in the silent night,
> *Now I will cease from sighes, lamentes, and teares,*
> And cease Parthenophe sweet *cease thy teares*
> [...] for we conjoyne this heavenly night. (*Sest.* 5:88–93, sig. U1ᵛ, my
>   emphasis)

This is a shocking fantasy of violence that extends beyond the physical, as Parthenophil dismantles Parthenophe's agency in order to reconstruct and protect his own. The same 'teares' that have threatened to disintegrate him are now forcibly transferred to Parthenophe, even as he attempts to contain and deny them. This is an extreme example of a broader tendency towards poetic violence in the lyric tradition, though the scale and extremity of Barnes's sequence, it must be said, does seem in keeping with the poet's broader personal and poetic style. As Thomas Nashe memorably reported, Barnes was neither a celebrated nor a subtle figure at court, as Nashe described one occasion on which, 'with a codpisse as big as Bolognian sawcedge', Barnes 'went up and downe Towne, and shewd himself in the Presence at Court, where he was generally laught out by the Noblemen and Ladies'.[39] As Wendy Wall notes, 'The image of Barnes seeking favor by such a hyperbolic breach of decorum acts as a correlate to his poetic sequence'.[40] 'Barnes's inappropriate literary and courtly displays', Wall observes, 'were

---

[39] Thomas Nashe, *Have With You to Saffron-Walden* (1596), in Ronald McKerrow (ed.), *The Works of Thomas Nashe*, rev. F.P. Wilson, 5 vols (Oxford: Basil Blackwell, 1958), 3: p. 109.

[40] Wall, p. 187.

Dramatic Reworkings of Poetic Pity

unsuccessful'.[41] It would however be a mistake to dismiss what we find in Barnes and in *Parthenophil and Parthenophe*, particularly since some critics have suggested that the rape of Parthenophe crystallises the core tensions of English Petrarchism. Jeffrey Nelson, for example, has read Parthenophe's rape as a realisation of 'the threat posed by courtiers who are given no satisfaction for the desire defined and created by the Elizabethan court and the Petrarchan conventions'.[42] Thomas Roche has called this scene 'the inevitable conclusion of the physical demands posited by the tradition'.[43] Both of these readings, it must be noted, seem inflected with a problematic willingness to explain or even justify an unforgivable violation. At the same time, both Nelson and Roche identify poetry and poetic convention as ineffective containers of sprawling feeling. The violence that seeps out, they suggest, is a bold testament to an unsustainable emotional landscape.

Emotionally-driven violence is easily traced in other sequences as well. William Smith's *Chloris*, for example, clearly outlines a prospective advantage to lashing out at the beloved:

> Tell me my deere what mooves thy ruthlesse minde
> To be so cruell, seeing thou art so faire?
> Did Nature frame thy beautie so unkinde?
> Or dost thou scorne to pitie my despaire?
> O no it was not natures ornament,
> But winged loves unpartiall cruell wound,
> Which in my hart is ever permanent,
> Untill my Chloris me whole and sound.
> O glorious love-god thinke on my harts griefe,
> Let not thy vassaile pine through deepe disdaine,
> *By wounding Chloris I shall finde reliefe,*
> *If thou impart to hir some of my paine.*[44]

Smith's speaker refigures violence as release, suggesting not that his emotion can dissipate but rather that it can and must be transferred and refigured onto the beloved. In one sense, this is a refusal to sit with insular emotion, an aggressive push to frame the lover's emotion in more social, shared terms. As Cynthia Marshall points out, in this poem Smith insists that 'where love is experienced as pain, wounding the beloved figures as the

---

[41]   Ibid., p. 187.

[42]   Jeffrey N. Nelson, 'Lust and Black Magic in Barnabe Barnes's *Parthenophil and Parthenophe*', *Sixteenth Century Journal*, 25 (1994), pp. 595–608 (p. 595).

[43]   Roche, p. 246.

[44]   William Smith, *Chloris, or The complaint of the passionate despised shepheard* (London: 1596), sonnet 11, ll. 1–12, sig. B1ᵛ, my emphasis.

Pity and Identity in the Age of Shakespeare

logical means towards mutuality'.[45] The poem assumes a system of emotional obligation that locks speaker and beloved together. It is a push towards a kind of emotional community, but a hostile one. Moreover, this is still a 'community' formed in sole service of the speaker's subjectivity, a 'mutuality' intended only to relieve the burden of the speaker's emotional overrun.

Astrophil and Stella imagines a turn to physical violation as well, when in Sonnet 73 Astrophil kisses the sleeping Stella:

> And yet my star, because a sugared kiss
> In sport I sucked, while she asleep did lie,
> Doth lour, nay chide; nay, threat for only this:
> Sweet, it was saucy Love, not humble I.
> But no 'scuse serves, she makes her wrath appear
> In beauty's throne; see now who dares come near
> Those scarlet judges, threat'ning bloody pain?
> O heav'nly fool, thy most kiss-worthy face
> Anger invests with such a lovely grace
> That anger's self I needs must kiss again. (ll. 5–14)

Astrophil's mention of Stella's 'wrath' makes clear that his advances on her sleeping form are understood as a violation, but the manner in which Astrophil displaces all culpability makes this an attack not just on Stella's body, but also upon her very selfhood. Astrophil blames 'saucy Love', and 'thy most kiss-worthy face', implying that he is the disempowered victim of his emotions, driven to act by inchoate forces, or by Stella herself. Of course, what looks like a renouncement of subjective agency is the very opposite. The poem ends with the lingering threat of future emotional overrun, and future physical violence directed not at Stella precisely, but her reconfiguration as 'anger's self': 'Anger invests with such a lovely grace | That anger's self I needs must kiss again'. With this Astrophil forwards an equally disturbing kind of violence, that kind narrated by Frances Howard when she denies any share in the responsibility for the consequences of Rodney's emotion.

As Frances Howard pointedly reminds Rodney, the lyric tradition strips women of their own emotional agency, forcibly applying new identities and unwanted responsibilities through male narratives of emotional obligation. 'Small cause have I, the owner, to rejoice' Howard writes, noting that 'for the fruitless painting of my cheeks', she must 'be termed "cruel"' (ll. 11–15). Howard's 'Answer' is also an account of her affective boundaries, a poetic expression that seeks to resituate a literary exchange in its real-life contexts: 'Divided in your sorrows have I strove | To pity that attempt I must not love' (ll. 1–2). Howard takes aim at the elements that Rodney aligns – pity

---

[45] Marshall, p. 83.

Dramatic Reworkings of Poetic Pity

and love – and severs the imagined link between them in order to deny her own place in the emotional landscape he constructs. She also takes the opportunity to bring Rodney back down to earth, by reminding him that someone else won the suit: 'The love that should have thanked you is bestowed!', she writes, 'So I must die in debt: my heart is gone. | You are not he, and I must have but one' (ll. 68–70). What Howard emphasises, what she wishes to remind Rodney of, are two significant divides. She is not the 'she' of Rodney's verse construction, and there is a striking difference between reality, and what is 'real' in poetry. At the same time, reading this exchange alongside its outcome makes obvious that the boundaries – between fiction and reality, emotional expressed and felt – are, for Rodney at least, less clearly defined than Howard imagines.

Nevertheless, Howard's 'Answer' could not be clearer in identifying the unfairness of lyric poetry's emotional methodology. Responding to Rodney's threat of self-harm, Howard writes:

[...] if one desperate in madness do it,
(Not yielding) are we accessory to it?
Is bondage then the happiness attends
On those whom everyone for "fair" commends? (ll. 17–20)

Howard is rejecting the systems of emotional obligation that underpin lyric, and offers an important counternarrative to the kind of emotional projection seen in works like *Astrophil and Stella*. We might particularly use Howard's insight here, for example, to reframe Astrophil's description of Stella's emotional capabilities in Sonnet 45. 'Stella oft sees the very face of woe | Painted in my beclouded stormy face', he observes, before noting that nevertheless she '*cannot skill to pity* my disgrace' (ll. 1–3, my emphasis). If there is an emotional misfiring happening here, Astrophil claims, it is Stella's failure, something she 'cannot skill' to do. Astrophil's failures are neatly reframed as Stella's, in what represents only a single moment in a larger campaign to control and dominate the emotional narrative of the sequence.

One of the great values of Frances Howard's 'Answer' is its timely anticipation of a much more contemporary line of feminist criticism that traces the problematic gender dynamics of the lyric tradition, and explores how, in Nona Fienberg's words, 'the poetry objectifies the beloved, translates her into metaphors of the poet's selfhood, and usurps her integrity to create his poetic corpus'.[46] The material I have quoted from Howard thus far is a testament to her keen awareness of the myriad ways in which male poetic speakers used the lyric tradition as a kind of weapon against women. This

---

[46] Nona Fienberg, 'The Emergence of Stella in *Astrophil and Stella*', *Studies in English Literature, 1500–1900*, 25.1 (1985), 5–19 (p. 5).

Pity and Identity in the Age of Shakespeare

extends not just to her objection to being cast as 'cruel', and held accountable for someone else's emotional unrest. As she turns also to the generic
conventions of lyric, Howard outlines a specifically *poetic* tradition of
emotional manipulation and deception. She notes:

> [...] poets, I have heard, in such a case,
> Hold flattery and lying the best grace;
> For they are men, forsooth, have words to pierce
> And wound a stony heart with softening verse.
> They can write sonnets, and with warbling rhymes
> Make women even as light as are the times. (ll. 123–130)

This vision of poetry and its agenda frames the tradition (somewhat reductively) in terms of its gender dynamics: poets are men, and they use their
craft to 'pierce' and 'wound' women. Howard's language, which acknowledges and rejects the violence embedded in this kind of work, clearly also
illustrates Howard's own understanding of the larger context in which she
receives Rodney's 'Elegia':

> Success and custom (to weak women, foes)
> Have made men wanton in our overthrows –
> Because the worser of our sex have granted.
> What is't in their attempts men have not vaunted?
> To weep, to threaten, flatter, beg, protest
> Is but in earnest, lust – and love in jest.
> [...]
> And can we be blamed (if, being harmed
> By sad experience) we be strongly armed
> With resolution to defend our wrongs
> Against the perjured falsehood of your tongues? (ll. 49–62)

Donald Foster suggests that here Howard is mocking 'not just the swan-
song of Sir George, but the patriarchalist assumptions and masculine
prerogatives that account for Rodney's Petrarchan language and patronizing
tone.'[47] This may be true, though Howard's own tone in this portion of 'The
Answer' does seem ill-suited to Rodney's particular situation, especially if
we take his ultimate fate as a confirmation of sincere feeling. Howard is
mindful of this later, and acknowledges Rodney more particularly in the
lines that follow: 'But whither range I in this vain dispute? | (Since what
you seek is of a different suit!)' (ll. 63–64). She is the first person to see that
Rodney is a poor fit for the tradition he adopts.

---

[47] Foster, p. 102.

Dramatic Reworkings of Poetic Pity

The self-awareness in these (and other) lines makes clear that Howard's 'Answer' is itself part socio-literary performance, as much an account of her own embeddedness in a culture and its literary modes as it is a response to Rodney himself and the 'Elegia'. In another sense however, Howard redirects generic tradition and context in order to contain and contextualise Rodney's overflowing emotion. Placing Rodney in his chosen genre and gesturing towards his faithful adherence to its language and emotional strategies, Howard also presents him an opportunity to cast real emotion and real distress as a literary performance. In doing so, she reminds him that his actions and reactions can also be safely contained within the lyric tradition. Howard summarises their respective positions, and offers her guidance, in this way:

In brief: whereas you write the fatal strife
'Twixt love and my disdain hath doomed your life,
Herein my mind is (and we'ld have you know it):
Poorly, methinks, you strive to play the poet-
[...]
Your last lines intimate you to be such.
If you be such, then I believe with ease
That you can die for love if so you please –
But die as poets do, in sighs (false fees
To corrupt trust!), in sonneting *ay-mes*,
With such-like pretty deaths, whose trim disguise
May batter yielding hearts and blind soft eyes. (ll. 119–138)

One of the central issues, both in the Rodney–Howard exchange and in the wider body of criticism around English lyric, is in determining the distance between poet and speaker, abjection and agency, literature and reality. In this moment, Howard denies the compatibility of the elements Rodney seeks to unite: poetry, genuine abjection, and the pressing threat of physical death as a result of that emotional burden. She points out here that death in poetry is 'pretty' – sanitised, safe, rhetorical. She assigns this kind of death only the slightest physicality: it happens 'in sighs', she points out, before moving back to an idea of purely textual, explicitly poetic death, rendered 'in sonneting ay-mes'. When she does revert to Rodney's own case, his own way of accounting for himself, it is under the cover of this generic reorientation of his emotion: 'I never yet could hear one prove | That there was ever any died for love', she writes, 'Nor would I have you be the man begin | The earnest dare to such a sportive sin'. 'For that', she warns him, 'would prove a laughter for an age, | Stuff for a play, fit matter for a stage'. Placed in the context of the social commentary that actually followed, Howard's suggestion of Rodney becoming a 'laughter' alludes to social judgement, a

Pity and Identity in the Age of Shakespeare

prophecy of Rodney's ruined reputation. Howard is also making an interesting generic suggestion that to take seriously the claims often made in lyric poetry – that a man left un-pitied may die of his emotional burden – is also to break a poetic boundary. Rodney's way of framing and navigating his emotion, Howard seems to suggest, highlights a point of generic incompatibility, and in this way, her advice is a warning both for the safety of his physical self, *and* his literary position. In his own account of Rodney, Arthur Wilson (himself a dramatist) also invokes the stage in various ways, commenting that Rodney comes to Wiltshire 'to *act*' his 'desperate attempt'; Wilson notes that through these events Rodney becomes 'desperate and sad *Spectacle* of Frailty'. It seems therefore that as his poetry and his story were received, Rodney's expression of his own emotional subjectivity also resulted in his being understood as *less* poetic and *more* dramatic.

These moments of generic boundary-marking from Howard and Wilson sit strangely alongside Rodney, a figure who expressed himself through poetry, and who is compelling in part because he so completely realises the language of lyric. There is no distance between Rodney's physical reality and the emotionally laden verse he directs at Howard: he physically realises the emotional threats that underpin and characterise so much of the poetry that he emulates. His response to Howard's explicit steer is in fact a doubling down on the themes that characterise the 'Elegia', a wilful refusal to engage with anything she has said. His final, shorter piece is an explicit account of fractured selfhood, and also, it seems, one final insistence that someone or something else is accountable for his misery:

> What shall I do that am undone?
> Where shall I fly, myself to shun?
> [Ay] me, myself my self must kill –
> And yet I die against my will.
> [...]
> [Ay] me, that love such woe procures! (ll. 1–13)

Donald Foster, the modern editor of the Rodney–Howard exchange, corrects 'Ah' – as it appears in British Library MS. Sloane 1446, fol. 66ᵛ ('Sr George Radney before hee killd himself') – to 'Ay' arguing that 'ah is clearly a corruption', and that with his response Rodney intends to volley back the very language that Howard has offered him. She advises him to die 'in sonneting ay-mes'; he offers that language back to her in the moments before his suicide. If that is the case, then Rodney's final offering to Howard is also a clear recommitment to the poetic genre, an indulgence in its clichés.

In committing so thoroughly however, it seems that Rodney violates the social and literary boundaries of English lyric. The obvious deviation is of course his turn to the physical, but the real violation of convention seems

Dramatic Reworkings of Poetic Pity

to be a more emotional one, the wilfulness with which Rodney literalises emotion that should remain purely literary. What the broader response to Rodney does confirm, however, is the social discomfort surrounding public emotion that is both unwieldy and uncontained. Wilson identifies the doomed poet's fate as 'desperate and sad', but also uses his story as a cautionary tale about the threat of emotional overflow, framing Rodney's plight as something of a personal failing attributable to his 'having drunk in too much affection, and not being able with his *Reason* to digest it'. The very boundaries of Rodney's self, by this description, are worryingly permeable to 'affection'. These accounts represent a clear effort to impose social and poetic distance from a truly troubled figure, but they are also seeking distance from a certain scale and intensity of feeling.

THE DRAMATIC VIEW

Regardless of its suggested theatricality, the realisation of Rodney's promised end sits very poorly with comedy. Nevertheless, it does seem that Howard was thinking of a stage comedy as she wrote her response to him. Her assertion, 'No, no, I never yet could hear one prove | That there was ever any died for love' neatly parrots comments that Rosalind makes to Orlando in *As You Like It*: 'The poor world is almost six thousand years old', Rosalind observes, 'and in all this time there was not any man died in his own person [...] in a love cause'.[48] 'Men have died from time to time and worms have eaten them', she continues, 'but not for love' (4.1.97–99). Like Howard, Rosalind directs this wisdom at someone who has attempted to channel his emotion through poetry. Orlando is, moreover, a very specific *kind* of poet, as Peter Hyland suggests in his description of the character as one 'entrapped by Petrarchism'.[49] Historically, it appears that Shakespeare's play is a compellingly close contemporary of the Rodney–Howard exchange. The mention of *As You Like It* in the Stationers' register in 1600 would position the play just before Howard and Rodney begin their poetic dialogue, which took place between May and July of 1601.[50] It is also quite tempting to read the parallels between Howard's 'Answer' and *As You Like*

---

[48] William Shakespeare, *As You Like It*, ed. by Juliet Dusinberre (London: Arden Shakespeare, 2006), 4.1.86–89. All references to *As You Like It* are to this edition.

[49] Peter Hyland, *An Introduction to Shakespeare's Poems* (Houndmills, Basingstoke: Palgrave Macmillan, 2003), p. 38.

[50] Martin Wiggins suggests 1600 as the best guess for *As You Like It's* date, noting also that the limits are likely 1598–1600. See: Martin Wiggins and Catherine Richardson, *British Drama 1533–1642: A Catalogue*, vol. IV (Oxford: Oxford University Press, 2014), p. 212.

Pity and Identity in the Age of Shakespeare

It in a straightforward way, and to conclude that Howard must have seen *As You Like It* before composing her 'Answer' to Rodney. It makes an appealing narrative of transmission, and influence, and one that perhaps makes Howard still more fascinating by virtue of suggesting a personal affinity for a well-known play. What is more significant to me, however, is the sense and significance of the generic interplay that seems to be at work in these materials. Howard may well be borrowing convenient or striking language – even language that Shakespeare himself reworked from a poetic tradition – but when it is rehoused in the generic context of her poetic exchange with Rodney, the results are devastating.

At the same time, the references to Rodney's dramatic impulses all seem, rather clearly, to privilege the poetic mode. Howard's suggestion that Rodney will become 'matter for a stage' reads as a kind of generic demotion, something specifically associated with disproportionate or poorly contained emotion. It is an example of one genre being invoked in service of another: Howard's reference to Rodney's theatricality is yet another way of shoring up her own position as the stronger and more controlled poet. But – as Howard's likely reference to *As You Like It* makes clear – drama was also invoking poetry in its own service. Like Rodney, Shakespeare is borrowing language from earlier work, an earlier time, and a different tradition. But for what purpose?

In her own work on the sonnetised body in *Romeo and Juliet,* Gayle Whittier traces the 'residual and fatal power' that might 'live on in the inherited poetic word'.[51] In *Romeo and Juliet*, she argues, Shakespeare 'transmutes [Petrarchan conventions] to serve the dramatic conspiracy between word and world'.[52] This crucially suggests a mode of generic interplay in which poetic convention was manipulated specifically to help define both drama's literary agenda and its impact. In what remains of this chapter, I want to extend these claims about the interplay between poetry and drama, particularly in the context of Howard's apparent turn towards comedy in her response to Rodney, her warning that he may become 'a laughter of an age', and her parroting of a well-known stage comedy. What does it mean to transplant into drama a mode of expression from another genre – one that, as Joel Fineman argued, had by this time introduced itself to England as 'an already achieved and foreign novelty, a poetic mode already done and

[51] Gayle Whittier, 'The Sonnet's Body and the Body Sonnetized in *Romeo and Juliet*', *Shakespeare Quarterly*, 40.1 (1989), 27–41 (p. 29).

[52] Ibid., p. 31.

Dramatic Reworkings of Poetic Pity

overdone elsewhere'?[53] What, in fact, is the significance of translating this mode into not one, but two new genres –drama, and comedy?

* * *

As You Like It shows a clear investment in expressions of generic identity, even as the play makes obvious its own position and allegiance. The characters repeatedly gesture towards the idea that the 'poetic' identity is something distinct and easily spotted, and that it is also not a well esteemed subjective position within the world of the play. Audrey's playful discussion with Touchstone in Act 3, scene 3 lays this out in very clear terms. Touchstone's comment, 'Truly, I would the gods had made thee poetical' (3.3.13–14) understands 'poetical' as a descriptor of receptiveness, a way of characterising someone that will respond in the expected way in the face of poetic overtures. Audrey's request for clarification – 'I do not know what "poetical" is' (3.3.15) – pushes beyond the notion of a literary community, with shared understandings of convention and ethos, and asks instead for an explanation situated in the 'real world'. 'Is it honest in deed and word?', she asks; 'Is it a true thing?' (3.3.15–16). Touchstone's response is direct: 'No, truly; for the truest poetry is the most faining, and lovers are given to poetry, and what they swear in poetry may be said, as lovers, they do feign' (3.3.17–19). Truth in poetry, by this description, is something quite different to truth of emotional expression. To put it another way: to be true to the genre is to be somehow distanced from the emotion it articulates. When Audrey asks, 'Do you wish then that the gods had made me poetical?', and Touchstone confirms: 'I do, truly, for thou swear'st to me thou art honest. Now if thou wert a poet I might have some hope thou didst feign' (3.3.20–24), he wishes for Audrey a different generic identity, imagining for the poetic identity a different set of conventions surrounding the relationship between language, emotion, and truth. Even beyond this, the turn to poetry here offers a positioning opportunity for both Touchstone and the play itself. Touchstone presents himself as the knowing authority on what it is to be 'poetical', as he suggests a confident knowledge of the poetic genre and its conventions. At the same time, through Audrey's questioning Touchstone is also able to separate 'poetical' expression as something constructed, something 'different' to the 'real world' – but their world is equally a literary fiction. Of course, it is also simply a very funny moment. One of *As You Like It*'s true comic exchanges – in which the play fulfils its own generic identity – is made possible by this drawing of generic boundaries against poetry.

---

[53] Joel Fineman, *Shakespeare's Perjured Eye: The Invention of Poetic Subjectivity in the Sonnets* (Berkeley, CA: University of California Press, 1986), p. 188.

Pity and Identity in the Age of Shakespeare

While *As You Like It* contributes to a broader social narrative questioning the emotional veracity of this type of poetry, as a comedy it also offers a certain generic security for the Rodney-like Silvius, who relies on Petrarchan cliché to express his emotion. The introduction of Silvius and Phoebe is immediately preceded by a moment of generic signposting that reminds us that we are at a play: Corin promises 'a pageant truly played | Between the pale complexion of true love | And the red glow of scorn and proud disdain' (3.4.48–50). Rosalind's reply: 'Bring us to this sight' (3.4.54) emphasises the spectacle of the form again, and her final line before Silvius's appearance onstage is still more explicit: 'I'll prove a busy *actor* in their *play*' (3.4.55). Nonetheless, when Silvius and Phoebe do appear, they give one of the most poetically minded exchanges in the play, with Silvius the champion of Petrarchan cliché ('Will you sterner be | Than he that dies and lives by bloody drops?' [3.5.6–7]), and Phoebe pushing his literary-ness into the literal ('Lie not, to say mine eyes are murderers. | Now show the wound mine eye hath made in thee' (3.5.18–20). The generic clashing is made all the more obvious as these two have an audience onstage, with Rosalind, Celia, and Corin standing witness.

This scene offers one of the most straightforward dramatic engagements with the pity appeal and its intended impact: 'Sweet Phoebe, pity me' (3.5.85), Silvius pleads. When she admits that she 'feels sorry', he continues (like Rodney, in iambic pentameter):

SILVIUS
Wherever sorrow is, relief would be:
If you do sorrow at my grief in love,
By giving love your sorrow and my grief
Were both extermined. (3.5.87–90)

Silvius makes clear that the aim of this language is total possession: 'I would have you' (3.5.92). Although he ends the play with Phoebe his, Silvius remains something of an outlier in *As You Like It*, a structural choice that underscores the rhetorical and emotional artifice of poetic courtship. Like Rodney, Silvius dedicates himself to his chosen form – speaking only in verse that becomes particularly regular if directed at Phoebe. Silvius is the subject of a social gaze – both Celia and Rosalind comment on his situation, classifying him according to his love suit and calling him, respectively, a 'poor shepherd' (4.3.64) and a 'fool' (4.3.22). He turns himself (to use Rosalind's words), 'into the extremity of love' (4.3.23). Of course, at the play's resolution it is not Silvius's words that have triumphed, but rather Rosalind's gender play. Silvius is notably silent at the play's conclusion and at Phoebe's acceptance of him: stripped of any lines, this would-be poet is remade as a non-verbal stage actor, finally assimilated by the genre in which he finds himself.

142

Dramatic Reworkings of Poetic Pity

Though *As You Like It* seems to wear its generic interests on its sleeve, these moments of generic posturing happen frequently enough across Shakespearean comedy to suggest a broader pattern in which the dramatic ethos is set out as something quite distinct from lyric poetry, particularly in its way of managing the interplay between genuine emotion, truth, and the pity appeal. At the same time, these dramatic interactions with the poetic genre consistently advance a comic theatrical agenda. For example, when Viola (as Cesario) offers Olivia the words 'I pity you', in *Twelfth Night*, Olivia reverts to the Petrarchan formula that equates and conflates pity and love: Viola's pity, Olivia responds, is 'a degree to love'.[54] But here again, the repurposing of this familiar language set produces comedy. Olivia retraces the Petrarchan modes, but they cannot function in the world of the play, where so many of the standard poetic elements have been subverted. When 'the lady' now bids for the emotional release of the 'male' beloved, Olivia reverses a familiar emotional trajectory. But of course, Olivia's appeal to Cesario only reminds the audience of Olivia's distance from the truth. She reverses the poetic structure, casting off her original position as the 'beloved' in order to furnish her own emotional venture. This move does not turn Cesario into the mute beloved, as we might expect: Orsino's emissary continues to participate in the dialogue. In this manoeuvre however, Olivia does successfully silence the disguised Viola, whose inability to convey her own truth is now both painfully and comically obvious (if only to the audience).

These examples from *As You Like It* and *Twelfth Night* are more thorough in terms of their generic posturing, but it is worth noting that this kind of literary manoeuvring happens in more passing moments in Shakespeare as well. Falstaff's poetic letter to Mistress Page in *The Merry Wives of Windsor*, for example, is so self-consciously over-poetic that it can hardly register as an earnest effort. Just like the poem's rudimentary rhyming patterns, the alignment of pity, love, and poetry in this inverted appeal is just another way that Falstaff overdoes it:

> *I will not say 'pity me' – 'tis not a soldier-like phrase – but I say 'love me'.*
> *By me, thine own true knight, by day or night,*
> *Or any kind of light, with all his might,*
> *For thee to fight. John Falstaff.*[55]

---

[54]   William Shakespeare, *Twelfth Night*, ed. by Keir Elam (London: Arden Shakespeare, 2008), 3.1.121–122.

[55]   William Shakespeare, *The Merry Wives of Windsor*, ed. by Giorgio Melchiori (Walton-on-Thames: Thomas Nelson and Sons Ltd., 2000), 2.1.11–15.

Pity and Identity in the Age of Shakespeare

Here again, the lack of innovation is powerfully reborn as comic posturing. Falstaff denies that he makes a pity appeal, since to do so would constitute a violation of his soldierly identity. But in place of pity he suggests 'love'. In spite of his own protestations it is – as the rhyming structure makes clear – an explicitly poetic appeal.

The Shakespearean examples I have offered here present a striking picture of poetic pity deployed in service of dramatic comedy. That said, this is by no means a uniquely Shakespearean mode. The turn to this kind of language, this particularly lyric way of deploying pity in romantic appeals, appears frequently in the work of other dramatists, and especially at the beginning of the seventeenth century. These examples largely blur together in sameness: each distinguishes itself only in its broad similarity to other instances. This kind of Petrarchan pity is present, for example, in a passing reference in John Marston's *The Malcontent*, when the courtier Ferneze makes his appeal to the adulterous duchess Amelia. 'Your smiles have beene my heaven, your frownes my hell', he claims, before moving to the familiar model of emotional exchange: 'O pitty then; Grace should with beauty dwell'.[56] The same language and emotional structures appear again in *The Thracian Wonder*, as a way of emphasising the comic character shift that happens to Tityrus, the cynic-turned-lover:

TITYRUS
Oh stay, oh turn, oh pitty me, that sighs, that sues for love of thee,
Oh lack I never loved before, if you deny, Ile nere love more.
No hope no help, then wretched I, must loose, must lack, must pine, and die,
Since you neglect when I implore,
Farewel hard, Ile nere love more.[57]

---

[56] John Marston, *The Malcontent* (London: 1611), sig. C1ʳ. Wiggins gives a date limit of 1602–1604 for this play. See: Martin Wiggins and Catherine Richardson, *British Drama 1533–1642: A Catalogue*, vol. V (Oxford: Oxford University Press, 2015), p. 16.

[57] John Webster and William Rowley, *The Thracian Wonder* (London: 1661), sig. E4ʳ. There is some debate over the likely dating and the authorship of *Wonder*. Most critics place it between 1610–1612. See Michael Nolan, 'Introduction', in William Rowley and Thomas Heywood, *The Thracian Wonder* (Salzburg: University of Salzburg, 1997), pp. xlviv–lvii. Authorial attribution ranges between anonymous designations, and arguments for William Rowley with a collaborator (typically Heywood). The attribution to Webster on the 1661 quarto (cited above) is an incorrect carry-over from a contemporary printing of *A Cure for a Cuckold*. See: Martin Wiggins and Catherine Richardson, *British Drama 1533–1642: A Catalogue*, vol. VII (Oxford: Oxford University Press, 2016), p. 324; O.L. Hatcher, 'The Sources and Authorship of *The Thracian Wonder*', *Modern Language Notes*, 23.1 (1908), pp. 16–20; and Michael Nolan, 'William Rowley and the Authorship of *The Thracian Wonder*', *Notes and Queries*, 44.4 (1997), 519–523.

Dramatic Reworkings of Poetic Pity

Tityrus' turn to pity here partly signals the scale of his character reversal: his sudden and complete emotional domination is narrated through these familiar structures and modes of description. The comedy of cliché is further emphasised visually and aurally by Tityrus' delivery: he enters the stage both physically and emotionally in pursuit of Ariadna, and singing the lines.

Even as drama seeks to stage and rework this familiar poetic language, these works often find a way of further containing or separating the material from dramatic dialogue, signalling that here is something distinct and different. Tityrus' turn to song disrupts the established patterns of conversation, further separating the ideas and language of the song from the supposed 'real world' of the play. This happens also in *Blurt Master Constable* (1602), in a song that reflects pity's central role in courtship. The song uses the word 'pitty' so often that it becomes almost meaningless in repetition:

> Pittie, pitty, pitty,
> Pitty, pitty, pitty,
> That word begins that endes a true-love Ditty,
> Your blessed eyes (like a paire of Sunnes,)
> Shine in the sphere of smiling,
> Your prettie lips (like a paire of Doves)
> Are kisses still com-piling.
> Mercy hangs upon your brow, like a pretious Jewell,
> O let not then,
> (Most lovely maide, best to be loved of men:)
> Marble, lye upon your heart, that will make you cruell:
> Pitty, pitty, pitty,
> Pitty, pitty, pitty:
> That word begins that ends a true-love ditty.[58]

What is especially striking about this song, aside from its emotional repetition, is that the flank of 'pitty' aurally (and in print, visually) frames the Petrarchan descriptive modes. This underscores the link between pity and the language of appeal, but also positions pity as a kind of governing structure. Pity gives the song its shape, but it also contains the hyperbolic emotional register of Petrarchan description. In a play that casts a cynical view on the authenticity of professed romantic emotion, the appearance

[58] Anonymous., *Blurt Master-Constable* (London: 1602), sigs. E1^r–E1^v. The authorship of *Blurt* is an unresolved issue, but the most recent scholarship has argued that the play is the work of Thomas Dekker. See: David J. Lake, *The Canon of Thomas Middleton's Plays* (Cambridge: Cambridge University Press, 1975); Thomas Leland Berger (ed.), *A Critical Old-Spelling Edition of Thomas Dekker's 'Blurt, Master Constable'* (1602), (Salzburg: University of Salzburg Press, 1979); MacDonald P. Jackson, *Studies in Attribution: Middleton and Shakespeare* (Salzburg: University of Salzburg Press, 1979).

Pity and Identity in the Age of Shakespeare

of this Petrarchan register further clarifies the distance between the poetic performance of courtship, and the more 'authentic' world of the play.

George Chapman's *May Day* (1604) more explicitly uses poetry to signal its own generic identity. The play's opening sequence sees Lorenzo in an odd kind of poetic dialogue: as he progresses through a stock Petrarchan account of Franceschina – 'Here have I put her face in rime' – Angelo undercuts the description at each line.[59] It is a moment that punctures both the reality of the lady and the manner of expression. Lorenzo's unimaginative opening, 'O haire, no haire but beames stolne from the Sunne', prompts Angelo's reflection: 'if it be shee that I thinke, shee has a Fox red cranion' (sig. A2ᵛ).[60] The scene progresses in much the same fashion, with poetic description immediately undercut by dramatic aside. The play returns to ideas of generic tension repeatedly, often as a way of signalling a character's distance from the 'real world' or society of the play. Poetic instincts in this way seem to place a character at a remove, expanding the distance between the lone poetic subject and the opportunity for meaningful interpersonal connection. In his efforts to bring the lovers Aurelio and Aemilia together, for example, Lodovico frequently cites Aurelio's poetic tendencies as an obstacle. Aurelio's description of Aemilia's home as a 'celestiall spheare, wherein more beauty shines' is in reality – at least according to Lodovico – merely 'the Tarrasse where thy sweet heart tarries' (sig. F3ᵛ). Though he invites Aurelio's turn to 'rime', for Lodovico it is a far cry for what will shortly unfold on the stage: 'I cannot abide this talking and undoing Poetry, leave your mellifluous numbers', he comments, 'yonder's a sight will steale all reason from your rime' (sig. F3ᵛ).

When he does begin courting Aemilia, Aurelio frames pity in a familiar way, highlighting the emotion as something that preserves, something that protects:

AURELIO
O sacred goddesse, what soe're thou art
That in meere pitty to preserve a soule
From undeserv'd destruction, hast vouchsaf't
To take *Aemiliaes* shape. (sig. G1ʳ)

---

[59] George Chapman, *May-day* (London: 1611), sig. A2ᵛ.

[60] Even Angelo's blazon suggests dramatic penetration and generic interplay in its language, mobilising the same descriptive pattern of Hieronimo's iconic speech – 'O eyes, no eyes' – in *The Spanish Tragedy*. See: Thomas Kyd, *The Spanish Tragedy*, ed. by Clara Calvo and Jesús Tronch (London: Bloomsbury Publishing, 2013), 3.2.1–4. At the same time, as Kyd's editors point out, Hieronimo's opening lines also recall Petrarch: '*oi occhi miei, occhi non già, ma fonti*' ('O eyes of mine, not eyes, but fountains now!' See Francesco Petrarca, *Canzoniere*, ed. by Gianfranco Contini (Turin: G. Einaudi, 1992), p. 217.

Dramatic Reworkings of Poetic Pity

As a rhetorical approach, this is a way of framing and approaching Aemilia that imposes distance between the lovers, not just in status (he is the lowly, piteous, and loving soul, she is the goddess in human form) but in spatial and social terms as well. Aurelio's poetic instincts delay the proper connection between the lovers, but they also crucially leave him socially and spatially exposed, as Lodovico comments: 'What a poeticall sheepe is this?', he asks. 'S'life, will you stand riming there upon a stage, to be an eye-marke to all that passe?' (sig. G1ʳ). What in one sense is a simple desire to conceal the lovers – Aemilia's father desires a different match for her – is in another sense a passing question about the poet's presence on the dramatic stage. In this moment, Aurelio's mode stands out: as a poet he holds the play's action back, rather than propelling it forward.

It is easy to see something of George Rodney in many of these dramatic characters, perhaps especially in the 'poetical sheepe' Aurelio. In spite of Aurelio's romantic success – a fact which itself might represent one of the benefits of his being transplanted from poetry onto the stage – he remains for a time a 'riming … eye-marke', a figure placed under a silent but pervasive social scrutiny, by virtue of his chosen modes of emotional expression. We might also think of Rodney in connection with Anthony's unsuccessful efforts to woo Phillis in *The Fair Maid of the Exchange* (c.1602):

> ANTHONY
> Within the centre of this paper square,
> Have I wrote downe in bloudy characters,
> A pretty poesie of a wounded heart,
> Such is loves force once burst into a flame,
> Doe what we can we cannot quench the same,
> Unlesse the teares of pitty move compassion,
> And so quench out the fire of affection,
> Whose burning force heats me in every vaine,
> That I to Love for safety must complaine:
> This is my Orator whose dulcet tongue
>   Must pleade my love to beauteous *Phillis*.[61]

The emotional structure is not new. All of the elements are there: an uncontained love that threatens violent outpouring and danger, the premise of

---

[61] Anonymous, *The Fayre Mayde of the Exchange* (London: 1607), sig. E3ᵛ. Wiggins offers date limits of 1601–1607, with a best guess date of 1602. The authorship of this piece is a matter of debate. Though the play has previously been attributed to Thomas Heywood, the most recent edition of the play leaves it unattributed. See: Wiggins and Richardson, *British Drama*, vol. IV, p. 377; and *The Fair Maid of the Exchange*, ed. by Genevieve Love, in Jeremy Lopez (ed.), *The Routledge Anthology of Early Modern Drama* (London: Routledge, 2020), pp. 816–831.

Pity and Identity in the Age of Shakespeare

'quenching' pity and the turn to verse. Anthony's reference to his 'bloudy characters' might call to mind Arthur Wilson's claim that Rodney's verse was composed in his own blood – a description that itself reads as an indulgence in literary cliché. In another sense however, Anthony is also reaching back to the poetic tradition when he calls his 'paper square' and 'pretty poesie' the 'Orator' that will represent him to Phillis. This is in fact not an agent-orator, but a textual stand-in of the kind that Sidney famously deploys in the opening lines *Astrophil and Stella's* first sonnet, in what Alex Davis calls a 'proleptic modelling of a scenario of readerly success'.[62] 'The poems' affective power and productivity', Davis argues, relies on Stella's readerly identity.[63] At the same time, that sense of a readerly identity is embedded in a particular poetic tradition and its limitations, as Joel Fineman has pointed out. 'The problem of [Sidney's] poet is explicitly poetical', Fineman writes, and wholly determined by this question of 'how to make his lady act according to Petrarchan formulas when those formulas are already registered as formulaic'.[64] Sidney gestures to the palimpsests of earlier poems that together create his current poetic obstacle, and yet the suggested solution is still more reading: the poet's approach here is self-consciously textual. This is a strategy Rodney copies as well, another way in which he signals his generic allegiance. Rodney's appeal for Howard's pity comes in a text to be read, and one which explicitly presents itself in those terms. 'Dear fair', he writes in the 'Elegia', 'receive this greeting to thee sent; | And still as oft as it is *read* by thee, | With some sad, deep-fetched sign, remember me' (ll. 2–4, my emphasis). Rodney imagines the poem as the future provocateur of Howard's emotion, a textual stand-in in a future emotional exchange. His poem is thus given a sort of physical agency, a physicality that will stand in for Rodney after he destroys himself. Though it appears on the stage as a prop, Anthony's 'paper square' is also a transparent poetic inheritance, just like Orlando's hanging verses. These are markers of an explicitly poetical mode of communication, presented newly on stage for its facilitation and extension of distance. This is a mode that places texts *between* people, and also asks the text to absorb much of the emotionality of the exchange.

Across all of these examples of dramatists apparently redeploying poetic moments, it is worth noticing the frequency with which these moments are in some way marked as different, set apart from the rest of the plays in which they sit. These comic reworkings often see the poetic pity appeal rendered explicitly, for example, as an on-stage poem, or performed as a song. Even Chapman's *May Day*, which seems more intent on blending

---

[62] Davis, p. 488.
[63] Ibid., p. 489.
[64] Fineman, p. 192.

Dramatic Reworkings of Poetic Pity

poetic description into the broader fabric of the play, and works the generic meditations into the dialogue, makes some effort to draw a structural distinction: the scene highlighted above, that brings together the poetic Aurelio with his love Aemilia, is set apart by virtue of its being the only substantive portion written in verse. Set apart in these ways, these dramatic moments should be read as part of a broader tradition of Petrarchan imitation, the same kind of activity that produces the plural notion of Petrarchisms even as it seems also to cement the Petrarchan 'mode' into canon. What is framed as a playful nod to a different literary mode is also a way of reinscribing that mode's patterns and emotional strategies. It is also, by extension, a way of defining difference, of signalling drama's own emotional strategies and ideologies as distinct.

Defined by his pursuit of emotional release through pity, the staged 'poetic' speaker becomes (to quote Rodney), 'a pyramis of pity': a monument to a narrow and unsatisfying application of the emotion. The transplant of this emotional framework into another genre appears to me a self-conscious acknowledgement of literary inheritance: it is made to stick out. However, whereas Howard marks Rodney's effort as somehow a generic violation – fundamentally different in its emotional veracity, in the weight of its promised violence, and therefore more dramatic than poetic – these dramatic examples seek to preserve and highlight the very elements of this appeal that were seen as clichéd. If the dramatic examples identify, contain, and separate one possible – if notorious – form of literary pity, they perhaps also create a space for a new understanding of pity's defining capacity as a broader mark of gentleness and humanity. In short: this borrowing helps dramatists create something newly and specifically dramatic. It is, of course, the weight of the poetic inheritance behind Silvius's plea for Phoebe's pity that marks the exchange as something quite different to Orlando's suggestion to Duke Senior, that to 'know what 'tis to pity and be pitied' (2.7.118) is to separate oneself from 'all things [...] savage' (2.7.108), to 'sit [...] down in gentleness' (2.7.125). In this way we might collectively read these other moments of genre comedy as performing a significant alternative function beyond mere entertainment. When placed on stage as a visible social outlier, the pitiful poet also contains one type of pity by marking it as obviously 'poetic'. By containing one form of pity within a strict generic framework, space is opened up to imagine a more complex and multivalent position for the emotion, to consider the very many other ways that pity might facilitate human connection.

However constructive this might be for drama, it is of course in another direction terribly reductive. The patterns of usage I identify here as belonging to English lyric are neither a full nor a just representation of early modern poetry, its modes of expression, and its emotional strategies.

149

Pity and Identity in the Age of Shakespeare

By the time the Petrarchan poet-lover began to appear regularly as a figure of comedy on the stage, the poetic conventions that characterised him were already being challenged, reworked, and reimagined in subsequent waves of English poetry.[65] The emotional structures I have outlined in English lyric have a certain notoriety by virtue of being so evocative of a particular moment: when these structures are reproduced on the stage they are (intentionally, I think) reduced even further. This is a vision of 'poetic' pity that is rooted in sexual and romantic connection, bound up in felicity of expression, and perhaps should also be read as a kind of social calculation. It is also, most importantly, a form of pity fully implicated in defining and protecting an isolated and predominantly masculine model of selfhood. The poetic speaker appeals for pity, remember, in a structure designed to overwrite and dismantle the subjectivity of the beloved. The speaker is in emotional conversation with himself certainly, and perhaps with the reader, but almost never with his beloved.

CONCLUSION

Much critical attention has been given specifically to Shakespeare's habit of bringing poetry into his dramatic work, not only in his use of poetic verse but also his frequent inclusion of (often original) songs and poems.[66] At the same time, it is difficult both to ignore and to reconcile what Ekbert Faas describes as the 'consistently negative portrayal of poets in [Shakespeare's] work'.[67] Peter Holbrook observes, for example, that 'throughout [Shakespeare's] oeuvre there is a repeated disowning of the merely "poetic"'.[68] As Katherine Duncan-Jones points out, the critical anxiety over Shakespeare's apparent poetry-scepticism may well be tied to the facts of production: 'How

---

[65] Furthermore, as Colin Burrow argues, the English engagement with epic suggests a separate poetic engagement with pity that is more nuanced and wider ranging, appears in more contexts, and weaves its way through a 'complex body of concerns' (p. 4). The *Iliad* and the *Odyssey*, Burrow contends, together presented a complex 'structure of emotion' (p. 3) that in different ways encompassed the full possible range of social interaction, and heavily influenced the emotional frameworks for the early modern epic that followed from Spenser, Chapman, Milton, and others. See: Colin Burrow, *Epic Romance: Homer to Milton* (Oxford: Clarendon Press, 1993).

[66] For more on these, see: Edward Hubler (ed), *Shakespeare's Songs and Poems* (New York, NY: McGraw Hill, 1959).

[67] Ekbert Faas, *Shakespeare's Poetics* (Cambridge: Cambridge University Press, 1986), p. xii.

[68] Peter Holbrook, 'Shakespeare and Poetry', in Mark Thornton Burnett, Adrian Streete, and Ramona Wray (eds.), *The Edinburgh Companion to Shakespeare and the Arts* (Edinburgh: Edinburgh University Press, 2011), pp. 37–48 (p. 41).

Dramatic Reworkings of Poetic Pity

do we reconcile Shakespeare's consistently scornful allusions to sonnets and sonneteering in his plays', she asks, 'with the fact of his having composed one of the longest sonnet sequences of the period?'[69] The surviving material offers a complicated picture: a writer who contributed substantial work as a poet; a playwright who relied heavily on poetic form to shape his dramatic expression, even as the characters he created seem to strain against a set of language and behaviours associated with being 'too poetic'. The critical response, moreover, suggests a profound discomfort with these contradictions for *Shakespeare* specifically. A number of appealing proposals have been offered to account both for his work in poetry, and for the mixed messages produced through his dramatic oeuvre. Patrick Cheney argues, for example, that many of Shakespeare's plays explicitly concern themselves with the generic interplay between poetry and drama.[70] Cheney sees these patterns of usage as evidence of Shakespeare as 'poet-playwright', a balanced and crucially multi-genre model of authorship that is 'fundamentally a sixteenth-century phenomenon'.[71]

At the same time, it is striking how frequently Cheney gestures towards poetic material being used as a point against which the dramatic genre is defined. He references, for example, 'the dramatic *utility* of [...] a poetic rehearsal', and observes that 'often [Shakespeare] inserts a *bad poem* in order to create *great drama*'.[72] This is a vision of generic interplay that specifically directs poetic cliché in the service of advancing, refining, and *defining* the dramatic mode. While the overwhelming critical impulse has been to emphasise Shakespeare's use of poetry in his dramatic work as a particular phenomenon, the dramatic interest in lyric's use of the pity appeal is more widely spread, and suggests a much broader network of playwrights engaging in this kind of generic posturing. Many of the dramatic examples I have offered in this chapter – *The Fair Maid of the Exchange*, *Blurt Master Constable*, and *The Thracian Wonder* – draw critical attention that focuses primarily on authorship dispute, or dating. Critics are united, however, in attributing these works to playwrights *other* than Shakespeare. In this respect these plays, and the range of playwrights associated with them, suggest that the dramatic impulse to borrow poetic

---

[69] Katherine Duncan-Jones (ed.), *Shakespeare's Sonnets* (London: Thomas Nelson and Sons Ltd, 1997), p. 45.

[70] Patrick Cheney, *Shakespeare, National Poet-Playwright* (Cambridge: Cambridge University Press, 2004).

[71] Ibid., p. 4

[72] Patrick Cheney, 'Poetry in Shakespeare's plays', in Patrick Cheney (ed.), *The Cambridge Companion to Shakespeare's Poetry* (Cambridge: Cambridge University Press, 2007), pp. 221–240 (p. 234, my emphasis; p. 236, emphasis in original).

Pity and Identity in the Age of Shakespeare

modes and then repurpose them in service of a dramatic agenda extends well beyond Shakespeare. When read together with Shakespeare's own work, the consistency of portrayal and the repeated repurposing of a noticeably poetic form of pity suggests a more cohesive effort at generic posturing. This habit of mining poetry's language, its emotional strategies, its characteristic features – and then turning these materials to dramatic comedy – must be understood as something more than a Shakespearean instinct. This is behaviour that does not distinguish Shakespeare so much as it situates him within a specific theatrical community. As a strategy, this way of engaging with lyric – while somewhat opportunistic – also significantly opens up the possibilities for rethinking the emotionality of interpersonal exchange. By setting aside one kind of pity and one way of articulating emotional subjectivity as the 'property' of another genre, vital space was created for imagining new ways in which pity might facilitate interpersonal connection, and how this emotion might newly situate the individual subject in their community. This is a tearing down of one kind of pity, but one that imagines its reconstruction and repositioning, in drama, as a more central function of human experience.

Chapter 4

THEORISING HUMANITY THROUGH PITY

'UNCAPABLE OF PITY, VOID AND EMPTY'

When, in *The Merchant of Venice,* the Duke describes Shylock to Antonio, he uses the language of pity and humanity to conjure the merchant's legal adversary:

> DUKE
> I am sorry for thee: thou art come to answer
> A stony adversary, an inhuman wretch
> uncapable of pity, void and empty
> From any dram of mercy.[1]

The Duke captures Shylock's character in terms of his *absent* qualities. Shylock *is* what he *lacks*; he is *un*capable, void, and empty. The connected category assessment – that Shylock is *in*human – acts as a kind of shorthand for his emotional shortcomings. By this description, inhumanity is defined partially as a missing capacity for pity; an emotional 'void' and emptiness that is filled in for 'full' humans. As I have argued throughout this book, this framing of pity as a vital component of humanity – something funda-mental to the human category – appears again and again in early modern English writing, and particularly in Shakespeare's dramatic work. That said, in *The Merchant of Venice*, it is easy to see that there is more at stake. The Duke uses pity (or rather, its absence) as a way of separating and isolating Shylock from the play's society. This is a multi-layered othering: if you are not like us in your emotions, the Duke seems to suggest, you are not like us in your taxonomy. The Duke's use of the negated term – *in*human – also silently constructs the positive counterpart: human. This is as much a state-ment about what Shylock lacks as it is a claim about what the Duke and the

---

[1] William Shakespeare, *The Merchant of Venice*, ed. by John Drakakis (London: Arden Shakespeare, 2010), 4.1.2–5.

Pity and Identity in the Age of Shakespeare

other Venetians possess. Language about emotional (in)capacity appears to prompt a moment of biological boundary marking, in which pity sits between human and *in*human subjects.

By using the term 'inhuman', the Duke engages in a long-established tradition of describing humanity by gesturing towards other categories. Even within *The Merchant of Venice*, of course, Shylock is repeatedly classified in animal terms: he is, over and over, a 'dog' (1.3.107; 2.8.14; 4.1.127); his desires are 'wolvish' (4.1.137). As Jean Feerick and Vin Nardizzi have argued, humankind's privileged position has always relied on relational terms. 'The story of humankind's complex embeddedness among creaturely life on the earth', they write, is 'marked by a kind of limping distinction in only *potentially* occupying a step up from his creaturely kin'.[2] And while 'inhuman' may suggest an inchoate population of creaturely otherness, in reality the Duke's comment is entirely focused on shades of difference and exclusion *within* human society. The spectre of 'inhumanity' is simply used as a way of clarifying Shylock's position beyond the Venetian community: the comment flirts with non-human language to degrade and clarify the socially othered.

Shakespeare routinely implies a permeable boundary between human and non-human behaviour. The use of non-human descriptors particularly emerges in the development of characters who otherwise resist straightforward classification, and who, for reasons of plotting, cannot exist sympathetically with the dominant society of a given play. Nonetheless, as I contend in this chapter, the turn towards the 'creaturely' or otherwise non-human is very rarely an earnest consideration of alternative subjectivities. Rather, it is way of highlighting humankind's tenuous privilege, a subjectivity position that, however dominant, is also acutely aware of the precarity of being *self*-determined and *self*-narrated. However useful the external marker of the non-human may be, this manner of delineating humankind's position is also implicitly antagonistic: the continuous narrating of humankind's distinct specialness becomes, on this reading, a mode of self-protection, a manner of inscribing and reinscribing defences that is inevitably exploitative. Attending to the use of pity in these discussions of distinction helps to clarify these problematic (and unstable) power structures. Tracing the muddy discourse that implicates humans and non-humans in systems of compassionate obligation makes clear the instability of the human category, and the violence of relational definition. It is here that imaginative material is again able to push harder on the tensions and impossibilities

---

[2]   Jean E. Feerick and Vin Nardizzi, 'Swervings: On Human Indistinction', in Feerick and Nardizzi (eds.), *The Indistinct Human in Renaissance Literature* (Basingstoke: Palgrave Macmillan, 2012), pp. 1–12 (pp. 2–3).

Theorising Humanity Through Pity

of contemporary practice, this time in the creation of a host of 'proximal' human characters: emotional subjects who challenge the delicate systems of distinction by existing in the problematic interstitial spaces between human and non-human.

'NO BEAST SO FIERCE BUT KNOWS SOME TOUCH OF PITY'

Much has been made about the significance of animals in early modern studies, particularly in regard to the period's manner of conceiving human subjectivity. Within this, Shakespeare has understandably figured prominently. As Karen Raber insists: 'as far as Shakespeare is concerned, it is impossible to know people without knowing them *through* or *as* animals.'[3] It would be difficult to deny the enduring material presence of animals in the work of Shakespeare and his contemporaries, and the seemingly endless appeal of animal language and reference in creating what are, typically, human stories. I however am less interested in dramatic animals themselves, and more interested in what they represent: a piece of a larger exploitative turn, a project of human definition that absorbs animals as part of a broader investment in the utility of non-human figures. As this chapter details, the spectre of non-humanity and the language of pity were both means of defining the human category, and creating a power hierarchy within it.

Consider, for example, Shakespeare's Richard III. Across the plays in which he features, Richard represents a quandary of kind. As characters attempt to categorise him, to define and understand his separate-ness, they return again and again to common ideas about pity, non-humanity, and lack. A standout example of this sits in what Greta Olson calls *Richard III*'s 'impossible scene', in which Richard (as the Duke of Gloucester) successfully courts the Lady Anne, despite having recently murdered both her husband and her father-in-law.[4] That he manages to do this over one of the bodies, having interrupted the funeral procession, confirms this scene as one of Shakespeare's most confounding: it is a veritable mess of social, emotional, and visual conflict. As Olson explains, 'Richard's person, his chosen object, and the setting all conspire to make this seduction appear inconceivable.'[5] The seeming impossibility of this union is at least partially marked by Anne's initial reaction to her suitor's presence, even as the pace of their exchange confirms, for some, 'the considerable virtuosity of Richard's

---

[3]   Karen Raber, *Animal Bodies, Renaissance Culture* (Philadelphia, PA: University of Pennsylvania Press, 2013), p. 99.

[4]   Greta Olson, 'Richard III's Animalistic Criminal Body', *Philological Quarterly*, 82.3 (2003), 301–323 (p. 305).

[5]   Ibid, p. 305.

performance'.[6] Although Anne's condemnation acknowledges, repeatedly, that he is man, she also deploys multiple non-human comparisons as a means of explaining the apparent absence of humanity:

> LADY ANNE
> Villain, thou know'st no law of God nor man:
> No beast so fierce but knows some touch of pity.
>
> GLOUCESTER
> But I know none, and therefore am no beast.
>
> LADY ANNE
> O wonderful, when devils tell the truth!
>
> GLOUCESTER
> More wonderful, when angels are so angry.
> Vouchsafe, divine perfection of a woman,
> Of these supposed-evils, to give me leave,
> By circumstance, but to acquit myself.
>
> LADY ANNE
> Vouchsafe, defused infection of a man,
> For these known evils, but to give me leave,
> By circumstance, to curse thy cursed self.[7]

Anne invokes multiple identity categories to separate Richard from the rest of humanity, to mark him as an aberration. Separate from the laws of both God and man, Anne places him beyond the social obligations of standard human community, and then invokes the image of the 'beast'. What is essentially a problem of classification – of determining Richard's *kind* – is framed here in explicitly emotional terms. Anne's claim that there is 'no beast so fierce but knows some touch of pity' uses pity to explain what Richard lacks. She casts pity as basic and fundamental, something so thoroughly accessible to humankind that even the most violent examples of the group most proximate to humankind – animals – can feel it.

Like the Duke in *The Merchant of Venice*, Anne is defining humanity by negation: hers is an account of Richard that can only understand him by describing what he is *not*. Anne is not saying that *all* beasts have the capacity for pity, but instead suggests that there are *no* beasts – even the worst – who *fail* to experience this emotion. The double negative of this linguistic framework creates the shape of Richard's failure, and clarifies the completeness of

---

[6] Donald R. Shupe, 'The Wooing of Lady Anne: A Psychological Inquiry', *Shakespeare Quarterly*, 29.1 (1978), 28–36 (p. 28).

[7] William Shakespeare, *Richard III*, ed. by James R. Siemon (London: Arden Shakespeare, 2009), 1.2.70–80.

Theorising Humanity Through Pity

his isolation. This way of defining Richard by his lack of emotional capacity also assumes a lower standard for animals: Richard's emotional failure, by this formulation, is a failure that breaches the human boundary to violate 'even' a beastly standard. The dexterity of Richard's response – what Linda Charnes memorably describes as one of many 'flip-side tosses of the same rhetorical coinage' – acknowledges the implied classification hierarchy in its evasion of the more unfavourable 'beastly' position.[8] Richard spins this same lack as evidence that he is, clearly, 'no beast', but in this denial he also definitively rejects a model of subjectivity predicated on pity. What follows is a messy catalogue of identity possibilities, in which classification categories are so crowded – God, man, beast, devil, angel, woman – that they cease to have any substantive material value: they are terms used only to define the aberrant human subject.

The scene captures the tensions at the heart of Richard's character: his ability, especially here, to transgress social and emotional boundaries in order to court Anne. At the same time, moments like these also confirm the stakes of Shakespeare's dramatic explorations of *kind*-ness. The non-human figures used here are used wholly in the service of defining humanity, conscripted to resolve a human category that is apparently unable to sustain and define itself independently. Anne's compulsion to define Richard, to identify a space where he fits, also goes some way to revealing the inherent privilege of the human category. Many kinds of beings are pulled into this consideration of what Richard is, but he remains obviously human – in form and rational capacity, if not in emotion. He is a man, even if a 'defused infection' of a man. Richard is not easily dismissed, because he is human, and what this exchange makes clear is that because he is human, other categories of kind will be used to make sense of him.

'THEY WHICH WANT REASON'

In her attempts to understand Richard as an aberration of humanity, it is worth noting that Anne never attacks him on the grounds of irrationality – nor could she, in a scene that demonstrates, 'as one of its main points', Richard's 'near-diabolical powers' of language and manipulation.[9] Her focus is on his (underdeveloped) emotional capabilities, and she attempts to define him by this different, affective standard. The standard Anne posits is one that frames pity as a defining characteristic that situates a person

---

[8]   Linda Charnes, *Notorious Identity: Materializing the Subject in Shakespeare* (Cambridge, MA: Harvard University Press, 1993), p. 39.

[9]   Denzell S. Smith, 'The Credibility of the Wooing of Anne in *Richard III*', *Papers on Language and Literature*, 7.2 (1971), 199–202 (p. 199).

Pity and Identity in the Age of Shakespeare

on a sliding scale between humanity and non-humanity. Richard's response, though it approaches the project of definition from another direction, uses the same standard. Working against the dominant intellectual instincts of Shakespeare's time, both of these characters use pity, rather than reason, as a means of shaping identity. Both situate pity between humanity and non-humanity; both use pity to destabilise or affirm a privileged human status.

The dominant early modern theories attempting to define and distinguish humankind, of course, focused on the human capacity for reason. The most famous of these, Descartes's *Discourse on the Method*, used the *cogito* to argue for the separation of men from the mindless existence of animals, by asserting humans as vessels of pure reasoning.[10] Although Shakespeare and his contemporaries wrote in a pre-Cartesian moment, they nevertheless lived and worked in a culture that preferred to define humanity in terms of reason and rational capacity. As Bruce Boehrer notes, even before Descartes there was a habit of viewing reason as 'the *definitive* feature of humanity'.[11] Further evidence of this perspective can be seen, for example, in the second edition of Daniel Widdowes's translated and abridged *Naturall Philosophy: Or A Description of the World, and of the Severall Creatures therein Contained*: 'All creatures are reasonable, or unreasonable', he observes, going on to note that 'They which *want* reason, are *Beasts*, who live on Land or in Water'.[12] As is obvious here, humanity is not defined in isolation but in opposition, here with the animal (or 'beast') category representing defining rational lack: this was the most common group against which humanity was constructed. Scipion Dupleix, Lord of Clarens, for example, neatly captures this view of humankind's rational (and relational) superiority:

> If the beasts had beene also infirme as men in their birth, the greatest part of them had beene lost, *neither having judgement, nor conduct, nor the commodities of men*, and being subject to be taken, and surprized by one another, as also by man; but in mans behalfe it was very expedient that he should be borne so weake, to the end that he should acknowledge his basenesse and his infirmity, and that he should be lesse proud.[13]

[10] René Descartes, *Discourse on Method* and *The Meditations*, trans. F.E. Sutcliffe (London: Penguin, 1968).

[11] Bruce Boehrer, *Shakespeare Among the Animals: Nature and Society in the Drama of Early Modern England* (New York, NY: Palgrave Macmillan, 2002) p. 9, my emphasis.

[12] Daniel Widdowes, *Naturall philosophy, or, A description of the world*, 2nd ed. (London: 1631), sig. K3ᵛ, my emphasis. As noted above, this volume is an abridged translation of an earlier work by Wilhelm Adolf Scribonius (active 1576–1583), entitled *Rerum naturalium doctrina methodica*.

[13] Scipion Dupleix, *The resolver; or Curiosities of nature* (London: 1635), sig. C7ʳ, my emphasis.

Theorising Humanity Through Pity

Dupleix intends to repackage human corporal vulnerability as a kind of esoteric advantage, but he nevertheless participates in a familiar model of defining humankind against non-human (in this case, animal) lack. What Dupleix's 'beasts' possess, they possess specifically because they do *not* enjoy 'the commodities of men'. Though outwardly Dupleix encourages human-kind to admit their 'basenesse' and 'infirmity', to 'be lesse proud', this is a statement of man's distinction and superiority. However, the exploitation of the non-human counterpart effectively means that 'containing' human-kind's superiority comes at the cost of reductively defining other groups. It also imagines this lack as something keenly felt: Widdowes' observation that beasts '*want* reason' (my emphasis) accounts for absence in a way that also projects desire, framing the non-rational creature as somehow incomplete.

This mode of thinking problematically assumes humanity as a perfect whole, a starting point that, on the level of individual subjects, can only produce varieties of failure to fully realise an ideal. The creation of sepa-rate and distinguishable 'non-human' categories therefore offers a way of explaining these failures of humanity. Though other categories are used (typically relating to spirit life or monstrosity), these discourses on humanity most often model the inherent appeal of animals as the explan-atory non-human other.[14] William Adlington's translation of Apuleius (1566), for example, explains that:

> When as we suffer our mindes so to be drowned in the sensuall lustes of the fleshe, and the *beastly* pleasure therof [...] we léese wholy the *use of reason and vertue (which proprely should be in man)* & play the partes of bruite and savage beastes.[15]

Here, rational thought is cast as the defining property of humankind. Reason is placed again in opposition to 'beastly' behaviour, which is framed in the more emotive terms of sensuality and pleasure. Although the passage gestures towards the fixed point of a separate *kind* – 'bruite and savage beasts' – there is no real suggestion of a definitive and permanent

[14] For more on early modern ideas about monstrosity, see: Surekha Davies, *Renais-sance Ethnography and the Invention of the Human: New Worlds, Maps and Monsters* (Cambridge: Cambridge University Press, 2016); Laura Lunger Knoppers and Joan B. Landes (eds.), *Monstrous Bodies/Political Monstrosities in Early Modern Europe* (Ithaca, NY: Cornell University Press, 2004); Mark Thornton Burnett, *Constructing 'Monsters' in Shakespearean Drama and Early Modern Culture* (London: Palgrave Macmillan, 2002); and Linda Woodbridge, 'Renaissance Bogeymen: The Necessary Monsters of the Age', in Guido Ruggiero (ed.), *A Companion to the Worlds of the Renaissance* (Malden, MA: Blackwell Publishing, 2002), pp. 444–459.

[15] Apuleius, *The. xi. bookes of the Golden asse [...]* trans. William Adlington (London: 1566), sig. A2ᵛ–A3ʳ, my emphasis.

Pity and Identity in the Age of Shakespeare

taxonomic change. The imagined subject who succumbs to the pleasures of the flesh remains essentially human: the invocation of non-humanity is only intended to clarify a perceived failure or lack of the human category. The emotional turn that is also imagined as a turn towards beastliness is, tellingly, explained as 'play'-ing a part.

Within this broad model that sets rationality against emotion-led sensation, there is some slippage when it comes to pity. Rational thought was imagined to confirm the distance between humankind and animals, but the capacity for fellow-feeling was also frequently described as a shared and broadly positive characteristic, a common ground that threatened to collapse any dividing border. Citing these shared sensitivities, Montaigne famously insisted that animals should be viewed as 'the fellow-brethren and compeers' of humans.[16] Thomas Wright, in his 1604 work *The Passions of the Mind in General*, observed that what 'we call Passions, and Affections, or perturbations of the mind' are 'common with us, and beasts'.[17] Joint possession of the sensitive soul, as Gail Kern Paster has pointed out, 'constituted the essential similarity between humans and animals'.[18] That said, closer inspection of the language surrounding the emotional lives of animals reveals the extent to which these discussions are all ultimately directed towards the project of clarifying and defining humanity.

In more than four hundred pages detailing the physical characteristics, habitats, and behavioural patterns of a veritable ark's worth of animals, Edward Topsell gives only one specific example of the animal capacity for pity, when discussing sheep. He writes:

[16] For Montaigne, the phrase 'Fellow brethren and compeers' is John Florio's translation: see Michel de Montaigne, *Essays*, trans. John Florio (London: 1613), sig. Y5ᵛ. See also: Arthur Kirsch, 'Virtue, Vice, and Compassion in Montaigne and *The Tempest*', *Studies in English Literature, 1500–1900*, 37.2 (1997), 337–352.

[17] Thomas Wright, *The Passions of the Mind in General* (London: 1604), sig. I2ᵛ.

[18] Gail Kern Paster, *Humoring the Body: Emotions and the Shakespearean Stage* (Chicago, IL: University of Chicago Press, 2004), p. 150. For more on the tension between human and animal categories in the early modern period, see: Rebecca Ann Bach, *Birds and Other Creatures in Renaissance Literature: Shakespeare, Descartes, and Animal Studies* (New York, NY: Routledge, 2018); Bruce Boehrer, *Animal Characters: Nonhuman Beings in Early Modern Literature* (Philadelphia, PA: University of Pennsylvania Press, 2010); Erica Fudge, *Perceiving Animals: Humans and Beasts in Early Modern English Culture* (Basingstoke: Macmillan, 2000), and *Brutal Reasoning: Animals, Rationality, and Humanity in Early Modern England* (Ithaca, NY: Cornell University Press, 2006); and Laurie Shannon, '"Poor, Bare, Forked": Animal Sovereignty, Human Negative Exceptionalism, and the Natural History of *King Lear*,' *Shakespeare Quarterly* 60.2 (2009), 168–196; and *The Accommodated Animal: Cosmopolity in Shakespearean Locales* (Chicago, IL: University of Chicago Press, 2013).

Theorising Humanity Through Pity

> Concerning the simplicity of sheep, I must say more, and also of their innocency, yet the simplicity thereof is such, and so much, that it may well be termed folly, [...] Without cause it wandereth into desert places, and in the winter time when the aire is filled with cold windes, and the earth hardened with hoare frostes, then it forsaketh and goeth out of his warme coate or stable, and being in the cold Snow, there it will tarry and perish, were it not for the care of the sheapheard, for he taketh one of the Rams by the hornes, and draweth him in a doores, then do all the residue follow after. [...] and no lesse is their love one toward another, every way commendable, for one of them pittieth and sorroweth for the harme of another, and when the heate of Sunne offendeth them, *Albertus* writeth, that one of them interposeth his body to shaddow the other.[19]

Many of the tensions underpinning this chapter are at work in this description. On the one hand, Topsell's account of sheep pity hints at the social baggage surrounding the emotion. Topsell's view is largely positive: he describes the fellowship of sheep as being in 'every way commendable', and cites the fact that sheep 'pittieth and sorroweth for the harme of another' as evidence of that fellowship. Pity in that sense brings a community (of sheep) together and defines it. There is however an individual cost, if one extends the description in the direction of its logical conclusion. The 'pity' that Topsell sees in sheep – the image of one sheep using his body to shelter another from the sun – is a physical act of responsive selflessness, a move that sacrifices the comfort of one sheep in the service of another. Although the stakes are relatively low here, it is easy to see the cost of compassion in this example: if this is pity, it is not obviously beneficial to the animal who offers it, except perhaps in the abstract sense of character definition. This compassionate drive seems, for Topsell, a practice unique to the sheep, a herd animal otherwise notable for a simplicity that borders on stupidity. In another sense therefore, the compassionate instinct informs both positive and negative character constructions that also contribute to power hierarchies.

However commendable, these pitying sheep require the protection of a rational being (the human shepherd) in order to avoid even the most obvious threats (in Topsell's example, inclement weather). While there is no necessary correlation between the pity of the sheep and its apparent helplessness, something about this combination of pity, simplicity, an incomplete sense of self and self-preservation also works to elevate the shepherd through his compassionate intervention. Moreover, to read clear evidence of sheep pity, Topsell must project intention and emotional agency onto physical action: that he does so without commenting on that projection

---

[19] Edward Topsell, *The Historie of Foure-Footed Beasts* (London: 1607), sig. Lll3ʳ.

reaffirms his privileged position, the authority he assumes in detailing other animals. Alongside the brief reference to Topsell's shepherd – a benevolent but authoritative protector figure – these are reminders that all of this classification work ultimately serves humanity, even if implicitly. Topsell only speaks of pity once, only in his description of one animal, and only in a way that clarifies human superiority.

Topsell's implicit emphasis on humanity is evident throughout the larger piece. The great majority of Topsell's animals are characterised either by their ferocity and cruelty, or by their innocuousness, and these qualities are often framed against the fixed position of humankind. He even goes so far as to highlight this pervasive cruelty as the reason many animals do not breed in large numbers:

> The cruell and malignant creatures which live only upon the devouring of their inferiours, as the Lyons, Wolves, Foxes, and Beares, conceive but verie seldome, because there is lesse use for them in the world, and God in his creatures keepeth downe the cruell and ravenous, but advanceth the simple, weake, and despised. (sig. Aa2^r)

Here and elsewhere, Topsell suggests that animals are primarily identified either as ferocious or harmless. What underpins this work is the implicit suggestion that animals derive their identity by their relation to humans: they are classified either by their utility, or the threat they may or may not pose. The suggestion that the ferocious beasts breed less because 'there is lesse use for them in the world' is clearly informed by a human perspective: the mild sheep is of far more use (to humans) than the wolves that eat them. What therefore looks like a straightforward account of pity in sheep also clarifies the value of embeddedness in human society. Sheep are described in more positive, sympathetic terms apparently because they demonstrate relatively little personal autonomy and therefore can be directed toward human advantage. Those animals who might be more antagonist to human society, like wolves, are put at a distance through their description as 'cruell and malignant'. Still it seems there is a very little way for any non-human animal to achieve a truly favourable position when humans remain at the top of the power structure: these animals are either 'cruell' and therefore set at a distance, like the wolf, or brought close and cast down through description: inferior, helpless, 'despised', like the sheep.

A brief return to Shakespeare's character Richard III helpfully illustrates the way pity is used to position subjects within or beyond the human community. Across plays, pity is repeatedly used to give shape to Richard's character. Each time, it stands as an indicator of emotional (in)capacity, a marker of humanity that Richard cannot (or will not) reach for. And, each time, non-human language looms around this failure of attainment,

Theorising Humanity Through Pity

shaping Richard's subjectivity even as it linguistically distances him from the human category. In the final moments of *3HenryVI*, as Richard kills Henry, he also gives this account of himself:

> RICHARD III
> Down, down to hell, and say I sent thee thither:
> *[Stabs him again]*
> *I, that have neither pity, love nor fear.*
> Indeed, 'tis true that Henry told me of,
> For I have often heard my mother say
> I came into the world with my legs forward.
> [...]
> The midwife wonder'd and the women cried,
> 'O, Jesus bless us, he is born with teeth!'
> And so I was, which plainly signified
> That I should snarl, and bite and play the dog.
> Then, since the heavens have shaped my body so,
> Let hell make crook'd my mind to answer it.
> I have no brother, I am like no brother.
> And this word 'love', which graybeards call divine,
> Be resident in men like one another
> And not in me: *I am myself alone.*[20]

Richard's turn to emotional language and non-human coordinates only make clear the instability of the human category. His 'I' is here defined by what it lacks: pity, love, and fear. This emotional positioning is the first part of a longer process by which Richard signals his difference, his separate-ness: he comes into the world differently, and his lack of belonging is physically marked by the 'teeth' he is born with, and by his shape. Richard uses animal language to quantify this social separateness, noting that his infant teeth were a clear indicator that he should 'snarl and bite and play the dog'. This way of framing himself positions Richard against the society of other humans, but it is not a straightforward move toward animality. Instead, Richard constructs his own subjectivity in terms of his aloneness, his isolation from the community of others. Here again, whatever Richard is, he remains human, and though he uses the dog to explain his anti-social perspectives, he is still only *playing* the dog, borrowing a different – and lower – set of behavioural expectations, and using them to define his own character. At the same time, Richard acknowledges that what he lacks emotionally is the very essence of what fosters kinship in, and defines,

---

[20] William Shakespeare, *King Henry VI pt. 3*, ed. by John D. Cox and Eric Rasmussen (London: Arden Shakespeare, 2001), 5.6.67–83, my emphasis.

Pity and Identity in the Age of Shakespeare

others: 'this word "love"', he observes 'Be resident in men *like one another* | and *not in me*' (my emphasis). Richard's is a picture of lone subjectivity, a vision of selfhood in isolation: 'I have no brother, I am like no brother', he admits, before finally concluding 'I am myself alone'. Richard does not lack rational capacity, but instead frames his emotional shortcomings as the isolating obstacle: he eschews the fellow-feeling that pity represents, but this is nevertheless a statement of the emotion's binding capabilities.

'NOTHING SO KIND, BUT SOMETHING PITIFUL'

These examples from *3Henry VI* (1591) and *Richard III* (1592–1594) make clear that Shakespeare was considering pity's role in defining humanity even at the earliest stages of his dramatic career. The ideas appear again in *Titus Andronicus* (1594), where Lavinia's desperate pleas to Tamora, Chiron, and Demetrius rely heavily on ideas of emotional transference in breeding, and in kind:

LAVINIA
When did the tiger's young ones teach the dam?
O, do not learn her wrath: she taught it thee.
The milk thou suckst from her did turn to marble;
Even at thy teat thou hadst thy tyranny.
Yet every mother breeds not sons alike:
(*To CHIRON*)
Do thou entreat her show a woman's pity.

CHIRON
What, wouldst thou have me prove myself a bastard?

LAVINIA
'Tis true; the raven doth not hatch a lark.
Yet have I heard – O, could I find it now –
The lion, moved with pity, did endure
To have his princely paws pared all away.
Some say that ravens foster forlorn children
The whilst their own birds famish in their nests.
O be to me, though thy hard heart say no,
Nothing so kind, but something pitiful. (2.2.141–156)

Central to Lavinia's appeal is the assumption that one's emotional capacities may be determined by one's parentage, either by instruction or by nature. Lavinia hopes however (for her own sake) that Tamora's pitilessness is an individual aberration, something can be isolated and therefore contained. She hopes that Chiron and Demetrius might yet prove to be of a

Theorising Humanity Through Pity

different, more pitying kind to their mother. Lavinia's emotional agenda – her pursuit of pity – therefore drives the muddled turn to animal language in the exchange. However, this is a move that creates more problems than it solves. The use of animal language complicates Lavinia's efforts to use pity to neutralise the threat posed by her tormentors, in part because it extends the assessment spectrum to open up a wider range of behavioural possibilities. Crucially, through the invocation of the animal, Lavinia introduces the possibility of human agents who hold themselves to lower social and emotional standards. As Mary Fawcett points out, Lavinia's mode of containing Tamora is to '[single] her out from the general category, womanhood', by relabelling her 'beastly creature' (2.2.182), but Chiron blocks the attempt with a testament of kind-ness.[21] When he denies Lavinia, he makes clear that an offer of pity would constitute a violation of kinship, and that this would in turn reclassify him: 'wouldst thou have me prove myself a bastard?'. It is a proclamation of allegiance, and of likeness, that hinges on pity. Whatever Chiron, Demetrius, and Tamora are, they are the same.

Although it is never in question that these characters are human, the metaphoric chaos of Lavinia's language here somehow still presses the question of how Tamora and her sons might be categorised. She invokes tigers, ravens, larks, and lions – even an animalistic reference to Tamora's 'teat' – in her efforts to capture a complex theory of emotional development that intersects with a system of human taxonomy. Like her bid to save herself, Lavinia's linguistic effort to capture and define the Goth queen is ineffective: metaphorically realigning Tamora with beastliness cannot explain her lack of pity, if in the same breath the lion is described as being 'moved with pity'. If anything, Lavinia's linguistic efforts only make obvious that Lavinia's actions isolate and separate her from the community of category. Perhaps what Lavinia is experiencing is a cognitive dissonance: the shock of Tamora's emotional disobedience, her deviation from assumed social norms. As Tamora explains however, her lack of pity is explicitly human, something she feels precisely *because* of her kinship with her sacrificed son, and because she herself has been confronted by pitiless humanity:

TAMORA
Even for his sake am I pitiless.
Remember, boys, I poured forth tears in vain
To save your brother from the sacrifice,
But fierce Andronicus would not relent. (2.2.162–165)

---

[21] Mary L. Fawcett, 'Arms/Words/Tears: Language and the Body in *Titus Andronicus*', *English Literary History* 50.2 (1983), 261–277 (p. 267).

Pity and Identity in the Age of Shakespeare

By her own account, Tamora's pitilessness is not natural, but learned, developed in human society. An example like *Titus* therefore highlights the complicated position that pity occupies in discussions and constructions of humanity. Lavinia's appeal proposes the emotion as an expression both of kindness and of *kind*: she uses it as a way of signalling Tamora as an unkind other, someone diminished by emotional (in)capacities. Moreover, it is clear that while Lavinia, in this moment, *wants* this theory of pitiful humanity to be true, it is less obvious that she *knows* it to be true: her theorising here is also an attempt to locate the protection she needs. Tamora's rejection, on the other hand, seems to confirm just how human pitilessness really is: she can refuse or reject the emotion precisely because another human (in this case, Titus himself) has shown her how, and in this it becomes clear to Lavinia just how dangerous the civilised world really is. For Tamora, for Chiron, and for Demetrius, this moment of approving or denying pity is also a crucial moment of articulating their subjectivity, a violation that expresses their proximal humanity even as it pushes on the human category, by implicating Titus.

'WHAT 'TIS TO PITY AND BE PITIED'

Reading these examples together, it becomes apparent that this kind of emotional theorising that invokes non-human figures like beasts, monsters, or devils is only ever intended to give further shape and clarity to the otherwise difficult-to-contain category of humanity. Power politics inevitably contribute to the instability of the human category. How, one might reasonably wonder, can ideas of core humanity truly exist alongside hierarchical systems of power and privilege? Invoking non-humanity – particularly with figures whose behaviours or capabilities place them in close proximity to humankind – also hints at a broader field of human identity. It gives the sense that is possible to be *indisputably* human, but also that it is possible, through thought and action, to move from centre and in the direction of a non-human identity. That said, indisputable humanity is invariably affirmed in community: to be embedded in a community is to be undeniably human; to be on the outskirts is to be constantly questioned. *As You Like It* presents this very clearly, late in Act 2, when Orlando intrudes upon Duke Senior's exiled court. As he roughly demands the food from their table, Orlando is surprised by the civility and ready hospitality of the forest dwellers:

> ORLANDO
> Speak you so gently? Pardon me, I pray you:
> I thought that all things had been savage here;
> And therefore put I on the countenance
> Of stern commandment. But whate'er you are

Theorising Humanity Through Pity

That in this desert inaccessible,
Under the shade of melancholy boughs,
Lose and neglect the creeping hours of time
If ever you have look'd on better days,
If ever been where bells have knoll'd to church,
If ever sat at any good man's feast,
If ever from your eyelids wiped a tear
And know what 'tis to pity and be pitied,
Let gentleness my strong enforcement be:
In the which hope I blush, and hide my sword. (2.7.107–120, my emphasis)

'I thought', Orlando admits, 'that all things had been savage here'. Orlando's manner of self-correction – of filling in secure humanity where he had expected and projected something *lesser* – presents an interesting catalogue of defining characteristics for human civility. Orlando imagines "better days" as days of social embeddedness, where both the landscape and the soundscape are marked by social gathering, signalled by the bells calling people to church. The invoked image of the feast underscores this view of humanity cultivated in community, as does the emotional turn of Orlando's final conditions: 'If ever from your eyelids wiped a tear | And know what 'tis to pity and be pitied'. Orlando's is a vision of humanity predicated on the condition of emotional capacity and obligation. For him, the experience of offering pity and receiving it is also a positive and explicit turn away from savage living, something which simultaneously defines, and distances.

Throughout this book I have traced the early modern English use of pity as a guiding social principle, a way of ordering social interaction and understanding social obligation. I have also argued that the period's drama consistently portrays pity as a core feature (however fraught) of the human experience. But here, Orlando is going a step further, specifically using pity as a way of theorising humanity, and in this case it allows Orlando to positively categorise these people who are removed from the obvious physical and social spaces surrounding humankind. Separated from these humane contexts, the Duke and his exiled court became – even if only for a moment – proximal humans: they were pushed (at least in Orlando's mind) towards savagery. What is also clear from this exchange is that processes of categorisation also guide behaviour. As Peter Erickson observes, in this speech Orlando 'effects as gracefully as possible a transition from toughness to tenderness', but the shift also confirms that his actions and attitude change significantly according to who (or what) he finds.[22] Orlando there-

---

[22] Peter B. Erickson, 'Sexual Politics and the Social Structure in *As You Like It*', *The Massachusetts Review, Inc.*, 23.1 (1982), 65–83 (p. 74).

Pity and Identity in the Age of Shakespeare

fore signals a complex system of social performance predicated on hierarchical humanity. The aggressive power language with which he enters the scene – believing the Duke and his company to be 'savage' – melts to gentleness when Orlando discovers they are of the same kind. The directness of Orlando's account perhaps also gives some insight into why early modern discourses of pity were so couched in the language of anxiety and worry. Orlando begs pardon for putting on the 'countenance | Of stern commandment', but not because the behaviour itself was poor (though it was). He apologises because the behaviour was misdirected, inappropriate for Duke Senior's *kind*. The stakes, therefore, are extremely high: if pity determines humanity, it equally determines how one behaves, and how one can expect to be treated in 'civil' society.

Early modern English drama often used the concept of pity to positively define human experience. As a way of glossing emotional permeability, expressions of pity and fellow-feeling clarified a model of dramatic subjectivity that understood the individual in context: separate and distinct, while also thoroughly embedded in systems of social obligation and support. Orlando's use of pity here, in the forest of Arden, uses pity to narrate humanity in a different way, this time using the emotion both to capture a particular kind of human experience (cultivated, privileged) and, crucially, to stabilise that humanity as protected/distanced from a worse but proximal category (in this case, 'savage').

Shakespeare favoured an emotionally-inflected manner of theorising humanity, a mode of exploration that appears in many of his plays. With the exception of Orlando's comments, the examples I have offered so far have themselves been of a kind, moments used to define a play's malevolents, of distinguishing moral otherness while simultaneously reinforcing the idea of a human community in which pity functions properly. The rest of this chapter, however, deals with the more extensive probing of emotional subjectivity in *The Tempest*, a play that explores a knotted relationship between pity, humanity, and social privilege. The emotional theorising that occurs throughout *The Tempest* clarifies the role of non-human or proximally human characters in defining humanity, by questioning conventional distinctions of kind-ness. Caliban, Ariel, and Miranda are all explicitly categorised according to their relationship to pity, and each of these characters, I suggest, articulate emotional subjectivity from a position of proximal humanity, of 'not-quite'-ness. As the play goes on, it also becomes clear that what these characters lack, the shape of their own incompleteness, relationally clarifies Prospero's privileged humanity, making him look more stable, more complete, and by extension more powerful. Shakespeare's play therefore places its meditation on human pity in what, for Prospero, is a self-serving system of power, privilege, and

Theorising Humanity Through Pity

self-definition. This is a play that highlights the vital role of non-humanity in defining the human characters of early modern drama, but it also problematises the profound emotional burden undertaken on their behalf. In the remainder of this chapter, I interrogate the ways in which *The Tempest* uses pity to navigate distinctions of *kind*: how the emotion both draws and blurs boundaries, how these classification systems work to reinforce problematic power hierarchies, and who (or what) is sacrificed in the service of 'humanity'.

ARIEL

For many Caliban is the obvious testament to Shakespeare's interest in the 'problem of distinctions', and the truest reflection of the early modern 'English cultural anxieties about the nature of humanity'.[23] That said, *The Tempest's* most explicit venture into what defines humanity actually comes in an exchange between Prospero and Ariel. With Stephano, Trinculo, and Caliban, 'Brimful of sorrow and dismay' (5.1.14), confined, tormented with reminders of their transgressions, and pushed towards madness, Ariel leaves to report the proceedings to his master. Urging Prospero to end his action against them, the spirit Ariel notes that:

ARIEL
Your charm so strongly works 'em
That, if you now beheld them, your affections
Would become tender.[24]

---

[23] Bruce Boehrer, 'Animal Studies and the Deconstruction of Character', *PMLA*, 124 (2009), 542–547, esp. p. 546; Tom Lindsay, '"Which first was mine own king": Caliban and the Politics of Service and Education in *The Tempest*', *Studies in Philology*, 113.2 (2016), 397–423, esp. p. 399. On *The Tempest's* broader posthumanist significance, Karen Raber has pointed to Ariel's occasional appearance as a harpy in the play as evidence of Shakespeare's interest in posthumanist hybridity. In *The Tempest* and elsewhere, Raber argues, 'entities are presented as composites, fusions of diverse types of both material and abstract being'. See: Karen Raber, *Shakespeare and Posthumanist Theory* (London: Bloomsbury, 2018), p. 103. On the significance of *The Tempest* as a posthumanist text, see: Julián Jiménez Heffernan, *Shakespeare's Extremes: Wild Man, Monster, Beast* (Basingstoke: Palgrave, 2015).

[24] All references to *The Tempest* (unless otherwise noted) are to: William Shakespeare, *The Tempest*, ed. Virginia Mason Vaughan and Alden T. Vaughan (London: Thomas Nelson and Sons Ltd, 1999), 5.1.17–19.

Pity and Identity in the Age of Shakespeare

'Your affections would become tender', he claims.[25] As one of the chief architects of these torments, Ariel's bid for Prospero's compassion marks an important shift in the play's action, a movement towards its resolution: this, he argues, is the moment to show pity. When Prospero presses him on this point of developing tender affections – 'Dost thou think so, spirit?' (5.1.19), Ariel replies: 'Mine would, sir, *were I human*' (5.1.20, my emphasis). Vitally, Ariel and Prospero use species classifications (spirit, human) rather than character names, a move that frames the exchange in generic terms rather than glossing it as a moment between familiars. Ariel is not Ariel, but 'spirit'; the pitying subject he imagines is not a known character, but instead someone of a specific *kind*: simply, 'human'.

Ariel's qualifying 'were I human' makes a claim about the human category even as it affords him an important distance from the emotion of the moment. As Seth Lobis has argued, it is significant that Ariel's emotional judgment can only been read as a 'spritely approximation' of compassion, more hypothetical than anything else.[26] Although Prospero later assumes that Ariel must experience 'a touch, a feeling | Of their afflictions' (5.1.21– 22), it is not clear that the spirit actually does feel anything towards those he has tormented: mine *would*, he suggests, *if*.[27] The comment is as much about conditions of membership as it is about emotional obligation: the moment presents the two as inextricably linked.

This scene sees Ariel articulate the defining capacity of the non-human in a number of ways. First, he makes explicit the link between compassion ('tender affections') and being human: he does not say, 'were I human *or animal*', but instead references the human as an insular category. In this way, he casts humanity as a condition specifically defined by compassion, clarifying that to be human is also to be emotionally implicated. But of course Prospero's emotion is a part of the problem: he is already emotionally implicated by his anger, unable to embrace pity unassisted. Moreover, he is out of practice, long-separated from the community of others. In delivering the external non-human perspective, Ariel is able to clarify the stakes for

[25] For another view of the importance of 'tenderness' in *The Tempest*, see Eric Langley, *Shakespeare's Contagious Sympathies: Ill Communications* (Oxford: Oxford University Press, 2018), esp. pp. 201–210.

[26] Seth Lobis, *The Virtue of Sympathy: Magic, Philosophy, and Literature in Seventeenth-Century England* (New Haven, CT: Yale University Press, 2015), p. 2.

[27] Ariel's proximity to compassion – however hypothetical – does fit oddly with his classification as a spirit, as Maurice Hunt points out: 'the Spirit strangely acts autonomously, teaching Prospero about a virtue – compassion – rarely associated with magic' (p. 64). Maurice Hunt, 'Shakespeare's *The Tempest* and Human Worth', *Ben Jonson Journal*, 20.1 (2013), 58–71.

Theorising Humanity Through Pity

Prospero. His comment makes clear that the magician must move on from his own feelings of wrath, to assume the desired position at the end of the play: compassionate, and therefore restored, powerful, socially embedded.

Taken in the context of other emotional exchanges between Ariel and Prospero, this moment understands compassion as operating within a very specific set of rules. The spirit appears to imagine compassionate connection as bound up in considerations of membership, or likeness: it is a theory that emphasises in particular the 'fellow' embedded in the term 'fellow-feeling'. At the same time, the play takes pains to blur Ariel's own category. Ariel is clearly not the kind of spirit imagined in the Great Chain of Being, a form understood to lack a sensitive soul.[28] Instead, elsewhere he is shown to be capable of both physical sensation *and* emotion. Prospero reminds Ariel that he 'didst *painfully* remain | A dozen years' (1.2.278, my emphasis) in Sycorax's prison; he is also described as 'moody' (1.2.244). These references to Ariel's emotional life pass quickly, and evoke no special reaction or reflection from either the spirit or his master. Ariel's later statement therefore uses compassion to facilitate what appears as an unusual moment of category definition in a play that otherwise tends to test or collapse boundaries. Ariel's ambiguity raises a number of questions about how compassion functions more broadly in the space of the island, and how the capacity for this kind of emotional connection determines the identities of its inhabitants. Either Ariel is unable to feel compassion because he understands the emotion as a uniquely human capacity, or he understands the emotion only as functioning between subjects of the same *kind*/category. One option defines the human; the other denies the possibility of cross-kind emotional communities. Both possibilities rely on compassion to draw species/category boundaries in some way.

Although Ariel is in other places (and by other characters) clearly identified as a spirit, in this moment all that matters is what he is *not*: human. At the same time, the conditions of the stage – his necessary portrayal by a human actor – ensure that the spirit retains an obvious proximity to the other human characters. Ariel frames himself explicitly as non-human only to reconfigure Prospero's own humanity, to remind him that he can

---

[28] Arthur O. Lovejoy, *The Great Chain of Being: A Study of the History of an Idea* (Cambridge, MA: Harvard University Press, 1936). The concept of the tripartite soul (of which the sensitive soul is one part) is developed in Aristotle's *De Anima*. For more see *De Anima* in Richard McKeon (ed.), *The Basic Works of Aristotle* (New York, NY: Random House, 1941), 535–603. For more on the tripartite soul, see: Katharine Park, 'The Organic Soul', in Charles Schmitt (ed.), *The Cambridge History of Renaissance Philosophy* (Cambridge: Cambridge University Press, 1988), pp. 464–484.

Pity and Identity in the Age of Shakespeare

only achieve his desired, privileged form of humanity *if* he produces the appropriate emotional response to the suffering of his enemies. In so doing, the spirit makes clear the utility of discrete-but-related category identities surrounding humanity, and the value of affective projection. What is happening here is, ultimately, not so much about distinguishing between different kinds of beings as it is about articulating one kind's superiority. This moment of theorising uses other kinds of creatures to give shape to Prospero's final form, his final position, and in this way it facilitates an important social hierarchy with his mode of humanity at the top.

Prospero's response to Ariel's report, his assurance that he will be moved to pity, also confirms this as the moment of his own elevation:

PROSPERO
Hast thou, which are but air, a touch, a feeling
Of their afflictions, and shall not myself
(*One of their kind*, that relish all as sharply,
Passion as they) *be kindlier* moved than thou art? (5.1.21–24, my emphasis)

In all of Shakespeare's work, this is the only use of 'kindlier'. It is a word that helps Prospero not just to compare two groups – of one's own kind versus *not* of one's own kind – but also helps to establish one of these as inherently *more*: the better, kindlier group.[29] Prospero makes the distinction between himself and Ariel explicit, agreeing that as 'one of their kind', he is either naturally inclined, or obligated, to 'be kind-*lier* moved' than Ariel. The play on 'kind' and 'kindlier' imagines a natural relationship between those of the same species (kind) and the capacity for shared emotion (kindness). It suggests the community and connectivity of social similarity, while equally making obvious the hierarchical thinking that underpins this theorising.

This particular way of thinking about compassionate community is present in Cicero's influential description of humankind as defined by the 'bonds of mutual obligation which tie us together in a *societas generis humani*' – or what Mike Pincombe calls 'the "fellowship of humankind"'.[30] As above, Ciceronian thought admits a broader application of 'tenderness' (to borrow Ariel's term), which operates across species boundaries. Nicholas Grimald's 1556 translation of Cicero, for example, makes clear that certain

---

[29] John Bartlett, *A New and Complete Concordance, or Verbal Index to the Words, Phrases, & Passages in the Dramatic Works of Shakespeare* (London: Macmillan, 1937), p. 829.

[30] Mike Pincombe, *Elizabethan Humanism: Literature and Learning in the Later Sixteenth Century* (Harlow: Longman, 2001), 15. For more on Cicero's significance in Renaissance humanism, see: Robin Headlam Wells, *Shakespeare's Humanism* (Cambridge: Cambridge University Press, 2005).

Theorising Humanity Through Pity

traits are 'given by nature', 'to every kinde of living creature', including 'a certayn tendernesse' for those in direct proximity, like offspring – but still he assigns a more elevated form of tenderness to humanity.[31] Cicero comments that man

> seeth sequels, beholdeth grounds, and causes of thinges, is not ignoraunt of their procedinges, and as it wer their foregoings: compareth semb-launces, & with thinges present joyneth, & knitteth thinges to come: dothe soone espye the course of his holle life, and to the leading therof purueieth thinges necessarie. (sig. A5^v)

These abilities, for Cicero, are the conditions required for a more complex (superior) application of tenderness, with capacity for a much broader scope and impact. This kind of tenderness also more closely approximates the kind of response that Ariel seeks from his master: the rational ability to understand cause and effect, to reflect on the past and the future, and to calculate from this the 'purueieth things necessarie'. For Cicero and Ariel alike, this is what defines 'the said nature' of humankind (sig. A5^v). This capacity, Cicero argues, 'winneth man to man, to a felowshippe bothe in talke, and also of life' (sig. A5^v). The stakes, as Cicero outlines them, give shape to the unspoken warning that Ariel is offering Prospero: 'Severed from common felowshippe, and neybourhod of men,' Cicero warns, '[there] muste needs bee a certein savagenesse, and beastly crueltie' (sig. H6^r). By this reading, humankind's ability to reason and to feel with one another defines humanity, and defines it specifically against non-human otherness. Ariel's figuring of compassion uses his own spirit-ness as the defining non-human counterpoint, but it is clear that if Prospero fails to feel compassion it will not push him toward a spiritly identity. Rather, it is Prospero's 'human-ness' that is under review. There is, moreover, no sense in Ariel's comment that his lack of 'tender affections' negatively impacts his own sense of self: if the comment prompts any existential reflection, it does so only for the human present. The identity threat for Prospero is, on a Ciceronian understanding, downward, to the 'certein savagenesse', the 'beastly crueltie'. This lack of emotion for a human subject almost always results in a move downward, toward the nonhuman animal – and, by extension, the increased likelihood of subjugation by 'superior' forms of humankind.

In both interpretations of this moment with Ariel, the absence of certain qualities or conditions in a proximate non-human projects shape and clarity on to the human counterpart. This positions humanity as a posi-tive presence articulated against an absence or void. However, as Erica

---

[31] Marcus Tullius Cicero, *Thre bokes of duties*, trans. Nicholas Grimald (London: 1556), sig. A5^r.

Pity and Identity in the Age of Shakespeare

Fudge, Ruth Gilbert, and Susan Wiseman have noted about this passage in *The Tempest*, the emotion in 4.1 is hypothetical for Prospero as well. As they point out, 'neither of the speakers claim to actually *experience* compassion – they imagine circumstances in which they would'.[32] The exchange, they note, 'articulates the desired qualities associated with the human', but *only* by pointing to the absence of those qualities in others.[33] The discussion gestures toward a concrete sense of human-ness, and yet that humanity does not materialise in its own right: it is worked toward, perhaps, but remains unconfirmed, still ever so slightly out of reach. Ariel's vision – and Prospero's understanding – of what it means to be human is defined relationally, hypothetically, and with Ariel's own non-human status shouldering all of the burden. As a result, Prospero's humanity is free to remain largely inchoate, enjoying the privilege of assumed superiority without the disadvantage of clear borders or expectation. Prospero's follow up comments are only effective in establishing his position because Ariel stands as a point of reference. Prospero does not imagine himself as independently 'kind', but instead he recognises an opportunity to be 'kindli*er*' than Ariel. He is unable to define himself without Ariel's non-human coordinates. In this way, compassion underscores the vital negative presence of the non-human, demonstrating that humanity is something that can only be created in dialogue. And yet, as the power dynamics of *The Tempest* make clear – as the very presence of Caliban confirms – these conversations only benefit the human interlocuters.

CALIBAN

The Tempest sees Caliban identified in myriad ways which, read together, make clear that 'indeterminacy is an essential feature of his character'.[34] He is, to begin with, the 'salvage, deformed slave' of the 1623 Folio's *dramatis personae*; a 'freckled whelp […] not honour'd with | A human shape' (1.2.283–284); an 'abhorred slave' (1.2.352); a 'strange fish' (2.2.27); and Prospero's 'thing of darkness' (5.1.275).[35] This seemingly never-ending enquiry into Caliban's ambiguous nature – and by extension, his position

---

[32] Erica Fudge, Ruth Gilbert, and Susan Wiseman, 'Introduction: The Dislocation of the Human', in Erica Fudge, Ruth Gilbert, and Susan Wiseman (eds.), *At the Borders of the Human: Beasts, Bodies and Natural Philosophy* (London: Macmillan, 1999), pp. 1–9 (p. 4).

[33] Ibid., p. 4.

[34] Deborah Willis, 'Shakespeare's Tempest and the Discourse of Colonialism', *Studies in English Literature, 1500–1900*, 29.2 (1989), 277–289 (p. 284).

[35] William Shakespeare, *Comedies, Histories & Tragedies* (London: 1623), sig. B4ʳ.

on the island – is perhaps what most clearly defines his character in *The Tempest*: we are only certain that we cannot be certain about him.[36]

Caliban plays a central role in *The Tempest's* larger exploration of classification boundaries, in part because his own position remains so resolutely uncertain. Caliban's humanity, as Julia Reinhard Lupton points out, 'remains a question rather than a given in the play'.[37] The play's first meditation on Caliban's ontological status – in his first appearance, in 1.2 – also uses the connection between kind and kindness to signal the ways in which all of the play's characters are positioned in relation to one another upon a human/non-human spectrum. Following the speech in which Caliban asserts his ownership of the island – 'This island's mine by Sycorax, my mother' (1.2.332) – Prospero neutralises the power threat of Caliban's claim by assigning him an inferior classification:

PROSPERO
Thou most lying slave,
Whom stripes may move, not kindness; I have used thee
(Filth as thou art) with humane care and lodged thee
In mine own cell, till thou didst seek to violate
The honour of my child. (1.2.345–349, my emphasis)

Though Caliban is othered from the moment that Prospero labels him with his social position ('slave'), the passage opens out into a rich description of how emotional considerations work to situate the characters on Shakespeare's variously populated island. Prospero's efforts here to construct a category difference in Caliban also highlights the perceived threat posed by cross-kind emotional relationships. Prospero's suggestion that 'stripes may move' Caliban, 'not kindness', emphatically displaces Caliban from the realm of emotional connection, labelling him as a physical being rather than an affective one. The timing of this moment makes clear that, for Prospero, this is a way of establishing a power hierarchy, rather than an impartial description. After all, Prospero is responding to one of Caliban's most emotionally-driven and sympathetic speeches:

CALIBAN
When thou cam'st first
Thou strok'st me and made much of me

---

[36] This lack of clarity is, as Mark Thornton Burnett argues, part of the point of Caliban's character, who is designed in such a way that 'Each character moulds Caliban in a different image, and the sum total of those imagined representations can never cohere' (*Constructing 'Monsters'*, pp. 133–134).

[37] Julia Reinhard Lupton, 'Creature Caliban', *Shakespeare Quarterly*, 51.1 (2000): 1–23 (p. 13).

Pity and Identity in the Age of Shakespeare

> [...] and [taught] me how
> To name the bigger light and how the less
> That burn by day and night. And then I loved thee [...] (1.2.333–337)

The early relationship Caliban refers to here is one predicated on kindness (or at least the appearance of it): Caliban narrates the experience of being moved by kindness in a moment of self-articulation that Prospero almost immediately denies and overwrites. This exchange however, which looks like a key moment of classification for Caliban, is more clearly designed to clarify Prospero's position: 'I have used thee', he notes, 'with humane care'. Prospero overwrites Caliban's subjectivity here with his own, in a move that neatly conflates the human with the humane. In designating Caliban a lying slave, as filth, as lacking honour, and as incapable of responding to emotional humanity, Prospero defines himself against that negative space, thereby clarifying his own difference, superiority, and humanity.

In this opening account of Caliban's many transgressions, the most significant offence implied is that he conflates emotional 'kindness' with physical or social 'kind-ness', or that he sees the two as inextricably linked. His attempted rape of Miranda has (rightly) been an obstacle to his finding a wholly sympathetic reception with audiences, but it is in another sense the play's clearest statement of Caliban's own sense of himself. His regret that he was unsuccessful in '[*peopling*] this isle with Calibans' (1.2.351–352) hinges on the apparent belief that it is biologically possible for him to procreate with her. As Lupton argues, Caliban's use of 'people' over 'increase' suggests that Caliban is 'rhetorically linking himself to the human kindness from which Prospero and Miranda would exclude him'.[38] For Caliban, this is the most problematic, but also the clearest possible expression of his belief that he is of the same *kind*. For Miranda and Prospero, this is the definitive evidence of his non-humanity. Prospero imagines that his efforts to treat Caliban humanely have been betrayed by Caliban's disrespect of the social (or perhaps, species) boundary that Prospero places between them.

The Tempest thus brings together two core concepts in its efforts to theorise humanity: the defining value of the non-human; and the significance of emotional capacity in identifying non-humanity. The play's emphasis on Caliban, however, also makes clear the importance of proximity: what makes Caliban an effective defining presence is precisely his 'not-quite'-ness. The play's inchoate 'human-animal amalgamation' helps to clarify the position of the other characters because he himself resists containment in a stable category.[39] Caliban seems to belong nowhere, and as a result he

---

[38] Ibid., p. 18.
[39] Raber, *Shakespeare and Posthumanist Theory*, p. 104.

Theorising Humanity Through Pity

is an unresolved presence that threatens to destabilise the positions of the more established human characters. However, what Caliban articulates is a very specific form of proximal humanity, located in a porous boundary between human and non-human. He is both closer and more unsettling, for example, than the largely overlooked and effectively partitioned animal life on the island, which he describes in his first encounter with Stephano and Trinculo:

> CALIBAN
> I prithee, let me bring thee where *crabs* grow,
> And I with my long nails will dig thee pignuts,
> Show thee a *jay*'s nest, and instruct thee how
> To snare the nimble *marmoset*. I'll bring thee
> To clust'ring *filberts*, and sometimes I'll get thee
> Young *scamels* from the rock. (2.2.164–169, my emphasis)

Prospero makes reference to additional animals in several of his exchanges with his servants. When threatening Caliban, Prospero promises that he will '[…] make thee roar, | That beasts shall tremble at thy din' (1.2.371–372); he reminds Ariel that when he released the spirit from his captivity under Sycorax, 'thy groan | Did make wolves howl and penetrate the breasts | Of ever-angry bears' (1.2.286–288). All of these examples suggest a vibrant and active animal community on the island – the crabs 'grow', the jays nest, the filberts 'cluster', and the wolves 'howl' – but this is a community that exists at a remove from the world of the play. When Prospero speaks of animals responding to Ariel's torment (or Caliban's promised torment), he does so in a way that reinforces distance: the noise of the torment, in both cases, is so loud that it reaches across physical distance as well as the distance between species. The 'ever-angry bear' will be emotionally penetrated; beasts shall tremble at Caliban's roar. The positioning of the island's animal life – clearly at a remove from the rest of the play – also importantly solidifies Caliban's in-between-ness, and confirms the role he plays in clarifying the other characters. Only Caliban frames the animal population as living productively and independently of the human storyline. As the native-guide figure, he is also the only character who speaks of closing the distance between human characters and the island's animal population. It is Caliban who can help facilitate access to these animals. Caliban's ability to recognise and narrate the agency of these island animals makes him the most sympathetically aligned to them, but his account also confirms their existence beyond the play's immediate scope. He stands somewhere between these animals and the island's humans. The contribution of the animals to the play's broader schedule of classification work, therefore, is

Pity and Identity in the Age of Shakespeare

only indirect: they confirm Caliban's own position, in a murky interstitial space between human and animal.

The relational value of Caliban's murky status is made explicit in his interactions with Trinculo and Stephano, where he is partially figured as the material of the island. In their first encounter Trinculo imagines Caliban as something he will use to define his own identity back at home:

TRINCULO
What have we here, a man or a fish? Dead or alive? A fish: he smells like a fish, a very ancient and fish-like smell, a kind of – not of the newest – poor-John. A strange fish! Were I in England now (as once I was) and had but this fish painted, not a holiday fool there but would give a piece of silver. *There would this monster make a man*; any strange beast there makes a man. (2.2.24–31, my emphasis)

As Trinculo describes it, Caliban's value is material: it is determined by his ambiguous status, his human-but-not-human presentation. Trinculo's meandering reflections on what 'makes a man' clarify the extent to which Caliban's own status shapes those near him. What Caliban *is* determines what Trinculo *will be* (in this case, a wealthier man). Stephano echoes this instinct as well, framing Caliban as the transferable material or goods that will be directed towards a privileged consumer audience: 'If I can recover him and keep him tame, and get to Naples with him', Stephano muses, 'he's a present for any emperor that ever trod on neat's leather' (2.2.64–69). Stephano imagines relocating Caliban to a place where privilege is marked by material (animal) commodity (neat's leather). Refigured as himself a kind of commodity, Caliban therefore becomes the means by which Stephano will access that privileged space and its society.

Throughout all these interactions, the principle and practice of compassion goes hand in hand with Caliban's definitional non-humanity. Although he is denied a stable sense of 'kind', he nevertheless acts as the barometer of each character's kind*ness* and social position. Stephano and Trinculo, who straightforwardly see Caliban as a 'fairground fantasy', and cultivate him as non-human commodity, ultimately finish the play at the bottom of the social hierarchy. Though Miranda and Prospero demonstrate varying degrees of compassion toward Caliban, they still end the play in a privileged position, top amongst the human characters. For Prospero and Miranda, Caliban offers the opportunity to perform compassion – and in so doing, they are able to consolidate a privileged social position. The unstable vision of humanity that Caliban represents, in these respects, reaches outward to shape those who encounter him, both in terms of wealth, status, and privilege, and in terms of emotional humanity. Caliban's utility as a categoriser of other characters is, moreover, specifically directed only at the human category: in spite of *The Tempest*'s variously populated island, the play only shows Caliban in dialogue with human characters.

These moments all testify to *The Tempest*'s interest what it means to be human, and to claim humanity. Here and elsewhere, the characters' own identities are shaped and clarified by their emotional reaction to other characters, characters who are either of the same kind, not of the same kind, or, in the case of Caliban, not obviously or firmly placed on a human/non-human spectrum. What is also clear is that this play sees a paradox in questions of what it means to be 'kind'. Kindness is at once the 'humane care' that Prospero mentions in 1.2, but it is equally being 'kindlier moved' with tender affection. This implies a reaching out; it imagines a compassionate connection between characters that is fundamentally social. At the same time, the kindness deployed here is also divisive, used to create boundaries and space between characters. With the line, 'shall not *myself* | one of their kind*'* (5.1.22–23, my emphasis), Prospero gestures towards his compassionate facilities as one equipped to 'relish all as sharply' (5.1.23). He uses this formulation to set himself apart from Ariel, both emotionally and physiologically: 'thou, *which art but air*' (5.1.21). Reaching out to another with compassion in this way becomes a marker of kind, but also a specific marker of *human*kind; it is an appropriate moment of posturing that separates Prospero from his island community and looks forward to his reintegration into more elite, homogenous Italian society whose promise looms in the background.

MIRANDA

While Ariel and Caliban are explicit in their proximal humanity, the more subtle not-quite-ness of Prospero's daughter makes obvious that what *The Tempest* seeks is a comprehensive exploration of the unsettling multivalency of the human category. Scholarship on *The Tempest* has tended to overlook Miranda in favour of Ariel and Caliban, who are typically seen as having the 'more vocal and dynamic roles'.[40] 'When she is mentioned at all', Jessica Slights observes, 'Miranda appears either as an archetype of pliant womanliness or as an allegorical, sentimentalized figure for the tender and fecund aspects of untamed nature'.[41] Miranda's particular brand of humanity – unformed, uncultured – is never questioned at the category

---

[40] Virginia Mason Vaughan and Alden T. Vaughan, 'Introduction', in William Shakespeare, *The Tempest*, ed. Virginia Mason Vaughan and Alden T. Vaughan (London: Thomas Nelson and Sons Ltd, 1999), pp. 1–138 (p. 27).

[41] Jessica Slights, 'Rape and the Romanticization of Shakespeare's Miranda', *Studies in English Literature, 1500–1900*, 41.2 (2001), 357–379 (p. 360).

Pity and Identity in the Age of Shakespeare

level but is rather confirmed, and in the most unequivocal terms by Ferdinand. It is another example of relational character construction, this time with Miranda's perfection and completeness coming at the cost of unseen women back in Italy. 'Full many a lady | I have eyed with best regard', Ferdinand reports, but

> never any
> With so full soul but some defect in her [...]
> But you, O you, |
> So perfect and so peerless, are created
> Of every creature's best. (3.1.39–48)

As a way of theorising humanity, the speech mobilises a familiar tension between fullness and defect, and it isolates Miranda in her excellence: she is both perfect *and* peerless. That excellence is an imagined composite, in which Miranda is the sum of parts borrowed from others, from 'every creature'. Though each represents a different end of the spectrum, in this composite-ness Miranda and Caliban occupy similar roles on the island. Each represents a kind of humanity that, because it exists beyond the confines of familiar social frameworks, prompts classification and description. These moments of definition make clear that describing humanity is a project that widely exploits non-human coordinates.

The juxtaposition of tenderness and unsocialised nature is a vital component of Miranda's role in *The Tempest*'s larger exploration of humanity. While Miranda models a specific vision of emotional subjectivity, her reception (both within the play and in criticism) confirms the connection between fellow-feeling and social vulnerability. Though 'perfect' and 'peerless', she is often discounted, especially by her father, as someone *not yet* fully formed, *not yet* fully socialised. 'Be collected; | No more amazement', Prospero advises as she reacts to the spectacle of the shipwreck: 'Tell your piteous heart | There's no harm done' (1.2.13–15). This rather unusual position, in which Miranda's demonstration of 'the very virtue of compassion' (1.2.27) is also evidence of her untrained humanity, sits at odds with Miranda's broader functional role in modelling subjectivity. As Melissa Sanchez points out, from the second scene of *The Tempest* 'we recognize that we have shared Miranda's perception of the storm and thus also occupy her role as spectator to be both manipulated and pleased'.[42] Her reaction to the shipwreck, Donald Wehrs argues, 'is akin to the socializing, civilizing feelings that humanist theatrical representation seeks to engender in audiences', and yet this moment is also the first that posits Miranda as an unpractised human,

---

[42] Melissa E. Sanchez, 'Seduction and Service in *The Tempest*', *Studies in Philology*, 105.1 (2008), 50–82 (p. 53).

Theorising Humanity Through Pity

still in need of her father's guidance.[43] In this sense, Miranda is both the compassionate ideal, and a cautionary tale that confirms that unchecked compassionate subjectivity might come at the cost of social power.

Miranda's connection to the audience is an affective one, and the reaction she narrates is emotional but also definitional. This mode of introducing Miranda both confirms her own emotional subjectivity and reflects it back to (and onto) the audience. It is an expression of individual character building, but equally another important mode of using emotion to theorise the human category. Miranda's first account of subjective experience – her first use of 'I' – is an expression of fellow-feeling: 'O, I have suffered | With those that I saw suffer' (1.2.5–6). This articulation of emotional receptiveness comes in a speech that also offers the play's first real consideration of kind-ness, and the limitations of category. As she comments on the 'Poor souls' (1.2.9), and her own feelings about what she has witnessed – 'O, the cry did knock | Against my very heart' (1.2.8–9) – she also reflects on her own limitation of response. 'Had I been any god of power', she notes

> [...] I would
> Have sunk the sea within the earth or ere
> It should the good ship so have swallowed and
> The fraughting souls within her. (1.2.10–13)

Her emotion confirms her category: in recognising her physical inability to follow her pity with effective response, she is also reminded of what she is not (in this case, a god with power to intervene).

Miranda is without question the most pitying character in the play, and if she has a guiding framework for the emotion, it seems to extend beyond considerations of kind. This perhaps is because she demonstrates only a limited understanding of species difference and hierarchy. Her removal from society and her isolated upbringing on the island lead to repeated classification failures, in which she seems unable to recognise those of her own kind. When she first sees Ferdinand she mislabels him, and looks to her father for guidance, asking 'What is't, a spirit?' (1.2.410). In so doing, she also invites the instruction and confirmation of kind that Prospero subsequently delivers. 'No, wench, it eats and sleeps and hath such senses | as we have' (1.2.413–414) he points out, all indications that 'thou mightst call him | A goodly person' (1.2.416–417). Though Prospero's own effort to capture Ferdinand's humanity is imprecise, it is Miranda who is frequently

---

[43] Donald R. Wehrs, 'Placing Human Constants within Literary History: Generic Revision and Affective Sociality in *The Winter's Tale* and *The Tempest*', *Poetics Today*, 32.3 (2011), 521–591, p. 547.

Pity and Identity in the Age of Shakespeare

reminded of her own lack of awareness in judging humanity, and subsequently dismissed. When she expresses her preference for Ferdinand, for example, her father answers:

PROSPERO
Hush.
Thou think'st there is no more such shapes as he,
Having seen but him and Caliban. Foolish wench,
To th' most of men, this is a Caliban,
And they to him are angels. (1.2.478–482)

By this account, judging humanity requires a broad exposure to the spectrum of humanness and multiple categories of kindness, to capture the available variety. Moreover, Prospero's framing of Caliban as a kind – 'this is *a* Caliban' – further demonstrates the myriad ways in which Caliban is used to determine the positions of the play's other characters.

If Ariel and Caliban each, in their own way, give shape to the fuzziness surrounding questions of kindness, then Miranda's compassionate activity pushes the play's philosophical enquiry still further. The staged action only shows Miranda expressing pity for characters who are indisputably human: her initial outlay of compassion at the sight of the shipwreck occurs without her knowing the identity of those on board, but these are later confirmed as human subjects. Ferdinand, a more intimate beneficiary of Miranda's compassion, has his category confirmed by her father. The only possible exception to this pattern of behaviour is, of course, Caliban, a moment of past compassion that is reported but not seen. This is also the only instance in which Miranda's pity – which remains unwieldy – explicitly puts her in danger. As she recounts her earlier relationship with Caliban:

MIRANDA
Abhorred slave,
Which any print of goodness wilt not take,
Being capable of all ill; *I pitied thee*,
Took pains to make thee speak, taught thee each hour
One thing or other. When thou didst not, savage
Know thine own meaning, but wouldst gabble like
A thing most brutish, I endowed thy purposes
With words that made them known. (1.2.352–358, my emphasis)[44]

---

[44] This speech has an uncharacteristically severe tone – an oddity that inspired many editions, starting with Dryden and Davenant's 1667 *Tempest* (published 1670) and continuing until the mid-twentieth century, to attribute this part of the dialogue to Prospero instead. The modern preference (which I observe here) follows the First

Theorising Humanity Through Pity

The passage reaffirms Miranda's broader capacity for pity: the emotion is cited here as a primary motivator in her early interactions with Caliban. It also suggests Miranda does not conceive of pity as an exchange occurring strictly between human beings. In the course of one speech she describes him both as 'savage' and 'a thing', each of which might imply a different category, and though we cannot guess with what language Miranda might have used to describe Caliban at the point in their relationship when she felt inclined to pity him, it is plain that he has never been immediately or obviously identifiable as human. Miranda's account of their early relationship, however, makes clear that in spite of this she saw no reason to withhold her pity. It is only after Caliban's attempted violation that Miranda seems to learn to conceive of him as a separate kind of creature: 'But thy vile race (Though thou didst learn) had that in't which good natures could not abide to be with' (1.2.359–360). By the time of the play's action Miranda believes that Caliban is fundamentally other in a way that renders him unfit for her society: this is a claim of categorical difference in kind, and one that contradicts Caliban's apparent belief that it is possible for them to have children.

Ultimately Miranda's habits of language suggest that she conceives of most (including herself) in strikingly general terms, avoiding even broad classifications like 'human', or 'animal' for the purposes of establishing difference. On one hand, this apparent reluctance to classify life on a hierarchical scale seems to produce a more expansive willingness to pity: one of the ways in which Miranda differs from *The Tempest*'s other human characters is that her pity is free-flowing and, in comparison, largely unfettered by a strict set of rules. As an emotional presence therefore, Miranda also highlights the restrictions that other characters place on their emotional outgoings. However, Miranda articulates mutable humanity in still another way, as her character cultivates a habit of naming and classifying that increases as she prepares to leave the island. At the play's conclusion, Miranda seems finally to gesture towards nuance of kindness when she is confronted with the full assembly of Italians:

MIRANDA
O wonder!
How many goodly *creatures* are there here!
How beauteous *mankind* is! O brave new world
That has such *people* in't. (5.1.182–185, my emphasis)

Folio in attributing the speech to Miranda. See: John Dryden, *The Tempest, or The Enchanted Island, A Comedy* (London: 1670), sig. C2ᵛ.

Pity and Identity in the Age of Shakespeare

As she moves through the description, she becomes more detailed: the generic 'creature' moves towards the implied civility of 'people'. It is another moment of classification that signals Miranda's imminent integration into Italian society: now effectively embedded into privileged human society, Miranda becomes more invested in the categorising process.

PROSPERO

Together Ariel, Caliban, and Miranda represent different iterations of the same triangulation between compassion, the borders of human identity, and the defining role of proximal humanity. Vitally, the definitional work these characters do is specifically directed – towards Prospero. Discounting the vibrant animal population that seems to exist beyond the reaches of the play, Ariel, Caliban, and Miranda represent the entirety of Prospero's de facto island kingdom. They are all used to facilitate his own social restoration, all directed towards Prospero's ultimate emergence as a specific *kind* of man: compassionate, merciful, benevolent, powerful. The relationship between Prospero and his island subjects makes clear the systems of social privilege and power underpinning these humanist explorations. As characters and ideals are absorbed into the project of clarifying the human category, however, both categories – human and non-human alike – become increasingly blurred, to the extent that the efforts ultimately unsettle rather than confirm the image of 'full' humanity. Prospero's great moment of posturing, following the fantastical pageantry of Ferdinand and Miranda's union in 4.1, offers a striking example. In a scene that explicitly stages the 'drolleries' that characterise life on the island, Prospero also offers the rather dreamy catalogue of the island's makeup:

> PROSPERO
> … Be cheerful, sir.
> Our revels now are ended. These our actors,
> As I foretold you, were all spirits and
> Are melted into air, into thin air;
> And – like the baseless fabric of this vision –
> The cloud-capped towers, the gorgeous palaces,
> The solemn temples, the great globe itself,
> Yea, all which it inherit, shall dissolve,
> And like this insubstantial pageant faded,
> Leave not a rack behind. We are such stuff
> As dreams are made on, and our little life
> Is rounded with a sleep. (4.1.147–158)

'We are such stuff,' he observes, 'As dreams are made on'. This comment on the 'stuff' of the play offers an insight into how most of the characters understand the island's material: utterly malleable, wholly invested in and shaped by the human characters. This is an account of Prospero's mastery – a signal that he has arranged and controls the pageantry – and yet he implicates himself in the midst of his posturing. When Prospero announces that '*we* are such stuff', he also blurs the line between the master and the materials that reaffirm his power, establishing a more intimate sense of community, and closer proximity via communal language.

Prospero's own move toward pity – if it does come – comes only at the end of the play, in the iconic moment of affiliation with Caliban. It is another moment that juxtaposes compassionate action with identity and category classification: 'this thing of darkness I | Acknowledge mine' (5.1.274–276, my emphasis). This has been read as a moment of compassion – however underwhelming – an extension and an expression of the 'tender affections' that Ariel has counselled. In one sense, the moment sees Prospero finally resist the instinct for retribution and instead shepherd the play towards its compassionate conclusion. At the same time, as Paul Brown points out, it is also a moment that 'powerfully designates the monster as [Prospero's] property, an object for his own utility, a darkness from which he may rescue self-knowledge'.[45] Prospero's acknowledgement of Caliban is a performance of the magician's new (or indeed, his old) identity as a social elite. Caliban's relationship to Prospero imitates the power dynamic between Stephano, Trinculo, and Alonso – as Prospero reminds Alonso that 'Two of these fellows you | Must acknowledge and own' (5.1.274–275) – and in this way Caliban becomes the material proof of Prospero's redeemed status. Moreover, if this acknowledgement means Caliban's fate is to return with Prospero to Italy, then it is actually Prospero who will realise Trinculo and Stephano's original vision of Caliban 'mak[ing] a man' back home.[46] The social/market value of these characters is assigned by those with a privileged humanity, and the capacity to perform these kinds of classification perpetuate that social privilege. By

---

[45]   Paul Brown, '"This thing of darkness I acknowledge mine": *The Tempest* and the Discourse of Colonialism', in Jonathan Dollimore and Alan Sinfield (eds.), *Political Shakespeare: Essays in Cultural Materialism* (Manchester: Manchester University Press, 1985), pp. 48–71, esp. p. 68.

[46]   Stephen Greenblatt has commented that 'Shakespeare leaves Caliban's fate naggingly unclear' (p. 570). Stephen J. Greenblatt, 'Learning to Curse: Aspects of Linguistic Colonialism in the 16th Century', in Fredi Chiapelli (ed.), *First Images of America: The Impact of the New World on the Old* (Berkeley, CA: University of California Press, 1970), pp. 561–580.

Pity and Identity in the Age of Shakespeare

this reading, Stephano, Trinculo, and Caliban make possible this moment, in which Prospero demonstrates – through compassionate posturing – that he and Alonso are the same *kind* of human.

Moments of posturing like these represent the bulk of Prospero's activity in the play. Though the story is his – a tale of a carefully executed revenge and redemption plan – the actual burden of labour falls to those who surround him and whom he controls: Ariel principally, in all displays of magic; Miranda and Caliban in a secondary sense. As one critic observes, *The Tempest* presents as one possibility that Prospero's authority 'derives not from magic power but from the civilized order which he stands atop'.[47] If Prospero is intended to model a superior form of humanity, then the play also makes clear that that superiority is unstable enough to require constant fortification. Prospero's position is constructed primarily in social terms, and consolidated in these moments of reflective theorising that seem always, only, to benefit and secure his position. As Stephen Orgel observes, Prospero's power 'is not inherited but self-created'.[48] *The Tempest*'s variously populated island, therefore, seems crafted to high-light a particular model of self-creation in which elite humanity must be defined against proximal otherness. Although the play does present and sustain a system of taxonomy, its interest is only in elevating and defining the privilege of a certain *kind* of humanity. When he gives up the magic that has supposedly defined his position on the island, Prospero admits:

> Now my charms are all o'erthrown,
> And what strength I have's mine own,
> Which is most faint. (Epi. 1–3)

These closing lines highlight the paradox of humanity as the play presents it. By his own account, Prospero is left only with the intrinsic power he possesses as a human; it is a declaration of the relative weakness of human-kind. But of course, at the same time – newly embedded in elite society after a masterful social manipulation – he has never been more powerful. Coming at the end of the play, Prospero's clearest moment of compassion signals the emotion as a tool for definition and self-definition: a mode of classifying the self through classifying others.

---

[47] David Adamson, 'Authority and Illusion: The Power of Prospero's Book', *Comitatus: A Journal of Medieval and Renaissance Studies*, 20.1 (1989), 9–19 (p. 10).

[48] Stephen Orgel, 'Prospero's Wife', *Representations*, 8 (1984), 1–13 (p. 8).

Theorising Humanity Through Pity

CONCLUSION: 'WHAT IS'T YOU LACK?'

While it would be easy to imagine this kind of compassionate theorising as a purely Shakespearean enterprise, a brief turn to Ben Jonson's *Bartholomew Fair* suggests a much broader application to this way of thinking. The ideological work of *The Tempest* manifests in Jonson's play: both test the boundaries of humanity, the definitional role of non-humans, and consider how principles of compassion both clarify and confuse definitions of kind. Jonson's reframing of these issues in *Bartholomew Fair* clarifies what is really at stake in *The Tempest*, and how socially exploitative these modes of posturing can be. Critics have tended to read very limited ideological sympathy between Shakespeare and Jonson as playwrights, but the reciprocity of these *particular* plays is also striking because Jonson took pains to distinguish *Bartholomew Fair* as an entirely different *kind* of play.

The 'most notorious passage' of *Bartholomew Fair*'s Induction reveals, for many, Jonson's distaste for Shakespeare's later work, and a particular objection to *The Tempest*:

> If there be never a servant-monster i'the Fair; who can help it? he says – nor a nest of antics? He is loath to make nature afraid in his plays, like those that beget *Tales, Tempests*, and such-like drolleries, to mix his head with other men's heels, let the concupiscence of jigs and dances, reign as strong as it will amongst you ...[49]

According to Jonson's definitive editors, this reference to the 'servant-monster' is 'a clear allusion to Caliban'; '*Tales* [and] *Tempests*,' they remark, 'can have only one meaning.'[50] The passage has also been recognised as an important (and intentional) moment of professional positioning, with varying understandings of Jonson's antagonism. As the author's mouthpiece, the scrivener has been described as 'tak[ing] up a carelessly superior tone' when referencing Shakespeare's work, while more recently, Simon Palfrey has argued that this part of *Bartholomew Fair*'s Induction

---

[49] Richard Dutton, *Ben Jonson: To the First Folio* (Cambridge: Cambridge University Press, 1983), p. 159. Ben Jonson, *Bartholomew Fair*, ed. by John Creaser, in *The Works of Ben Jonson*, vol. 4, ed. by David Bevington, Martin Butler, and Ian Donaldson (Cambridge: Cambridge University Press, 2012), pp. 253–428, Ind. 95–100. All other references to *Bartholomew Fair* are to this edition unless otherwise noted.

[50] C.H. Herford, Percy Simpson, and Evelyn Simpson (eds.), *Ben Jonson: Play and Masque Commentary*, vol. X (Oxford: Clarendon, 1950), pp. 175–176. This connection was so obvious to Herford and the Simpsons that they felt inclined towards more pointed comment: 'Yet [William] Gifford, and – what is very remarkable – so accurate a scholar as Alexander Dyce [editors of the 1816 and 1853 editions of *Bartholomew Fair*, respectively] closed their eyes to the allusion' (p. 176).

Pity and Identity in the Age of Shakespeare

advertises Jonson's commitment 'to a career as the corrective superego to the monstrous id-child, Shakespeare'.[51] The passage certainly takes aim at the theatrical culture in which Jonson found himself, and more broadly the Induction insists on classifying the play in terms of what it is *not*: Jonson's fair is not like the real fair, Jonson is not like other playwrights in terms of what he will tolerate from his audience. Nonetheless, the body of criticism surrounding *Bartholomew Fair*'s Induction suggests that of all the things the play self-consciously poses itself as 'un-like', it is particularly unlike *The Tempest*. With this act of distancing – or so many critics have it – Jonson also similarly positions himself as most particularly, most unlike, Shakespeare.[52]

The language of the Induction has significantly contributed to an overarching critical narrative in which Jonson and Shakespeare are positioned as irretrievably and fundamentally different playwrights. Within this framework, Jonson is seen as consciously cultivating the distance between them. The metaphor employed in his self-stated refusal 'to mix his head with other men's heels' typifies this twin pursuit of difference and distance, with Jonson's work representing not just a different part in the larger body of dramatic work, but also one that spatially is as far removed from the 'heels' as possible. And yet Jonson's use of compassion, to classify the characters of *Bartholomew Fair* and to arrange the social hierarchy of his play, suggests a closer proximity to the ideological work of *The Tempest*.[53] As Ian McAdam has pointed out, while 'Jonson partly parodies Shakespeare's "romantic" approach in *The Tempest* [...] thematically his own play develops, rather

---

[51] Richard Dutton, *Ben Jonson: Authority: Criticism* (Basingstoke: Macmillan, 1996), p. 161. Simon Palfrey, *Shakespeare's Possible Worlds* (Cambridge: Cambridge University Press, 2014), p. 53.

[52] David Bevington has written on Jonson's habit of 'using Shakespeare implicitly as his opposite example on a number of scores' (p. 3). David Bevington, 'Jonson and Shakespeare: A Spirited Friendship', *Ben Jonson Journal*, 23.1 (2016), 1–23. Kevin Pask speaks specifically of Caliban's 'unnaturalness' as 'the central example of Jonson's own distinction from William Shakespeare' (p. 739). Kevin Pask, 'Caliban's Masque', *English Literary History*, 70.3 (2003), 739–756.

[53] Criticism linking these plays together has tended to do so on generic rather than ideological grounds, emphasising the play as a satiric reworking of Shakespeare's romance form. See: Thomas Cartelli, who reads in Jonson 'an active preoccupation with the relatively recent romances and earlier comedies of his master and nemesis' (p. 152); Richard Dutton (1996), who argues that Jonson 'systematically parodies the romance conventions of lost-and-found, the vindication of innate nobility, and the wondrous working of divine providence' (pp. 148–149); and Kevin Pask, who calls *Bartholomew Fair* 'a reconstituted and thoroughly urban version of Shakespearean pastoral' (p. 749). Thomas Cartelli, '*Bartholomew Fair* as Urban Arcadia: Jonson responds to Shakespeare', *Renaissance Drama*, 14 (1983), 151–172.

Theorising Humanity Through Pity

than contradicts, themes inherent in Shakespeare'.[54] This sense of development particularly relates to these questions of what defines humankind: *Bartholomew Fair* is also a testament to Jonson's interest in the kinds of characters who inhabit *The Tempest*, their relation to one another, and how issues of kindness – both in terms of species classification and in terms of compassion – inform the emotional landscape of Shakespeare's play. This interest in classifications of kind extends well beyond Jonson's explicit engagement with Caliban in his Induction, though critical commentary that identifies *Bartholomew Fair* as a 'correction' of perceived faults in *The Tempest* has tended to figure this character as the locus of Jonson's issue.[55] Jonson's reduction of Caliban into Shakespeare's 'servant-monster' also serves as another type of shorthand, an early indication of the kinds of questions that Jonson will pick up in his own play: questions of what makes up 'human' identity, what role non-humans play in defining humanity, and how emotional capacities – compassion specifically – flow throughout and between questions of kind in both plays. Jonson indicates that the 'servant-monster' will make no appearance at his Fair, and this moment is one of many that has established Jonson and Shakespeare as 'mighty opposites'.[56] Nonetheless, *Bartholomew Fair* is more implicated than it admits.

Bartholomew Fair often (and pointedly) echoes *The Tempest*, repeatedly prompting recollection at the level of plot and language. Like Shakespeare, Jonson brings us to a place 'full of noise' (Ind. 62; see also *The Tempest* at 3.2.135). Like Shakespeare's Italians, the hapless Bartholomew Cokes finds himself trapped within an artificially controlled landscape. And of course, like *The Tempest*, in *Bartholomew Fair* the brokering of marriage plays a central role. Like Prospero, Justice Overdo expects to further his own position by marrying off his young ward. These similarities are easy to overlook

---

[54] Ian McAdam, 'The Puritan Dialectic of Law and Grace in *Bartholomew Fair*', *Studies in English Literature 1500–1900*, 46.2 (2006), 415–433, esp. p. 426.

[55] The critical emphasis on Caliban stems from Jonson's comment in the Induction, but also occasionally includes the character Mooncalf, whose name recalls Stephano's classification of Caliban at 2.2.106. Jonson and Shakespeare, however, seem to be working to different definitions. For Shakespeare, a 'mooncalf' is 'A deformed animal; a monster' (*OED*, 'mooncalf, n.', definition 3), but Jonson's usage veers back to the human: his Mooncalf is 'A born fool; a congenital idiot; a simpleton' (definition 2c). Jonson's imagined distinction between mooncalves and monsters is made explicit in Jonson's later masque, *Newes from New World Discovered in the Moon*, when one character asks 'Moone-Calves! what Monster is that?' and is quickly corrected by another: 'Monster? *None at all*; a very familiar thing, like our foole here on earth' (sig. G2ʳ, my emphasis). Ben Jonson, *The Works of Benjamin Jonson* (London: 1641).

[56] Cartelli, p. 151.

Pity and Identity in the Age of Shakespeare

because Jonson's play – a satirical, openly cynical city comedy – feels and looks so different to Shakespeare's island romance. Nonetheless, the connection between these works is made clearer by what Jonson's play admits that it lacks: Caliban. Here again is an example of using *lack* to define, of using a character's unstable or proximal humanity to give something else a more definitive shape. In spite of Caliban's famous indeterminacy, Jonson's description of him in *Bartholomew Fair* is strikingly precise: he assigns one concrete identity, the servant-monster, and moves on, apparently without giving the matter another thought. Jonson is, moreover, true to his word: there is no servant-monster in *Bartholomew Fair*. By identifying Caliban as the 'servant-monster' Jonson, like so many of *The Tempest's* characters, passes judgment on what Caliban is. At the same time, in raising the spectre of Caliban, Jonson participates in another tradition – both within *The Tempest* and in its long history of reception – of directing an evaluative gaze at Shakespeare's character, and using him for categorisation and classification. This moment, which mirrors similar evaluative moments in *The Tempest*, signals Jonson's engagement with the issues surrounding indeterminant humanity.

Because it is so clearly signalled, the absence of Caliban's 'not-quite'-ness in *Bartholomew Fair* importantly emphasises the difficulty of defining humanity without a proximal, non-human other. Without the clarifying comparative presence of non-human others, it is difficult to see the play's human characters as belonging to a distinct and separate category at all. The vast majority of Jonson's characters are, after all, described not in human but in animal terms: they are named as animals, marked by animal traits, and surrounded by animated objects. As Neil Rhodes has noted, for example, a character like Ursula is 'inseparable from the pigs which are her trade'; she is the 'pig-woman' (2.2.59), the 'walking Sow of tallow' (2.5.59), and of course also the 'she-bear' (2.3.1).[57] Mooncalf is marked by his 'grasshopper's thighs' (2.2.56); Wasp is, like his name, a 'pretty insect!' (1.4.34); the singer Nightingale uses his 'hawk's eye' (2.4.37) and his 'beak' (2.4.39) to help Edgeworth, the cutpurse, identify victims; and Littlewit calls himself 'a silkworm' (1.1.2). Quarlous casts Winwife as the stag when he asks 'Oh, sir, ha' you ta'en soil here? (1.3.1), and later imagines a time when Winwife might 'walk as if thou had'st borrow'd legs of a spinner and voice of a cricket' (1.2.64). The hapless Bartholomew Cokes is labelled 'one that were made to catch flies, with his Sir Cranion [crane-fly] legs' (1.5.80); Ursula assures Knockem that he 'shall not fright me with [his] lion-chap, sir, nor [his] tusks' (2.3.37–38). Busy describes the delights of the fair as 'hooks, and baits, very baits' designed to catch its visitors 'by the gills' (3.2.34–36); Winwife describes Busy guiding his party

[57] Neil Rhodes, *Elizabethan Grotesque* (London: Routledge and Kegan Paul, 1980), p. 146.

Theorising Humanity Through Pity

through the fair as 'driving 'em to the pens' (3.2.43). This overwhelming reliance on animal language initially presents as a stock method of de-humanising the characters – framing them as animals in order to signal mutual rapacity, and thereby removing entirely the notion of *humanitas* from the fair. There is however more to see here, precisely because there are virtually no living animals in the play, either in terms of presence or reference. Jonson offers approximations of animals – the human characters he describes in animal terms, the animal products that define the identities of those human characters (as in the case of Ursula's pigs), and other material goods fashioned after animals (such as Leatherhead's hobbyhorses) – but the actual animal population is negligible. The 'animal' in *Bartholomew Fair* therefore becomes just the 'stuff' – the language, the meat, the commodities – that creates the characters; it becomes another expression of the defining role of the non-human other. In this Jonson introduces his own version of the slippage between human and non-human categories, intensifying the point that Shakespeare makes in *The Tempest*, that everything is absorbed into the project of defining humanity.

Within this landscape Jonson places only one substantive reference to compassion and its defining capacity, applied to the Prospero-like Justice Overdo.[58] Overdo shares Prospero's link to 'charm' language: Leatherhead notably comments to Joan that Overdo 'is the man must charm you' (2.2.22–23). Like Prospero, Overdo spends the bulk of the play at a remove from the society into which he will later reappear (as he imagines, in a newly acquired position of authority). After overhearing Bristle and Haggis describe him as 'a severe justicer' (4.1.58) with a reputation for being 'angry, be it right or wrong' (4.1.65), Overdo makes a calculated commitment to be more compassionate. 'I will be more tender hereafter' he vows, reflecting that 'I see compassion may become a justice, though it be a weakness, I confess; and nearer a vice than a virtue' (4.1.67–68). This resolution is also prompted by Bristle's account of Trouble-All's madness, a condition Bristle attributes to Overdo's earlier ill treatment. 'If this be true', Overdo comments, 'this is *my* greatest disaster!' (4.1.63–64, my emphasis). Overdo's comment figures the self as constructed in social terms, particularly the kind of public selfhood that Overdo imagines for himself. It is within this model of social subjectivity that Overdo frames his sense of emotional obligation: 'How am I bound to satisfie this poore man, that is, of so good

---

[58] Margaret Tudeau-Clayton notes that through Overdo, Jonson 'engages critically with Shakespeare's figure of the learned (over)seer, Prospero' (p. 178). Margaret Tudeau-Clayton, '"I do not know my selfe": The Topography and Politics of Self-Knowledge in Ben Jonson's *Bartholomew Fair*', in Margaret Tudeau-Clayton and Philippa Berry (eds.), *Textures of Renaissance Knowledge* (Manchester: Manchester University Press, 2003), pp. 177–198.

Pity and Identity in the Age of Shakespeare

a nature to me, out of his wits' (4.1.64–65). Overdo's subsequent commitment to pity is apparent in the vow to 'be more tender', but this resolution is importantly tied to his own desire for self-fashioning, and his feeling that he is a different kind of person (and in fact, a better kind) than those who populate the fair. This re-working of Prospero's own move towards compassion is striking, down to the re-deployment of Ariel's key word, 'tender' and the use of the future tense. Like Prospero, Overdo *will* be more tender, though what *Bartholomew Fair* actually stages is his misguided attempts to show compassion to the pickpocket Edgeworth, and the mad Trouble-All. This moment of self-reflection references the compassion's capacity for self-fashioning: 'I see compassion may *become* a justice', he notes: it is expected, attractive, a commodity. But the word also implies a more active moment of self-creation: to become. Compassion is, in short, a necessity for the kind of man Overdo aspires to be. As in *The Tempest*, here is a way to 'make' a certain type of man. Here again, the question of kindness corresponds to questions of *kind*, specifically the kind of position Overdo wants to hold in the world of the play. Through Overdo, Jonson casts compassion explicitly as a social performance, a mode of self-creation that – if executed properly – serves the compassionate performer first, and their target perhaps not at all. In this case, however, Overdo's attempts at compassion are also effectively his un-doing: these fairly empty gestures are what lead to his sustained humiliation in the fair, where he is repeatedly beaten and eventually put into the stocks. His attempt to model compassion to Trouble-All by giving him – but really, giving the disguised Quarlous – his warrant eventually costs Overdo his wardship of Grace, or, part of 'the stuff' that he has used to define his position in the play.

The conclusion of the play stresses that Overdo's mismanagement of his own emotional self-fashioning has had concrete social costs. As Quarlous outlines it:

> Sir [...] I'le helpe you: harke you Sir, i' your eare, your *Innocent young man*, you have tane such care of, all this day, is a *Cutpurse*; that hath got all your brother *Cokes* his things, and help'd you to your beating, and the stocks; if you have a minde to hang him now, and shew him your *Magistrates* wit, you may: but I should think it were better, recovering the goods, and to save your estimation in him.[59] I thank you, S^r. for the gift of your *Ward*, M^{rs}. *Grace*: look you, here is your hand & seale, by the way. (5.6.73–83)

[59] The Oxford Edition alters this line slightly: 'but I should think it were better, recovering the goods, and to save your estimation in *pardoning* him'; this only supports the notion of Overdo as a reworked Prospero, given that the latter's pardoning of Caliban is a significant moment in that play's conclusion. See Ben Jonson, *Bartholomew Fair*, in *The Alchemist and Other Plays*, ed. by Gordon Campbell (Oxford: Oxford University Press, 1995), V.vi.78.

Theorising Humanity Through Pity

This has all been made possible by Overdo's overzealous use of pity as a mode of social posturing. This moment – the final assembly of characters, the resolution of the action – should be a moment of triumph for Overdo: it is one he has imagined, the obvious moment to re-establish his authority, and to reveal his control over this community. Of course this is impossible, in part because he so consistently misreads his social context: the final moments only confirm the extent to which he lacks authority, his failure to manipulate the social hierarchy in his own favour. Instead it is Quarlous who ultimately defines Overdo and pushes the play to its conclusion: 'remember you are but Adam, flesh and blood! You have your frailty; forget your other name of Overdo, and invite us all supper' (5.6.104–106). In the end, Overdo is unable to establish himself as a different, superior kind of human, unable to effectively harness pity as a tool to perform these feats of distinction. Prospero recognises his own frailty and its fundamental vulnerability: by manipulating the emotional landscape of his own play, he ends in a privileged position, in which he metes out pity along carefully measured considerations of kind. Overdo's mismanagement of his play's emotional landscape, by contrast, makes him the fool of *Bartholomew Fair*. The supposedly 'wise Justice of Peace' that Jonson promises in the Induction, ultimately becomes the fairground attraction, an exploited source of public entertainment.

* * *

If Prospero's self-defining 'we are such stuff' speech in 4.1 gazes upwards towards 'cloud-capped towers', then Jonson's hobby-horse seller Leatherhead brings the vision back down to earth, making it clear that for Jonson, the 'stuff' that defines humankind is neither lofty nor harmless. Leatherhead's discussion with Trash mobilises this same question, 'what stuff [things] are made on', but situates itself in the material reality of the Fair, which is anything but dream-like:

LEATHERHEAD
The Fair's pest'lence dead, methinks; people come not abroad to day, whatever the matter is. Do you hear, Sister Trash, Lady o' the basket? Sit farther with your gingerbread-progeny there, and hinder not the prospect of my shop, or I'll ha' it proclaimed i'the Fair *what stuff they are made on.*

TRASH
Why, *what stuff are they made on,* Brother Leatherhead? Nothing but what's wholesome, I assure you.

> LEATHERHEAD
> Yes, stale bread, rotten eggs, musty ginger, and dead honey, you know.[60]

Leatherhead's account of Trash's gingerbread casts a knowing eye on what's behind the spectacle of her seemingly appealing wares: 'stale bread, rotten eggs, musty ginger, and dead honey'. The description of the gingerbread as her 'progeny' also makes clear the intimate connection between Trash and her wares: she is of the same 'stuff', and defined by it. Moreover, that stuff is lacking something – goodness, in this case, though Trash assures us it is '*whole*some'. Like *The Tempest*, *Bartholomew Fair* shares an interest in the 'stuff' that defines us, and Jonson emphasises that humanity is defined as much by what 'stuff' is lacking. The possible lack of compassion threatens Prospero's humanity, and Jonson's Leatherhead carries this threat of 'lack' into his repeated call in the fair: 'What do you lack, gentlemen, what is't you lack? A fine horse? A lion? A bull? A bear? A dog or a cat? An excellent fine Barthol'mew-bird? Or an instrument? What is't you lack?' (2.5.3–5). The stuff he proposes imagines a broad spectrum of non-humanity, ranging from the 'animal', to the animal/human whores of the fair, to the purely material instrument. For Jonson, as for Shakespeare, this is all the 'stuff' of self-fashioning. It is a vision of humankind defined by the non-human material surrounding it, by the opportunity that 'lack' represents: to define, to distinguish, to elevate – and in so doing, to subjugate.

---

[60] 2.2.1–8, my emphasis. Surprisingly, I have found no edition of *Bartholomew Fair* that makes note of Jonson's clear borrowing of Prospero's phrase here.

CONCLUSION

> War is waged over the matter of pity. This war probably has no age but, and here is my hypothesis, it is passing through a critical phase. We are passing through that phase and it passes through us.[1]

When Derrida references a war over pity in 'The Animal That Therefore I Am', he is partly recognising emotional obligation as a contentious concept, a malleable thing that changes according to the very many follow-up questions that might arise: in what context, for whom, how much, at what cost? For Derrida these considerations are foundational to his larger questions surrounding the ontology of nonhuman animals. The conflict over these issues, he notes, is as much determined by one's understanding of pity's reach as it is about 'the unequal forces' (human and non-human) locked in 'an unequal struggle'.[2] The battle lines are therefore drawn 'between those who violate not only animal life but *even and also this sentiment of compassion* and, on the other hand, those who appeal to an irrefutable testimony to this pity'.[3] This moment acknowledges that injustice might be produced as a result of an emotional misfiring, but it also more importantly frames emotion as a concept that *itself* might be violated. To accept the history of violence against pity is also to extend the reach of what happens *in the name of* pity, what happens when pity is wilfully rejected: these are moments that reach beyond the immediate to have a broader conceptual resonance. What is also striking to me about Derrida's comments is that they imagine a much larger historical arc to this particular conflict over a specific emotion. This war over pity, he observes, 'probably has no age', perhaps has no clear start or finish, and yet still might have moments of crystallisation, eras of particular impact or clarity. These are defining moments not just in the history of pity but also in the history of subjectivity: 'we are passing through that phase', he suggests, before adding that 'it passes through us'.

---

[1] Jacques Derrida and David Wills, 'The Animal That Therefore I Am (More to Follow)', *Critical Inquiry*, 28.2 (2002), 369–418 (p. 397).

[2] Ibid., p. 397.

[3] Ibid., p. 397.

Pity and Identity in the Age of Shakespeare

Derrida's insistence on his own moment as 'a critical phase' of the war over pity should remind us that many other eras have made the same claim, and many others have interpreted their own anxieties about pity as being of peculiar significance in the broader history of that emotion. Throughout this book I have pointed to early modern England as itself one such moment in the histories both of pity and of subjectivity. At the same time, it is worth remembering that Nietzsche uses the Renaissance as a counterpoint in his attack on the pitying tendencies, the 'sensitive humanity' of his own period:

> We modern men, very vulnerable, very sensitive, giving and taking hundreds of things into consideration, we actually imagine that the sensitive humanity we represent, the achieved unanimity in caring, in helpfulness, in mutual trust, is a sign of positive progress that puts us far ahead of men of the Renaissance. But this is what every age thinks, what it has to think. What is certain is that we cannot place ourselves in Renaissance conditions, not even in our imaginations: our nerves could not stand that reality.[4]

Pity is central to Nietzsche's thesis of acquired weakness and vulnerability, an instinct that 'makes suffering into something infectious' by 'preserv[ing] things that are ripe for decline' and 'keeping alive an abundance of failures of every type.'[5] Nietzsche's is a vision of corrosive compassion, a dark threat delivered under the apparently innocent pose of tender mutuality. Noting that 'Strong ages, noble cultures see pity, "neighbour love", and the lack of self and self-feeling as something contemptible', he identifies the Renaissance as 'the last *great* age.'[6] In this Nietzsche echoes his good friend Jacob Burckhardt by returning to a notion of Renaissance subjectivity that is both stable and insular. Where Burckhardt uses the Renaissance to define what came before, positioning it as a clear development from medieval communal subjectivity, Nietzsche points to the period as a high-water mark, an earlier standard that emphasises the slippage that follows. Both men look to this period as a defining era; both invoke the history of emotions to frame their evolutions of subjectivity.

Nietzsche's vision of Renaissance man is one of strength and emotional resilience, but this model of subjectivity is also characterised by a certain freedom that comes from denying pity as valuable or desirable. The work of

---

[4]   Friedrich Nietzsche, *Twilight of the Idols*, in *The Anti-Christ, Ecco Homo, Twilight of the Idols, and Other Writings*, ed. by Aaron Ridley and Judith Norman, trans. Judith Norman (Cambridge: Cambridge University Press, 2005), pp. 153–230 (p. 211), my emphasis. For Burckhardt, see: *The Civilization of the Renaissance in Italy*, trans. S.G.C. Middlemore (London: Penguin, 1990).

[5]   Nietzsche, *The Anti-Christ*, pp. 1–68 (p. 6).

[6]   Nietzsche, *Twilight*, p. 212, emphasis in original.

Conclusion

this book has been to dismantle this foundational premise, and instead to trace a model of early modern subjectivity that is, at its very core, emotionally encumbered. It is here, I suggest, that the value of imaginative material asserts itself, most particularly in the dramatic work of Shakespeare and his contemporaries. Here we see the full range of expression needed to understand the complex intersections of individual subjectivity, social selfhood, the weight of emotional vulnerability and obligation, and the perceived threat of emotional outliers. This material makes clear the social importance of pity, its centrality: this is an emotion that appears over and over, and in many different community settings. Even when pity fails to materialise, its absence is heavily discussed. The overwhelming emphasis on pity that I have traced in the period's drama registers the intense and intimate perceived vulnerability of individual selfhood. It documents an instinct to turn to this very social emotion as a means of organising and assuaging that vulnerability. And still, this material pushes at the weakness of pity as an organising principle, showing the very many ways that pity can falter. Close attention to pity also makes clear the interdependence of the histories of emotion and subjectivity: here is a constant reminder of our emotional interconnectedness and interdependence, a call to remember that we are always emotionally and socially exposed.

If the intimate relationship between pity and identity feels historically distant, I suggest the following sentence can help us understand why: *I pity you*. It is a sentence that neatly demonstrates Karen Gerdes's observation that 'the conventional understanding of "pity" has drifted far from its original meaning' of shared tenderness, of the goodness and kindness embedded in its Latin root *pietas*.[7] The mental image likely prompted by those words is a charged scene, with an emotional register wholly different to the early modern interactions I have traced in this book. We might even picture the words being thrown at someone, a form of weaponised language. It is a way of establishing distance. Although the word pity, psychologist Jesse Geller notes, 'is still very much a part of our living language', its register has changed entirely, moving away from 'original positive meanings' to become something almost 'misanthropic'.[8] Linguistic convention is at least partially to blame for this: it is simply no longer fashionable to use the word 'pity' when we mean something like 'compassion', 'sympathy', or 'fellow-feeling'. The term is no longer used, I would argue, precisely because we

---

[7]   Karen E. Gerdes, 'Empathy, Sympathy, and Pity: 21st-Century Definitions and Implications for Practice and Research', *Journal of Social Service Research*, 37.3, 230–241 (p. 232).

[8]   Jesse D. Geller, 'Pity, Suffering, and Psychotherapy', *American Journal of Psychotherapy*, 60.2 (2006), 187–205 (pp. 190–191).

Pity and Identity in the Age of Shakespeare

have developed this notion that pity is a negative emotion, something from which we should naturally attempt to gain distance. It is not obvious how we may have progressed from one point to another, but there are, I think, some important observations to make about what has changed in our understanding of what is 'bad' about pity. As I argue throughout this book, early modern worries about pity for the most part emphasise problems of vulnerability and individual compromise. Pity is worrying because it produces emotional vulnerability in the person who *offers* it: they are weakened by what they encounter, susceptible to and overrun by the suffering of others. They are also, potentially, in danger of being manipulated. In the modern interpretation however, pity has become the problem of the *recipient*. We do not want pity now, because it indicates that someone else has identified something objectionable in us – something unsavoury, something requiring distance. There is no connection imagined in this kind of exchange. In fact, it produces a clean break between two separate entities: the pitied, now isolated in his own objectionability, and the pitier, who uses pity specifically to sever ties. These two models of exchange look very different, and in fact, they are polar opposites: one is entirely about connection, the other about separation. If the modern interpretation has, in fact, lost this sense of forming connection, it is easy to see how the emotion lost its appeal.

I began this book with Robert Aylett's description of Man as 'the weakest creature God hath made', a figure reliant, both for defence and distinction, on the 'loving kind and tender heart from whence | Flow Pitie, Mercy, Love, Benignity'.[9] Aylett's is a description of compassionate subjectivity that recognises pity as something fundamental, but also places pity firmly within a framework of personal vulnerability. In this framework, pity is something that defines, something that soothes, a positive formulation of humankind's goodness. At the same time, it is intimately and unavoidably connected to the very many threats to which an individual subject might be exposed, an instinct made necessary by the human condition. Aylett's vision – and it is a vision confirmed by the rest of the material in this book – imagines a tight relationship between compassionate feeling and anxiety. The idea of pity soothes, but its obvious unreliability introduces a worrying precarity. Relying on principles of universal pity to organise social interaction itself requires a kind of community vulnerability – in which everyone is vulnerable to the outliers, the compassionate failings and misfirings of individual agents. For all that this book traces the early modern obsession with (and anxiety about) pity, it is also clear that, for all its complications, principles of pity did facilitate forms of relation, and helped the early moderns define

---

[9]   Robert Aylett, *Peace with her foure garders* (London: 1622), sig. C6ʳ.

Conclusion

themselves in important and positive ways. These pages present early modern English pity as a prominent source of struggle, doubt, and vulnerability, *but also* something that prompted mutual connection and shared community. There is something vital and constructive in this type of fellow-feeling, in spite of it seeming, again and again, so fundamentally problematic and messy. Nietzsche was correct in identifying the Renaissance as an important period in the history of pity, but for a different reason: people in this era were acutely aware of the challenges posed by pity, even as they continued to conceive of the emotion as a vital element of their identities. So how, then, can this view of early modern England inform our broader understanding of pity's history? As David Konstan notes in his own study of Classical pity, 'the idea and expression of pity changed in accord with broad historical and intellectual movements, in the course of which one or another aspect of pity came to the fore while others receded into the background, where they were not extinguished but remained latent'.[10] To consider the shifting place of pity over time is to consider that we may have lost the sense of just how central emotional vulnerability is to human experience. It is also a stark reminder of how exposure to the feeling or experience of others can work both to construct and erode a discrete sense of self. Perhaps we have allowed this aspect of pity to recede from the collective consciousness. If so, it is my hope that the emotional landscapes traced here will facilitate a rediscovery of some of pity's more positive and productive elements. Perhaps pity is never quite enough, never quite secure, but in another sense is it all we have: something that captures the inherent messiness of social subjectivity, defining us through a shared sense of individual shortcomings and common vulnerability.

[10] David Konstan, *Pity Transformed* (London: Bloomsbury, 2001), p. 126.

BIBLIOGRAPHY

PRIMARY

Apuleius, *The. xi. bookes of the Golden asse [...]* trans. William Adlington (London: 1566)

Aristotle, *De Anima*, in Richard McKeon (ed.), *The Basic Works of Aristotle* (New York, NY: Random House, 1941), 535–603

Aristotle, *A briefe of the art of rhetorique*, unnamed translator (London: 1637)

—— *Poetics*, trans. D.W. Lucas (Oxford: Clarendon Press, 1968)

Augustine, *Of the Citie of God* (London: 1610)

Aylett, Robert, *Peace with her foure garders* (London: 1622)

Barlow, William, *A proper dyaloge, betwene a gentillman and a husbandman[n] eche complaynynge to other their miserable calamite, through the ambicion of the clergye. An A.B.C. to the spiritualte* (Antwerp: 1530)

Barnes, Barnabe, *Parthenophil and Parthenophe, Sonnettes, Madrigals, Elegies and Odes* (London: 1593)

Berger, Thomas Leland (ed.), *A Critical Old-Spelling Edition of Thomas Dekker's 'Blurt, Master Constable'* (1602), (Salzburg: University of Salzburg Press, 1979)

Blake, William, 'The Human Abstract', in *The Complete Poetry and Prose of William Blake*, ed. by David V. Erdman (Berkeley, CA: University of California Press, 1982)

Blurt Master-Constable (London: 1602)

Bullokar, John, *An Englis[h] Expositor[;]teaching the in[ter]pretation of the harde[st] words [used] in our language* (London: 1621)

Brooke, Humphrey, *Ugieine or A conservatory of health* (London: 1650)

Campion, Thomas, *Observations in the Art of English Poesie* (London: 1602)

Chamberlain, John, *Letters of John Chamberlain*, ed. by Norman Egbert McClure, vol. I (Philadelphia, PA: The American Philosophical Society, 1939)

Chapman, George, *May-day* (London: 1611)

Chaucer, Geoffrey, *The Legend of Good Women*, ed. by the Rev. Walter W. Skeat (Oxford: Clarendon Press, 1889)

Cicero, Marcus Tullius, *Thre bokes of duties*, trans. Nicholas Grimald (London: 1556)

Daniel, Samuel, *Delia*, in Gordon Braden (ed.), *Sixteenth-Century Poetry* (Oxford: Blackwell Publishing, 2005)

Day, John, 'The P[rinter]. To the Reader', in Thomas Norton, *The Tragidie of Ferrex and Porrex* (London: 1570)

Descartes, René, *Discourse on Method* and *The Meditations*, trans. F.E. Sutcliffe (London: Penguin, 1968)

Bibliography

Dryden, John, *The Tempest, or The Enchanted Island, A Comedy* (London: 1670)

Dupleix, Scipion, *The resolver; or Curiosities of nature* (London: 1635)

Everyman, from *Everyman and Mankind,* ed. by Douglas Bruster and Eric Rasmussen. (London: Arden Shakespeare, 2009)

The Fayre Mayde of the Exchange (London: 1607)

—— *The Fair Maid of the Exchange,* ed. by Genevieve Love, in Jeremy Lopez (ed.), *The Routledge Anthology of Early Modern Drama* (London: Routledge, 2020), pp. 816–831

Fish, Simon, *A supplicaycon of beggers* (London: 1529)

Frith, John, *A disputacio[n] of purgatorye* (Antwerp: 1531)

Golding, William, *The xv bookes of P. Ovidius Naso, entytuled Metamorphosis* (London: 1567)

Gower, John, *Confessio Amantis,* ed. by Russell A. Peck, trans. Andrew Galloway (Kalamazoo, MI: Consortium for the Teaching of the Middle Ages, 2006–)

Heywood, Thomas, *The Rape of Lucrece* (London: 1608)

Hobbes, Thomas, *The Art of Rhetoric, with A Discourse of the Laws of England* (London: 1681)

Hyckescorner (London: 1515)

—— *Hickscorner,* in Ian Lancashire (ed.), *Two Tudor Interludes* (Manchester: Manchester University Press, 1980), pp. 153–238

Jonson, Ben, *Bartholomew Fair,* in *The Alchemist and Other Plays,* ed. by Gordon Campbell (Oxford: Oxford University Press, 1995)

—— *Bartholomew Fair,* ed. by John Creaser, in *The Works of Ben Jonson,* vol. 4, ed. by David Bevington, Martin Butler, and Ian Donaldson (Cambridge: Cambridge University Press, 2012), pp. 253–428

—— *The Works of Benjamin Jonson* (London: 1641)

Kyd, Thomas, *The Spanish Tragedy,* ed. by Clara Calvo and Jesús Tronch (London: Bloomsbury Publishing, 2013)

Latimer, Hugh, *Fruitfull sermons* (London: 1562)

—— *A notable sermo[n] of ye reverende father Maister Hughe Latemer which he preached in ye Shrouds at paules church in Londo[n], on the xviii. daye of January. 1548.* (London: 1548)

Lipsius, Justus, *Two Bookes of Constancie* (London: 1595)

Livy, *The Romane Historie,* trans. Philemon Holland (London: 1600)

—— *Livy,* vol. I, trans. B.O. Foster (London: William Heinemann, 1919)

Lodge, Thomas, *Phillis* (London: 1593)

Lowe, Peter, *The whole course of chirurgerie* (London: 1597)

Lydgate, John, *Fall of Princes,* ed. by Henry Bergen, vol. 1 (London: Published for the Early English Text Society by Oxford University Press, 1924)

Lyly, John, *Euphues and his England* (London: 1580)

Lyndwood, William, *Provinciale seu constitutiones Angliae* (Oxford: 1679, repr. Farnborough: 1968)

'The maner of the world now a dayes', Huntington Library Britwell HEH 18348, EBBA 32588. Accessed 30 April 2020, <http://ebba.english.ucsb.edu/ballad/32588/xml>

Marston, John, *The Malcontent* (London: 1611)

Mathews, Richard, *The Unlearned Alchymist* (London: 1660)

Bibliography

Middleton, Thomas, *The Ghost of Lucrece* (London: 1600)

Montaigne, Michel de, *Essayes*, trans. John Florio (London: 1613)

Nashe, Thomas, *Christs Teares over Jerusalem* (London: 1613)

—— *Have With You to Saffron-Walden*, in Ronald McKerrow (ed.), *The Works of Thomas Nashe*, rev. F.P. Wilson, vol. 3 (Oxford: Basil Blackwell, 1958)

Nietzsche, Friedrich, *The Anti-Christ, Ecco Homo, Twilight of the Idols, and Other Writings*, ed. by Aaron Ridley and Judith Norman, trans. Judith Norman (Cambridge: Cambridge University Press, 2005)

—— *Daybreak*, in *The Nietzsche Reader*, ed. by Keith Ansell Pearson and Duncan Large (Oxford: Blackwell Publishing, 2006)

Ovid, *Fasti*, trans. Sir James George Frazer (London: William Heinemann Ltd, 1931)

—— *Ovid's Festivalls, or Romane Calendar*, trans. John Gower (Cambridge: 1640)

—— *Metamorphoses*, trans. Frank Justus Miller (London: William Heinemann, 1977)

Painter, William, *The Palace of Pleasure*, vol. 2 (London: 1566)

Petrarca, Francesco, *Canzoniere*, ed. by Gianfranco Contini (Turin: G. Einaudi, 1992)

Pliny, *The History of the World*, trans. Philemon Holland (London: 1634)

Puttenham, George, *The Arte of English Poesie* (London: 1589)

Quintilian, *The Declamations of Quintilian*, trans. John Warr (London: 1686)

Rousseau, Jean-Jacques, *Emile* (Middlesex: Echo Library, 2007)

Rowley, William and Thomas Heywood, *The Thracian Wonder*, ed. by Michael Nolan (Salzburg: University of Salzburg, 1997)

Schopenhauer, Arthur, *On the Basis of Morality*, trans. E.F.J. Payne (Providence, RI: Berghahn Books, 1995)

Seneca, Lucius Annaeus, *Seneca's Morals*, trans. by Sir Roger L'Estrange (Philadelphia, PA: Gregg and Elliot, 1834)

Shakespeare, William, *The Arden Complete Works of William Shakespeare*, ed. by Richard Proudfoot, Ann Thompson, and David Scott Kastan (Walton-on-Thames: Thomas Nelson and Sons Ltd., 1998)

—— *As You Like It*, ed. by Juliet Dusinberre (London: Arden Shakespeare, 2006)

—— *King Henry VI pt. 3*, ed. by John D. Cox and Eric Rasmussen (London: Arden Shakespeare, 2001)

—— *King Lear*, ed. by R.A. Foakes (London: Arden Shakespeare, 1997)

—— *The Merchant of Venice*, ed. by John Drakakis (London: Bloomsbury, 2010)

—— *The Merry Wives of Windsor*, ed. by Giorgio Melchiori (Walton-on-Thames: Thomas Nelson and Sons Ltd., 2000)

—— *The Rape of Lucrece*, in *Shakespeare's Poems*, ed. by Katherine Duncan-Jones and H.R. Woudhuysen (London: Bloomsbury Arden, 2007)

—— *Richard III*, ed. by James R. Siemon (London: Bloomsbury Arden, 2009)

—— *The Tempest*, ed. Virginia Mason Vaughan and Alden T. Vaughan (London: Thomas Nelson and Sons, 1999)

—— *Titus Andronicus*, ed. by Jonathan Bate (London: Bloomsbury Arden, 1995)

—— *Twelfth Night*, ed. by Keir Elam (London: Arden Shakespeare, 2008)

—— *Comedies, Histories & Tragedies* (London: 1623)

—— *The Rape of Lucrece* (London: 1655)

Bibliography

—— *Titus Andronicus* (London: 1594)

—— *Titus Andronicus* (London: 1600)

—— *Titus Andronicus* (London: 1611)

Sidney, Philip, *An Apologie for Poetry* (London: 1595)

—— *Astrophil and Stella*, in Katherine Duncan-Jones (ed.), *The Oxford Authors: Sir Philip Sidney* (Oxford: Oxford University Press, 1989), pp. 153–211

Smith, Adam, *The Theory of Moral Sentiments*, ed. by D.D. Raphael and A.L. Macfie (Oxford: Oxford University Press, 1976)

Smith, William, *Chloris, or The complaint of the passionate despised shepheard* (London: 1596)

Spinoza, Baruch, *Complete Works*, ed. by Michael L. Morgan, trans. Samuel Shirley (Indianapolis, IN: Hackett Publishing, 2002)

Stow, John, *A survay of London* (London: 1598)

Stubbes, Philip, *The second part of the anatomie of abuses* (London: 1583)

Topsell, Edward, *The Historie of Foure-Footed Beasts* (London: 1607)

Tyndale, William, *The practyse of prelates* (London: 1548)

Walkington, Thomas, *The Opticke Glasse of Humors* (London: 1607)

Webster, John, *Appius and Virginia* (London: 1654)

Webster, John and William Rowley, *The Thracian Wonder* (London: 1661)

Widdowes, Daniel, *Naturall philosophy, or, A description of the world*, 2nd ed. (London: 1631)

Wilson, Arthur, *The History of Great Britain* (London: 1653)

Wright, Thomas, *The Passions of the Mind in Generall* (London: 1604)

Wyatt, Thomas, *Collected Poems*, ed. by Joost Daalder (London: Oxford University Press, 1975)

SECONDARY

Adamson, David, 'Authority and Illusion: The Power of Prospero's Book', *Comitatus: A Journal of Medieval and Renaissance Studies*, 20.1 (1989), 9–19

Aers, David, and Nigel Smith, 'English Reformations', *Journal of Medieval and Early Modern Studies*, 40.3 (2010), 425–438

Aggeler, Geoffrey, 'Good Pity in *King Lear*: The Progress of Edgar', *Neophilologus*, 77.2 (1993), 321–331

Airlie, Stuart, 'The History of Emotions and Emotional History', *Early Medieval Europe*, 10 (2001), 235–241

Archer, Ian W., 'The Charity of Early Modern Londoners', *Transactions of the Royal Historical Society*, 6.12 (2002), 223–244

—— 'The Nostalgia of John Stow', in D.M. Smith and R. Strier (eds.), *The Theatrical City: Culture, Theatre, and Politics in London, 1576–1649* (Cambridge: Cambridge University Press, 1995), pp. 18–34

Bach, Rebecca Ann, *Birds and Other Creatures in Renaissance Literature: Shakespeare, Descartes, and Animal Studies* (New York, NY: Routledge, 2018)

Baines, Barbara, *Thomas Heywood* (Boston, MA: Twayne, 1984)

Baldwin, T.W.,*William Shakspere's Small Latine and Lesse Greeke* (Urbana, IL: University of Illinois Press, 1944)

Bibliography

—— *On the Literary Genetics of Shakespeare's Poems and Sonnets* (Urbana, IL: University of Illinois Press, 1950)

Bartlett, John, *A New and Complete Concordance, or Verbal Index to the Words, Phrases, & Passages in the Dramatic Works of Shakespeare* (London: Macmillan, 1937)

Bate, Jonathan, *Shakespeare and Ovid* (Oxford: Clarendon Press, 1993)

Bates, Catherine, *Masculinity, Gender and Identity in the English Renaissance Lyric* (Cambridge: Cambridge University Press, 2007)

Battenhouse, Roy, *Shakespearean Tragedy: Its Art and Its Christian Premises* (Bloomington, IN: University of Indiana Press, 1969)

Beckwith, Sarah, *Signifying God: Social Relation and Symbolic Act in the York Corpus Christi Cycles* (Chicago, IL: University of Chicago Press, 2001)

Beier, A.L., *The Problem of the Poor in Tudor and Early Stuart England* (London: Routledge, 1983)

Belsey, Catherine, 'Invocation of the Visual Image: Ekphrasis in *Lucrece* and Beyond', *Shakespeare Quarterly*, 63.2 (2012), 175–198

—— 'Tarquin Dispossessed: Expropriation and Consent in *The Rape of Lucrece*', *Shakespeare Quarterly*, 53 (2001), 315–335

Bennett, Judith M., 'Conviviality and Charity in Medieval and Early Modern England', *Past & Present*, 134 (1992), 19–41

Berry, Philippa, 'Women, Language, and History in *The Rape of Lucrece*', *Shakespeare Studies*, 44 (1992), 33–39

Bevington, David, *From Mankind to Marlowe* (Cambridge, MA: Harvard University Press, 1962)

—— 'Jonson and Shakespeare: A Spirited Friendship', *Ben Jonson Journal*, 23.1 (2016), 1–23

—— *Medieval Drama* (Boston, MA: Houghton Mifflin, 1975)

Bloom, Harold, *Shakespeare: The Invention of the Human* (London: Fourth Estate, 1999)

Boehrer, Bruce, *Animal Characters: Nonhuman Beings in Early Modern Literature* (Philadelphia, PA: University of Pennsylvania Press, 2010)

—— "Animal Studies and the Deconstruction of Character," *PMLA*, 124 (2009), 542–547

—— *Shakespeare Among the Animals: Nature and Society in the Drama of Early Modern England* (New York, NY: Palgrave Macmillan, 2002)

Bossy, John, *Christianity in the West, 1400–1700* (Oxford: Oxford University Press, 1985)

Breitenberg, Mark, 'Reading Elizabethan Iconicity: *Gorboduc* and the Semiotics of Reform', *English Literary Renaissance*, 18.2 (1988), 194–217

Bretz, Andrew, 'Sung Silence: Complicity, Dramaturgy, and Song in Heywood's *Rape of Lucrece*', *Early Theatre*, 19.2 (2016), 101–118

Brigden, Susan, *London and the Reformation* (Oxford: Clarendon Press, 1989; repr. London: Faber & Faber Ltd., 2014)

—— 'Religion and Social Obligation in Early Sixteenth-Century London', *Past & Present*, 103 (1984), 67–112

Brockman, Sonya L., 'Trauma and Abandoned Testimony in *Titus Andronicus* and *Rape of Lucrece*', *College Literature*, 44.3 (2017), 344–378

Bibliography

Brown, Paul, "'This thing of darkness I acknowledge mine": *The Tempest* and the Discourse of Colonialism', in Jonathan Dollimore and Alan Sinfield (eds.), *Political Shakespeare: Essays in Cultural Materialism* (Manchester: Manchester University Press, 1985), pp. 48–71

Burckhardt, Jacob, *The Civilization of the Renaissance in Italy*, trans. S.G.C. Middlemore (London: Penguin, 1990)

Burke, Peter, 'Is there a Cultural History of the Emotions?', in Penelope Gouk and Helen Hills (eds.), *Representing Emotions: New Connections in the Histories of Art, Music and Medicine* (Aldershot: Ashgate, 2005), pp. 35–48

Burnett, Mark Thornton, *Constructing 'Monsters' in Shakespearean Drama and Early Modern Culture* (London: Palgrave Macmillan, 2002)

Burrow, Colin, *Epic Romance: Homer to Milton* (Oxford: Clarendon Press, 1993)

Butler, Martin, *Theatre and Crisis, 1632–1642* (Cambridge: Cambridge University Press, 1984)

Camino, Mercedes Maroto, *"The Stage am I": Raping Lucrece in Early Modern England* (Lewiston, NY: Edwin Mellen Press, 1995)

Campbell, Oscar J., 'The Salvation of Lear', *English Literary History*, 15 (1948), 93–109

Cartelli, Thomas, '*Bartholomew Fair* as Urban Arcadia: Jonson responds to Shakespeare', *Renaissance Drama*, 14 (1983), 151–172

Cauthen, I.B. Jr., '*Gorboduc, Ferrex and Porrex*: The First Two Quartos', *Studies in Bibliography*, XV (1962), 231–233

Charnes, Linda, *Notorious Identity: Materializing the Subject in Shakespeare* (Cambridge, MA: Harvard University Press, 1993)

Cheney, Patrick, 'Poetry in Shakespeare's plays', in Patrick Cheney (ed.), *The Cambridge Companion to Shakespeare's Poetry* (Cambridge: Cambridge University Press, 2007), pp. 221–240

—— *Shakespeare, National Poet-Playwright* (Cambridge: Cambridge University Press, 2004)

Coleridge, Samuel Taylor, *Coleridge's Shakespearean Criticism*, ed. by T.M. Raysor (Cambridge, MA: Harvard University Press, 1930)

Colie, Rosalie L., 'The Energies of Endurance: Biblical Echo in *King Lear*', in Rosalie L. Colie and F.T. Flahiff (eds.), *Some Facets of* King Lear: *Essays in Prismatic Criticism* (Toronto: University of Toronto Press, 1974), pp. 117–144

Condron, Stephanie, 'Not for the Fainthearted', *The Telegraph*, 03 June 2006 <http://www.telegraph.co.uk/news/uknews/1520196/Not-for-the-fainthearted.html> [10 December 2011].

Cooper, Helen, *Shakespeare and the Medieval World* (London: Methuen, 2010)

Craik, Katharine, *Reading Sensations in Early Modern England* (Basingstoke: Palgrave Macmillan, 2007)

Craik, T.W., *The Tudor Interlude* (Leicester: Leicester University Press, 1958)

Crewe, Jonathan, *Trials of Authorship: Anterior Forms and Poetic Reconstruction from Wyatt to Shakespeare* (Berkeley, CA: University of California Press, 1990)

Culhane, Peter, 'Livy in Early Jacobean Drama', *Translation and Literature*, 14 (2005), 21–44

Bibliography

Cunningham, Karen, '"Scars Can Witness": Trials by Ordeal and Lavinia's Body in *Titus Andronicus*', in Katherine Anne Ackley (ed.), *Women and Violence in Literature: An Essay Collection* (New York, NY: Garland, 1990), pp. 139–162

Daniel, Christopher, *Death and Burial in Medieval England, 1066–1550* (London: Routledge, 1997)

Daniels, Charles B., and Sam Scully, 'Pity, Fear, and Catharsis in Aristotle's *Poetics*', *Noûs*, 26.2 (1992), 204–217

Davenport, William Anthony, *Fifteenth-Century English Drama: The Early Moral Plays and their Literary Relations* (Cambridge: D.S. Brewer, 1970)

Davies, Surekha, *Renaissance Ethnography and the Invention of the Human: New Worlds, Maps and Monsters* (Cambridge: Cambridge University Press, 2016)

Davis, Alex, 'Revolution by Degrees: Philip Sidney and *Gradatio*', *Modern Philology*, 108.4 (2011), 488–506

Davis, Natalie Zemon, 'Boundaries and the Sense of Self in Sixteenth-Century France', in Thomas C. Heller, Morton Sosna, and David E. Wellbery (eds.), *Reconstructing Individualism: Autonomy, Individuality and the Self in Western Thought* (Stanford, CA: Stanford University Press, 1986), pp. 53–63

Davis, Nicholas, 'The Meaning of the Word "Interlude"', *Medieval English Theatre*, 6 (1984), 5–15

de Grazia, Margreta, Maureen Quilligan, and Peter Stallybrass, 'Introduction', in Margreta de Grazia, Maureen Quilligan, and Peter Stallybrass (eds.), *Subject and Object in Renaissance Culture* (Cambridge: Cambridge University Press, 1996), pp. 1–13

De Sousa, Ronald, *The Rationality of Emotion* (Cambridge, MA: MIT Press, 1987)

Derrida, Jacques, and David Wills, 'The Animal That Therefore I Am (More to Follow)', *Critical Inquiry*, 28.2 (2002), 369–418

Dessen, Alan C., 'Homilies and Anomalies: The Legacy of the Morality Play to the Age of Shakespeare – Review Article', *Shakespeare Studies*, 11 (1978), 243–258

—— *Shakespeare and the Late Moral Plays* (Lincoln, NE and London: University of Nebraska Press, 1986)

Diehl, Huston, 'Religion and Shakespearean Tragedy', in Claire McEachern (ed.), *The Cambridge Companion to Shakespearean Tragedy* (Cambridge: Cambridge University Press, 2003), pp. 86–102

Distiller, Natasha, *Desire and Gender in the Sonnet Tradition* (Houndmills: Palgrave Macmillan, 2008)

Dixon, Thomas, *From Passions to Emotions: The Creation of a Secular Psychological Category* (Cambridge: Cambridge University Press, 2003)

—— *Weeping Britannia: Portrait of a Nation in Tears* (Oxford: Oxford University Press, 2015)

Dolan, Frances E., *True Relations: Reading, Literature, and Evidence in Seventeenth-Century England* (Philadelphia, PA: University of Pennsylvania Press, 2013)

Dollimore, Jonathan, *Radical Tragedy*, 2nd edn (London: Harvester Wheatsheaf, 1989)

Donaldson, Ian, *The Rapes of Lucretia: A Myth and its Transformation* (Oxford: Clarendon Press, 1982)

Bibliography

Dubrow, Heather, *Captive Victors: Shakespeare's Narrative Poems and Sonnets* (Ithaca, NY: Cornell University Press, 1987)

—— *Echoes of Desire: English Petrarchism and its Counterdiscourses* (Ithaca, NY: Cornell University Press, 1995)

Duffy, Eamon, *The Stripping of the Altars: Traditional Religion in England, 1400–1580* (New Haven, CT: Yale University Press, 1992)

Duncan-Jones, Katherine, 'Introduction', in *Shakespeare's Sonnets* (London: Thomas Nelson and Sons Ltd, 1997), pp. 1–105

—— 'Ravished and Revised: The 1616 *Lucrece*', *The Review of English Studies*, 52.208 (2001), 516–523

Dutton, Richard, *Ben Jonson: Authority: Criticism* (Basingstoke: Macmillan, 1996)

—— *Ben Jonson: To the First Folio* (Cambridge: Cambridge University Press, 1983)

Ekman, Paul, and Richard J. Davidson (eds.), *The Nature of Emotion: Fundamental Questions* (Oxford: Oxford University Press, 1994)

Elton, William R., *King Lear and the Gods* (San Marino, CA: The Huntington Library, 1968)

Enterline, Lynn, *The Rhetoric of the Body from Ovid to Shakespeare* (Cambridge: Cambridge University Press, 2000)

—— *Shakespeare's Schoolroom: Rhetoric, Discipline, Emotion* (Philadelphia, PA: University of Pennsylvania Press, 2012)

Erickson, Peter B., 'Sexual Politics and the Social Structure in *As You Like It*', *The Massachusetts Review, Inc.*, 23.1 (1982), 65–83

Faas, Ekbert, *Shakespeare's Poetics* (Cambridge: Cambridge University Press, 1986)

Fawcett, Mary Laughlin, 'Arms/Words/Tears: Language and the Body in *Titus Andronicus*', *English Literary History*, 50.2 (1983), 261–277

Febvre, Lucien, 'Sensibility and History: How to Reconstitute the Emotional Life of the Past', in *A New Kind of History: From the Writings of Febvre*, ed. by Peter Burke, trans. K. Folca (London: Routledge and Kegan Paul, 1973), pp. 12–26

Feerick, Jean E., and Vin Nardizzi, 'Swervings: On Human Indistinction', in Jean E. Feerick and Vin Nardizzi (eds.), *The Indistinct Human in Renaissance Literature*, (Basingstoke: Palgrave Macmillan, 2012), pp. 1–12

Fernie, Ewan, *Shame in Shakespeare* (London: Routledge, 2002)

Ferry, Anne, *The "Inward" Language: Sonnets of Wyatt, Sidney, Shakespeare, Donne* (Chicago, IL: University of Chicago Press, 1983)

Fienberg, Nona, 'The Emergence of Stella in *Astrophil and Stella*', *Studies in English Literature, 1500–1900*, 25.1 (1985), 5–19

Findlater, Richard, 'Shakespearean Atrocities', *The Twentieth Century* (October 1955), 364–372

Fineman, Joel, *Shakespeare's Perjured Eye: The Invention of Poetic Subjectivity in the Sonnets* (Berkeley, CA: University of California Press, 1986)

—— 'Shakespeare's Will: The Temporality of Rape', *Representations*, 20 (1987), 25–76

Floyd-Wilson, Mary, and Garrett A. Sullivan, Jr. (eds), *Environment and Embodiment in Early Modern England* (Basingstoke: Palgrave, 2007)

Forrest, Ian, *Trustworthy Men: How Inequality and Faith Made the Medieval Church* (Princeton, NJ: Princeton University Press, 2018)

Bibliography

Fortin, René E., 'Hermeneutical Circularity and Christian Interpretations of *King Lear*', *Shakespeare Studies*, 12 (1979), 113–125

Forster, Leonard, *The Icy Fire: Five Studies in European Petrarchism* (Cambridge: Cambridge University Press, 1969)

Foster, Donald, '"Against the perjured falsehood of your tongues": Frances Howard on the Course of Love', *English Literary Renaissance*, 24 (1994), 72–103

Freud, Sigmund, *On Sexuality*, ed. by Angela Richards, trans. James Strachey (Harmondsworth: Penguin, 1977)

Frye, Roland M., *Shakespeare and Christian Doctrine* (Princeton, NJ: Princeton University Press, 1963)

Fudge, Erica, Ruth Gilbert, and Susan Wiseman, 'Introduction: The Dislocation of the Human', in Erica Fudge, Ruth Gilbert, and Susan Wiseman (eds.), *At the Borders of the Human: Beasts, Bodies and Natural Philosophy*, (London: Macmillan, 1999), pp. 1–9

Fudge, Erica, *Brutal Reasoning: Animals, Rationality, and Humanity in Early Modern England* (Ithaca, NY: Cornell University Press, 2006)

—— *Perceiving Animals: Humans and Beasts in Early Modern English Culture* (Basingstoke: Macmillan, 2000)

Garber, Marjorie, *Shakespeare's Ghost Writers: Literature as Uncanny Causality* (New York and London: Methuen, 1987)

Geller, Jesse D., 'Pity, Suffering, and Psychotherapy', *American Journal of Psychotherapy*, 60.2 (2006), 187–205

Gerdes, Karen E., 'Empathy, Sympathy, and Pity: 21st-Century Definitions and Implications for Practice and Research', *Journal of Social Service Research*, 37.3, 230–241

Goldie, Peter (ed.), *Understanding Emotions: Minds and Morals* (Burlington, VT: Ashgate, 2002)

Green, Douglas E., 'Interpreting "her martyr'd signs": Gender and Tragedy in *Titus Andronicus*', *Shakespeare Quarterly*, 40.3 (1989), 317–326

Greenblatt, Stephen J., 'Learning to Curse: Aspects of Linguistic Colonialism in the 16th Century," In Fredi Chiapelli (ed.), *First Images of America: The Impact of the New World on the Old* (Berkeley, CA: University of California Press, 1970), pp. 561–580

—— *Renaissance Self-Fashioning: From More to Shakespeare* (Chicago, IL: University of Chicago Press, 1980)

Greene, Roland, *Post-Petrarchism: Origins and Innovations of the Western Lyric Sequence* (Princeton, NJ: Princeton University Press, 1991)

Greg, Sir Walter, *A Bibliography of the English Printed Drama to the Restoration*, vol. 1 (London: Bibliographical Society, 1970)

Gross, Daniel M., *The Secret History of Emotion: From Aristotle's Rhetoric to Modern Brain Science* (Chicago, IL: University of Chicago Press, 2006)

Guilfoyle, Cherrell, 'The Redemption of King Lear', *Comparative Drama*, 23.1 (1989), 50–69

Hadfield, Andrew, *Shakespeare and Renaissance Politics* (London: Arden Shakespeare, 2004)

Bibliography

—— 'The Summoning of *Everyman*', in Thomas Betteridge and Greg Walker (eds.), *The Oxford Handbook of Tudor Drama* (Oxford: Oxford University Press, 2012), pp. 93–108

Haigh, Christopher, *English Reformations: Religion, Politics, and Society under the Tudors* (Oxford: Clarendon, 1993)

Hamilton, A.C., '*Titus Andronicus*: The Form of Shakespearian Tragedy', *Shakespeare Quarterly*, 14 (1963), 201–213

Harding, Jennifer, and Deirdre Pribram (eds.), *Emotions: A Cultural Studies Reader* (New York, NY: Routledge, 2009)

Hatcher, O.L., 'The Sources and Authorship of *The Thracian Wonder*', *Modern Language Notes*, 23.1 (1908), pp. 16–20

Heal, Felicity, *Hospitality in Early Modern England* (London: Clarendon Press, 1990)

Heffernan, Julián Jiménez, *Shakespeare's Extremes: Wild Man, Monster, Beast* (Basingstoke: Palgrave, 2015)

Herford, C.H., Percy Simpson, and Evelyn Simpson (eds.), *Ben Jonson: Play and Masque Commentary*, vol. X (Oxford: Clarendon, 1950)

Holbrook, Peter, 'Shakespeare and Poetry', in Mark Thornton Burnett, Adrian Streete, and Ramona Wray (eds.), *The Edinburgh Companion to Shakespeare and the Arts* (Edinburgh: Edinburgh University Press, 2011), pp. 37–48

Holmes, Rachel E., and Toria A. Johnson, 'Introduction: In Pursuit of Truth', *Forum for Modern Language Studies*, 54.1 (2018), 1–16

Hubler, Edward (ed.), *Shakespeare's Songs and Poems* (New York, NY: McGraw Hill, 1959)

Hulse, S. Clark, 'Wresting the Alphabet: Oratory and Action in *Titus Andronicus*', *Criticism*, 21 (1979), 106–118

Hunt, Maurice, 'Shakespeare's *The Tempest* and Human Worth', *Ben Jonson Journal*, 20.1 (2013), 58–71

Hutson, Lorna, *Circumstantial Shakespeare* (Oxford: Oxford University Press, 2015)

—— *The Invention of Suspicion: Law and Mimesis in Shakespeare and Renaissance Drama* (Oxford: Oxford University Press, 2007)

—— 'Series Editor's Preface' in James Kuzner, *Open Subjects: English Renaissance Republicans, Modern Selfhoods, and the Virtue of Vulnerability* (Edinburgh: Edinburgh University Press, 2011)

—— 'Rethinking the "Spectacle of the Scaffold": Juridical Epistemologies and English Revenge Tragedy', *Representations*, 89 (2005), 30–58

Hyland, Peter, *An Introduction to Shakespeare's Poems* (Houndmills, Basingstoke: Palgrave Macmillan, 2003)

Hynes, Sam, 'The Rape of Tarquin', *Shakespeare Quarterly*, 10 (1959), 451–453

Jackson, MacDonald P., *Studies in Attribution: Middleton and Shakespeare* (Salzburg: University of Salzburg Press, 1979)

James, Heather, 'Cultural Disintegration in *Titus Andronicus*: Mutilating Titus, Virgil, Rome', in James Redmond (ed.), *Violence in Drama* (Cambridge: Cambridge University Press, 1991), pp. 123–140

James, Henry, and Greg Walker, 'The Politics of *Gorboduc*', *The English Historical Review*, 110.435 (1995), 109–121

Jayne, Sears, 'Charity in *King Lear*', *Shakespeare Quarterly*, 15.2 (1964), 277–288

Bibliography

Jed, Stephanie, *Chaste Thinking: The Rape of Lucretia and the Birth of Humanism* (Bloomington, IN: Indiana University Press, 1989)

Jones, Norman, *The English Reformation: Religion and Cultural Adaptation* (Oxford: Blackwell, 2002)

Jordan, W.K., *The Charities of London, 1480–1660: The Aspirations and Achievements of the Urban Society* (London: George Allen & Unwin Ltd., 1960)

—— *Philanthropy in England, 1480–1660: A Study of the Changing Pattern of English Social Aspirations* (Westport, CT: Greenwood Press, 1978)

Kagan, Jerome, *What is Emotion?: History, Measures, and Meanings* (New Haven, CT: Yale University Press, 2007)

Kahn, Coppélia, 'The Rape in Shakespeare's *Lucrece*', *Shakespeare Studies*, 9 (1976), 45–72

Kennedy, Gwynne, *Just Anger: Representing Women's Anger in Early Modern England* (Carbondale, IL: Southern Illinois University Press, 2000)

Kennedy, William, 'Petrarchan Poetics', in Glyn P. Norton (ed.), *The Cambridge History of Literary Criticism*, vol. 3 (Cambridge: Cambridge University Press, 1999), pp. 119–126

Kerrigan, William and Gordon Braden, *The Idea of the Renaissance* (Baltimore, MD: Johns Hopkins University Press, 1989)

Kewes, Paulina, 'Roman History and Early Stuart Drama: Thomas Heywood's *The Rape of Lucrece*', *English Literary Renaissance*, 32 (2002), 239–267

Kirsch, Arthur, 'Virtue, Vice, and Compassion in Montaigne and *The Tempest*', *Studies in English Literature, 1500–1900*, 37.2 (1997), 337–352

Knoppers, Laura Lunger and Joan B. Landes (eds.), *Monstrous Bodies/Political Monstrosities in Early Modern Europe* (Ithaca, NY: Cornell University Press, 2004)

Konstan, David, 'Senecan Emotions', in Shadi Bartsch and Alessandro Schiesaro (eds.), *The Cambridge Companion to Seneca* (Cambridge: Cambridge University Press, 2015), pp. 174–186

—— *Pity Transformed* (London: Bloomsbury, 2001)

Kott, Jan, *Shakespeare Our Contemporary*, trans. Boleslaw Taborski, 2nd ed. rev. (London: Methuen, 1967)

Lacan, Jacques, *The Four Fundamental Concepts of Psycho-Analysis*, ed. by Jacques-Alain Miller, trans. Alan Sheridan (New York, NY: Norton, 1978)

Lake, David J., *The Canon of Thomas Middleton's Plays* (Cambridge: Cambridge University Press, 1975)

Lancashire, Ian (ed.), *Two Tudor Interludes* (Manchester: Manchester University Press, 1980)

Langley, Eric, *Narcissism and Suicide in Shakespeare and His Contemporaries* (Oxford: Oxford University Press, 2009)

—— 'Plagued by Kindness: Contagious Sympathies in Shakespearean Drama', *Medical Humanities* 37 (2011), 103–109

—— *Shakespeare's Contagious Sympathies: Ill Communications* (Oxford: Oxford University Press, 2018)

—— 'Standing on a Beach: Shakespeare and the Sympathetic Imagination', in Kristine Steenbergh and Katherine Ibbett (eds.), *Compassion in Early Modern Literature and Culture* (Cambridge: Cambridge University Press, 2021), pp. 197–216

Bibliography

Lawrence, Séan, "'Gods That We Adore": The Divine in *King Lear*', *Renascence*, 56 (2004), 143–159

Lehnhof, Kent R., 'Relation and Responsibility: A Levinasian Reading of *King Lear*', *Modern Philology*, 111.3 (2014), 485–509

Lewis, C.S. *The Allegory of Love* (Oxford: Clarendon Press, 1936)

Lindsay, Tom, "'Which first was mine own king": Caliban and the Politics of Service and Education in *The Tempest*', *Studies in Philology*, 113.2 (2016), 397–423

Little, Arthur L., *Shakespeare Jungle Fever: National-Imperial Re-visions of Race, Rape, and Sacrifice* (Stanford, CA: Stanford University Press, 2000)

Lobis, Seth, *The Virtue of Sympathy: Magic, Philosophy, and Literature in Seventeenth-Century England* (New Haven, CT: Yale University Press, 2015)

Loewenstein, David, 'Agnostic Shakespeare?: The Godless World of *King Lear*', in David Loewenstein and Michael Witmore (eds.), *Shakespeare and Early Modern Religion* (Cambridge: Cambridge University Press, 2015), pp. 155–171

Lovejoy, Arthur O., *The Great Chain of Being: A Study of the History of an Idea* (Cambridge, MA: Harvard University Press, 1936)

Lupton, Julia Reinhard, 'Creature Caliban', *Shakespeare Quarterly*, 51.1 (2000), 1–23

Lynch, Stephen J., 'Sin, Suffering, and Redemption in *Leir* and *Lear*', *Shakespeare Studies*, 18 (1986), 161–174

Lyons, Bridget Gellert, 'The Subplot as Simplification in *King Lear*', in Rosalie L. Colie and F.T. Flahiff (eds.), *Some Facets of* King Lear: *Essays in Prismatic Criticism* (Toronto: University of Toronto Press, 1974), pp. 23–38

Mack, Maynard, *King Lear in Our Time* (Berkeley, CA: University of California Press, 1965)

Marshall, Cynthia, *The Shattering of the Self: Violence, Subjectivity, and Early Modern Texts* (Baltimore, MD: Johns Hopkins University Press, 2002)

Marshall, Peter, *Beliefs and the Dead in Reformation England* (Oxford: Oxford University Press, 2002)

—— *Religious Identities in Henry VIII's England* (Aldershot: Ashgate, 2006)

Matt, Susan J., 'Current Emotion Research in History: Or, Doing History from the Inside Out', *Emotion Review*, 3.1 (2011), 117–124

Maus, Katharine Eisaman, *Inwardness and Theater in the English Renaissance* (Chicago, IL: University of Chicago Press, 1995)

—— 'Taking Tropes Seriously: Language and Violence in Shakespeare's *Rape of Lucrece*', *Shakespeare Quarterly*, 37.1 (1986), 66–82

Martines, Lauro, 'The Politics of Love Poetry in Renaissance Italy', in Janet Levarie Smarr (ed.), *Historical Criticism and the Challenge of Theory* (Urbana, IL: University of Illinois Press, 1993), pp. 129–144

Mazzio, Carla, and David Hillman (eds), *The Body in Parts: Emotions and the Shakespearean Stage* (New York, NY: Routledge, 1999)

McAdam, Ian, 'The Puritan Dialectic of Law and Grace in *Bartholomew Fair*', *Studies in English Literature 1500–1900*, 46.2 (2006), 415–433

McEachern, Claire, *Believing in Shakespeare: Studies in Longing* (Cambridge: Cambridge University Press, 2018)

McIntosh, Marjorie Keniston, *Controlling Misbehavior in England, 1370–1600* (Cambridge: Cambridge University Press, 1998)

Bibliography

—— *Poor Relief in England, 1350–1600* (Cambridge: Cambridge University Press, 2012)

Meek, Richard, *Narrating the Visual in Shakespeare* (Surrey: Ashgate, 2009)

—— 'O, What a Sympathy of Woe is This': Passionate Sympathy in *Titus Andronicus*, 287–297

Meek, Richard, and Erin Sullivan (eds.), *The Renaissance of Emotion: Understanding Affect in Shakespeare and His Contemporaries* (Manchester: Manchester University Press, 2015)

Miller, Christopher W.T., 'Confusion of Tears: The Deadened Oedipal Couple and Predatory Identifications in *The Rape of Lucrece*', *American Imago*, 75.4 (2018), 489–515

Moyer, Ann E., 'Sympathy in the Renaissance', in Eric Schliesser (ed.), *Sympathy: A History* (Oxford: Oxford University Press, 2015), pp. 70–101

Mueller, Janel, 'Literature and the Church', in David Loewenstein and Janel Mueller (eds.), *The Cambridge History of Early Modern English Literature: The Tudor Era from the Reformation to Elizabeth I* (Cambridge: Cambridge University Press, 2003), pp. 257–310

Mullaney, Steven, *The Reformation of Emotions in the Age of Shakespeare* (Chicago, IL and London: University of Chicago Press, 2015)

Mulvey, Laura, 'Visual Pleasure and Narrative Cinema', *Screen*, 16 (1975), 6–18

Neely, Carol Thomas, 'The Structure of English Renaissance Sonnet Sequences', *English Literary History*, 45.3 (1978), 359–389

Nelson, Jeffrey N., 'Lust and Black Magic in Barnabe Barnes's *Parthenophil and Parthenophe*', *Sixteenth Century Journal*, 25 (1994), pp. 595–608

Newman, Jane, 'And Let Mild Women to Him Lose Their Mildness: Philomela, Female Violence, and Shakespeare's *The Rape of Lucrece*', *Shakespeare Quarterly*, 45.3 (1994), 304–326

Nohrnberg, James, 'About Suffering and On Dying: Shakespeare's Reinvention of a Theater of Eschatological Identity in King Lear', in Kathy Lavezzo and Roze Hentschell (eds.), *Essays in Memory of Richard Helgerson: Laureations* (Newark, DE: University of Delaware Press, 2011), pp. 107–129

Nolan, Michael, 'William Rowley and the Authorship of *The Thracian Wonder*', *Notes and Queries*, 44.4 (1997), 519–523

Nordlund, Marcus, *The Dark Lantern: A Historical Study of Sight in Shakespeare, Webster, and Middleton* (Goteburg: Acta Universitatis Gothoburgensis, 2006)

Nussbaum, Martha, *Upheavals of Thought: The Intelligence of Emotions* (Cambridge: Cambridge University Press, 2001)

O'Connell, Michael, '*King Lear* and the Summons of Death', in Curtis Perry and John Watkins (eds.), *Shakespeare and the Middle Ages* (Oxford: Oxford University Press, 2009), pp. 199–216

O'Hagan, Sean, 'Interview: Marina Abramović' *The Observer*, 3 October 2010, <http://www.guardian.co.uk/artanddesign/2010/oct/03/interview-marina-abramovic-performance-artist> [28 September 2011]

Oakley-Brown, Liz, '*Titus Andronicus* and the Cultural Politics of Translation in Early Modern England', *Renaissance Studies*, 19 (2005), 325–347

Oatley, Keith, *Emotions: A Brief History* (Malden, MA: Blackwell, 2004)

—— *The Psychology of Emotions* (Cambridge: Cambridge University Press, 1992)

Bibliography

Olson, Greta, 'Richard III's Animalistic Criminal Body', *Philological Quarterly*, 82.3 (2003), 301–323

Orgel, Stephen, 'Prospero's Wife', *Representations*, 8 (1984), 1–13

Ortony, Andrew, and Terence J. Turner, 'What's Basic About Basic Emotions?', *Psychological Review*, 97 (1990), 315–331

Palfrey, Simon, *Shakespeare's Possible Worlds* (Cambridge: Cambridge University Press, 2014)

Park, Katharine, 'The Organic Soul', in Charles Schmitt (ed.), *The Cambridge History of Renaissance Philosophy* (Cambridge: Cambridge University Press, 1988), pp. 464–484

Parker, Patricia, *Literary Fat Ladies: Rhetoric, Gender, Property* (London: Methuen, 1987)

Pask, Kevin, 'Caliban's Masque', *English Literary History*, 70.3 (2003), 739–756

Paster, Gail Kern, *Humoring the Body: Emotions and Shakespeare's Stage* (Chicago, IL: University of Chicago Press, 2004)

Paster, Gail Kern, Katherine Rowe, and Mary Floyd-Wilson, 'Introduction: Reading the Early Modern Passions', in Gail Kern Paster, Katherine Rowe, and Mary Floyd-Wilson (eds.), *Reading the Early Modern Passions: Essays in the Cultural History of Emotion* (Philadelphia, PA: University of Pennsylvania Press, 2004), pp. 1–20

Patterson, Annabel, *Reading Between the Lines* (London: Routledge, 1993)

Percy, Thomas, *Relics of Ancient English Poetry*, vol. I (London: Bickers, 1876–1877)

Perry, Curtis and John Watkins, 'Introduction', in Curtis Perry and John Watkins (eds.), *Shakespeare and the Middle Ages* (Oxford: Oxford University Press, 2009), pp. 1–20

Plamper, Jan, *The History of Emotions: An Introduction* (Oxford: Oxford University Press, 2015)

Pinch, Adela, 'Emotion and History: A Review Article', *Comparative Studies in Society and History*, 37 (1995), 100–109

Pincombe, Mike, *Elizabethan Humanism: Literature and Learning in the Later Sixteenth Century* (Harlow: Longman, 2001)

Pineas, Rainier, 'The English Morality Play as a Weapon of Religious Controversy', *Studies in English Literature 1500–1900*, 2.2 (1962), 157–180

Potter, Robert, *The English Morality Play: Origins, History and Influence of a Dramatic Tradition* (London: Routledge & Kegan Paul, 1975)

Prince, F.T., 'Introduction', in *The Poems* (London: Methuen, 1960), xi–xlvi

Punter, David, *The Literature of Pity* (Edinburgh: Edinburgh University Press, 2014)

Raber, Karen, *Animal Bodies, Renaissance Culture* (Philadelphia, PA: University of Pennsylvania Press, 2013)

—— *Shakespeare and Posthumanist Theory* (London: Bloomsbury, 2018)

Reddy, William M., *The Navigation of Feeling: A Framework for the History of Emotions* (Cambridge: Cambridge University Press, 2001)

Reiss, Timothy, *Mirages of the Selfe: Patterns of Personhood in Ancient and Early Modern Europe* (Stanford, CA: Stanford University Press, 2003)

Rhodes, Neil, *Elizabethan Grotesque* (London: Routledge and Kegan Paul, 1980)

Roche, Thomas P., *Petrarch and the English Sonnet Sequences* (New York, NY: AMS Press, Inc., 1989)

Bibliography

Rosenthal, Joel T., *The Purchase of Paradise* (London: Routledge & Kegan Paul, 1972)

Rosenwein, Barbara, *Emotional Communities in the Early Middle Ages* (Ithaca, NY: Cornell University Press, 2006)

—— 'Worrying about Emotions in History', *The American Historical Review*, 107 (2002), 821–845

Rowe, Katherine, 'Dismembering and Forgetting in *Titus Andronicus*', *Shakespeare Quarterly*, 45.3 (1994), 279–303

Rubin, Miri, *Charity and Community in Medieval Cambridge* (Cambridge: Cambridge University Press, 1987)

Ryan, Lawrence V., 'Doctrine and Dramatic Structure in *Everyman*', *Speculum*, 32.4 (1957), 722–735

Rycroft, Eleanor, '*The Interlude of Youth* and *Hick Scorner*', in Thomas Betteridge and Greg Walker (eds.), *The Oxford Handbook of Tudor Drama* (Oxford: Oxford University Press, 2012), pp. 465–481

Sanchez, Melissa E., 'Seduction and Service in *The Tempest*', *Studies in Philology*, 105.1 (2008), 50–82

Sartre, Jean-Paul, *Being and Nothingness*, trans. Hazel E. Barnes (London: Routledge, 1989)

Schen, Claire S., *Charity and Lay Piety in Reformation London, 1500-1620* (Farnham: Ashgate, 2002; repr. Abingdon: Routledge, 2016)

Schoenfeldt, Michael C., *Bodies and Selves in Early Modern England: Physiology and Inwardness in Spenser, Shakespeare, Herbert, and Milton* (Cambridge: Cambridge University Press, 1999)

Seigel, Jerrod, *The Idea of the Self: Thought and Experience in Western Europe Since the Seventeenth Century* (Cambridge: Cambridge University Press, 2005)

Selleck, Nancy, *The Interpersonal Idiom in Shakespeare, Donne, and Early Modern Culture* (Houndsmills: Palgrave Macmillan, 2008)

Shannon, Laurie, *The Accommodated Animal: Cosmopolity in Shakespearean Locales* (Chicago, IL: University of Chicago Press, 2013)

—— '"Poor, Bare, Forked": Animal Sovereignty, Human Negative Exceptionalism, and the Natural History of *King Lear*', *Shakespeare Quarterly* 60.2 (2009), 168–196

Sheehan, Michael M., *The Will in Medieval England* (Toronto: Pontifical Institute of Mediaeval Studies, 1963)

Shell, Alison, *The Arden Critical Companion to Shakespeare and Religion* (London: Methuen, 2010)

Shrank, Cathy, 'Disputing Purgatory in Henrician England: Dialogue and Religious Reform', in Andreas Höfele, Stefan Laqué, Enno Ruge, and Gabriela Schmidt (eds.), *Representing Religious Pluralization in Early Modern Europe* (Berlin: Lit Verlag, 2007), pp. 45–61

Shugar, Debora K., 'Subversive Fathers and Suffering Subjects: Shakespeare and Christianity', in Donna B. Hamilton and Richard Strier (eds.), *Religion, Literature, and Politics in Post-Reformation England, 1540–1688* (Cambridge: Cambridge University Press, 1996), pp. 46–69

Shupe, Donald R., 'The Wooing of Lady Anne: A Psychological Inquiry', *Shakespeare Quarterly*, 29.1 (1978), 28–36

Bibliography

Sierhuis, Freya, 'Autonomy and Inner Freedom: Lipsius and the Revival of Stoicism', in Quentin Skinner and Martin Van Gelderen (eds.), *Freedom and the Construction of Europe*, 2 vols (Cambridge: Cambridge University Press, 2013), II (2013), pp. 46–64

Simpson, James, *Reform and Cultural Revolution: 1350–1547* (Oxford: Oxford University Press, 2004)

Slights, Jessica, 'Rape and the Romanticization of Shakespeare's Miranda', *Studies in English Literature, 1500–1900*, 41.2 (2001), 357–379

Smith, Denzell S., 'The Credibility of the Wooing of Anne in *Richard III*', *Papers on Language and Literature*, 7.2 (1971), 199–202

Smith, Helen, '"This one poore blacke gowne lined with white": The Clothing of the Sixteenth-Century English Book', in Catherine Richardson (ed.), *Clothing Culture 1350–1650* (London: Routledge, 2004), pp. 195–208

Solomon, Robert, *The Passions: Emotions and the Meaning of Life* (Indianapolis, IN: Hackett, 1993)

Sponsler, Claire, *Drama and Resistance: Bodies, Goods and Theatricality in Late Medieval England* (Minneapolis, MN: University of Minnesota Press, 1997)

St. Hilaire, Danielle, 'Allusion and Sacrifice in *Titus Andronicus*', *Studies in English Literature, 1500–1900*, 49.2 (2009), 311–331

—— 'Pity and the Failures of Justice in Shakespeare's *King Lear*', *Modern Philology*, 113.4 (2016), 482–506

Stampfer, Judah, 'The Catharsis of *King Lear*', *Shakespeare Survey*, 13 (1960), 1–10

Stearns, Peter N., and Carol Z. Stearns, 'Emotionology: Clarifying the History of Emotions and Emotional Standards', *The American Historical Review*, 90 (1985), 813–836

Steffes, Michael, 'Medieval Wildernesses and *King Lear*: Heath, Forest, Desert', *Exemplaria*, 28.3 (2016), 230–247

Stockholder, Kay, 'Yet Can he Write: Reading the Silences in *The Spanish Tragedy*', *American Imago*, 47 (1990), 93–124

Sullivan, Erin, *Beyond Melancholy: Sadness and Selfhood in Renaissance England* (Oxford: Oxford University Press, 2016)

—— 'The History of Emotions: Past, Present, Future', *Cultural History*, 2.1 (2013), 93–96

Taylor, Charles, *Sources of the Self: The Making of Modern Identity* (Cambridge: Cambridge University Press, 1989)

Thomson, J.A.F., 'Piety and Charity in Late Medieval London', *Journal of Ecclesiastical History*, 16.2 (1965), 178–195

Tricomi, Albert, 'The Aesthetics of Mutilation in *Titus Andronicus*', *Shakespeare Survey*, 27 (1974), 11–19

Tudeau-Clayton, Margaret, '"I do not know my selfe": The Topography and Politics of Self-Knowledge in Ben Jonson's *Bartholomew Fair*', in Margaret Tudeau-Clayton and Philippa Berry (eds.), *Textures of Renaissance Knowledge* (Manchester: Manchester University Press, 2003), pp. 177–198

van Dijkhuizen, Jan Frans, *Pain and Compassion in Early Modern English Literature and Culture* (Cambridge: D.S. Brewer, 2012)

Bibliography

Vaughan, Virginia Mason, and Alden T. Vaughan, 'Introduction', in William Shakespeare, *The Tempest*, ed. Virginia Mason Vaughan and Alden T. Vaughan (London: Thomas Nelson and Sons Ltd, 1999), pp. 1–138

Vaught, Jennifer C., *Masculinity and Emotion in Early Modern English Literature* (Aldershot: Ashgate, 2007)

Vickers, Nancy, 'The Blazon of Sweet Beauty's Best: Shakespeare's *Lucrece*', in Patricia Parker and Geoffrey Hartman (eds.), *Shakespeare and the Question of Theory* (New York, NY: Methuen, 1985), pp. 95–116

—— 'This Heraldry in Lucrece's Face', *Poetics Today*, 6 (1985), 171–184

—— 'Vital Signs: Petrarch and Popular Culture', *Romantic Review*, 77 (1988), 184–195

Villeponteaux, Mary, '*Semper Eadem*: Belphoebe's Denial of Desire', in Claude J. Summers and Ted-Larry Pebworth (eds.), *Renaissance Discourses of Desire* (Columbia, MO: University of Missouri Press, 1993), pp. 29–45

Waith, Eugene, 'The Metamorphosis of Violence in *Titus Andronicus*', *Shakespeare Survey*, 10 (1957), 39–49

Walker, Greg, *Plays of Persuasion: Drama and Politics at the Court of Henry VIII* (Cambridge: Cambridge University Press, 1991)

Wall, Wendy, *The Imprint of Gender: Authorship and Publication in the English Renaissance* (Ithaca, NY and London: Cornell University Press, 1993)

Waller, Marguerite, 'The Empire's New Clothes: Refashioning the Renaissance', in Sheila Fisher and Janet E. Halley (eds.), *Seeking the Women in Late Medieval and Renaissance Writings* (Knoxville, TN: University of Tennessee Press, 1989), pp. 160–183

Warkentin, Germaine, 'Sidney and the Supple Muse: Compositional Procedures in Some Sonnets of *Astrophil and Stella*', in Dennis Kay (ed.), *Sir Philip Sidney: An Anthology of Modern Criticism* (Oxford: Clarendon, 1987), pp. 171–184

Wasson, John, 'The Morality Play: Ancestor of Elizabethan Drama?', *Comparative Drama*, 13 (1979), 210–221

Watkins, John, 'Moralities, Interludes, and Protestant Drama', in David Wallace (ed.), *The Cambridge History of Medieval Literature* (Cambridge: Cambridge University Press, 1999), pp. 767–692

Weaver, William, '"O, teach me how to make mine excuse": Forensic Performance in *Lucrece*', *Shakespeare Quarterly*, 59 (2008), 421–449

Weber, William W., '"Worse Than Philomel": Violence, Revenge, and Meta-Allusion in *Titus Andronicus*', *Studies in Philology*, 112.4 (2015), 698–717

Wehrs, Donald R., 'Placing Human Constants within Literary History: Generic Revision and Affective Sociality in *The Winter's Tale* and *The Tempest*', *Poetics Today*, 32.3 (2011), 521–591

Wells, Robin Headlam, *Shakespeare's Humanism* (Cambridge: Cambridge University Press, 2005)

Wesley, John, 'Rhetorical Delivery for Renaissance English: Voice, Gesture, Emotion, and the Sixteenth-Century Vernacular Turn', *Renaissance Quarterly*, 68.4 (2015), 1265–1296

Whittier, Gayle, 'The Sonnet's Body and the Body Sonnetized in *Romeo and Juliet*', *Shakespeare Quarterly*, 40.1 (1989), 27–41

Bibliography

Wickberg, Daniel, 'What is the History of Sensibilities?: On Cultural Histories, Old and New', *The American History Review*, 112 (2007), 661–684

Wierzbicka, Anna, *Emotions across Languages and Cultures: Diversity and Universals* (Cambridge: Cambridge University Press, 1999)

Wiggins Martin, and Catherine Richardson, *British Drama 1533–1642: A Catalogue*, vol. IV (Oxford: Oxford University Press, 2014)

—— *British Drama 1533–1642: A Catalogue*, vol. V (Oxford: Oxford University Press, 2015)

—— *British Drama 1533–1642: A Catalogue*, vol. VII (Oxford: Oxford University Press, 2014)

Wilkinson, L.P., *Ovid Recalled* (Cambridge: Cambridge University Press, 1955)

Willbern, David, 'Rape and Revenge in *Titus Andronicus*', *English Literary Renaissance*, 8 (1978), 159–182

Williams, Carolyn D., '"Silence, like a Lucrece knife": Shakespeare and the Meanings of Rape', *The Yearbook of English Studies*, 23 (1993), 93–110

Williams, Marilyn, 'Moral Perspective and Dramatic Action in the Tudor Interlude', *NEMLA Newsletter*, 2.2 (1970), 29–37

Willis, Deborah, 'Shakespeare's Tempest and the Discourse of Colonialism', *Studies in English Literature, 1500-1900*, 29.2 (1989), 277–289

Wilson, Dover, 'Introduction', in *Titus Andronicus* (Cambridge: Cambridge University Press, 1948), pp. i–lxxii

Wilson, Scott, 'Racked on the Tyrant's Bed': The Politics of Pleasure and Pain and the Elizabethan Sonnet Sequences', *Textual Practice* 3 (1989), 234–249

Woodbridge, Linda, 'Renaissance Bogeymen: The Necessary Monsters of the Age', in Guido Ruggiero (ed.), *A Companion to the Worlds of the Renaissance* (Malden, MA: Blackwell Publishing, 2002), pp. 444–459

Wulff, Helena (ed.), *The Emotions: A Cultural Reader* (Oxford: Berg, 2007)

INDEX

abjection 19 n.51, 31–2, 109, 119–21, 123, 128–31, 137
Abramović, Marina 31, 113–14
Adamson, David 186
Adlington, William 159
Aers, David 36 n.1
agency *see* subjectivity
Aggeler, Geoffrey 71
aggression *see* violence
Airlie, Stuart 15 n.38
anger 9, 14, 134, 170
animals *see under* non-humanity
anxiety 22, 25, 28, 31, 42–3, 46, 63, 168, 169, 196, 198
Apuleius 159
Archer, Ian W. 40, 44 n.32, 48 n.44, 49
Aristotle 4–7, 11, 24 n.70, 171 n.28
Augustine, St 95 n.33
Aylett, Robert 1–3, 5–8, 20, 27, 198

Bach, Rebecca Ann 160 n.18
Baines, Barbara 101 n.48
Baldwin, T.W. 96 n.34
Barlow, William
    An A.B.C. to the spiritualte 45–6
Barnes, Barnabe 132–3
    *Parthenophil and
        Parthenophe* 123–4, 131–3
Bartlett, John 172 n.29
Bate, Jonathan 97 n.36
Bates, Catherine 19 n.51, 120, 130
Battenhouse, Roy 80 n.7
Beckwith, Sarah 51 n.50
Beier, A.L. 42 n.24
Belsey, Catherine 81 n.7, 107 n.54
Bennett, Judith M. 41 n.18, 46
Berry, Philippa 107 n.54
Bevington, David 51 n.50, 58 n.60, 188 n.52
Blake, William 9
Bloom, Harold 86
Blurt Master Constable 145–6

Boehrer, Bruce 158, 160 n.18, 169
Bossy, John 44 n.30
Braden, Gordon 21 n.56, 130
Breitenberg, Mark 78 n.6
Bretz, Andrew 101 n.48
Brigden, Susan 38, 41, 49
Brockman, Sonya L. 87, 93
Brooke, Humphrey 17
Brown, Paul 185
Bullokar, John 12
Burkhardt, Jacob 20–1, 196
Burke, Peter 13
Burnett, Mark Thornton 159 n.14, 175 n.36
Burrow, Colin 150 n.65
Butler, Martin 101 n.48

Camino, Mercedes Maroto 101 n.48
Campbell, Oscar J. 62 n.67
Campion, Thomas 118
Cartelli, Thomas 188 n.53, 189
Catholicism *see* 'religion'
Cauthen, I.B. 77 n.4
Chamberlain, John 127–8
Chapman, George
    May Day 146–9
charity 27–9, 39–72
Charnes, Linda 157
Chaucer, Geoffrey 95 n.33
Cheney, Patrick 151, 151 n.72
Cicero 172–3
clemency *see under* 'pity'
Coleridge, Samuel Taylor 83–4
Colie, Rosalie L. 64 n.72
communities 2–3, 8, 15, 18–31, 35, 37–8, 49–50, 52, 55, 63, 78–82, 87, 96, 99, 114–15, 121, 134, 141, 152, 156, 161–79, 185, 197–99
compassion *see under* pity
Condron, Stephanie 84 n.16
Cooper, Helen 62 n.68
Craik, Katharine 19, 23 n.65

Index

Craik, T.W.   62 n.68
Crewe, Jonathan   131 n.36
cruelty   13, 64, 68, 69, 71, 83, 123, 124,
    131–6, 145, 162, 173
Culhane, Peter   102 n.49
Cunningham, Karen   91 n.30

Daniel, Christopher   41
Daniel, Samuel
    Delia   123–4
Daniels, Charles B.   24 n.70
Davenport, William Anthony   59
Davies, Surekha   159 n.14
Davis, Alex   124, 148
Davis, Natalie Zemon   22
Davis, Nicholas   57 n.59
Day, John (printer)   30, 75, 77–82, 86,
    94–101, 105–6, 109, 111–12
de Grazia, Margreta   21 n.60
Dekker, Thomas   32, 145 n.58
Derrida, Jacques   195–6
Descartes, René   21, 158
Dessen, Alan C.   57 n.59
De Sousa, Ronald   14 n.35
Diehl, Huston   67
Distiller, Natasha   129
Dixon, Thomas   14 n.35, 90–1
Dolan, Frances E.   16 n.42
Dollimore, Jonathan   68
Donaldson, Ian   101 n.48, 112
Dryden, John   182 n.44
Dubrow, Heather   107 n.24, 122, 125
Duffy, Eamon   41–2, 46, 51 n.50
Duncan-Jones, Katherine   101 n.48,
    150–1
Dupleix, Scipion, Lord of
    Clarens   158–9
Dutton, Richard   187, 188

Ekman, Paul   14 n.35
Elckerlijc   50, 52
Elton, William R.   64 n.72
emotion
    critical methodologies
        surrounding   13–19
    emotional confrontation   28–9, 31,
        46, 74, 81–2, 114
    passions   16–19, 160
Enterline, Lynn   19 n.51, 88 n.26, 107
    n.54
Erickson, Peter B.   167
Everyman   28, 50–6, 61–2, 73

Faas, Ekbert   150
Fair Maid of the Exchange, The   147–8,
    151
Fawcett, Mary Laughlin   165
Febvre, Lucien   13
Feerick, Jean E.   154
fellowship   56, 161, 172 *see also*
    Everyman
Fernie, Ewan   19 n.51
Ferry, Anne   130 n.36
Fienberg, Nona   135
Findlater, Richard   84 n.16
Fineman, Joel   107 n.54, 140–1, 148
Fish, Simon   43, 47
Florio, John (translator) see Montaigne,
    Michel de
Floyd-Wilson, Mary   14 n.35, 16 n.43
Forrest, Ian   42–3
Fortin, René E.   64 n.72
Forster, Leonard   130
Foster, Donald   117 n.1, 136, 138
Freud, Sigmund   98
Frith, John   46
Frye, Roland M.   64 n.72
Fudge, Erica   160 n.18, 173–4

Galen *see* humoral theory
Garber, Marjorie   86
Geller, Jesse D.   197
gender dynamics   117, 119, 121, 125,
    130, 135–6
generic interplay (poetry and
    drama)   139–52
generic posturing   126, 143
Gerdes, Karen E.   197
Gilbert, Ruth   174
Goldie, Peter   14 n.35
Golding, William (translator)   *see* Ovid
good works *see* charity
Gower, John   95 n.33
    as translator   97–8, 100 *see also* Ovid
Green, Douglas E.   85
Greenblatt, Stephen J.   20–1, 185 n.46
Greene, Roland   125
Greg, Sir Walter   77 n.4
Gross, Daniel M.   14 n.35
Guilfoyle, Cherrell   65 n.79

Hadfield, Andrew   52, 96 n.34, 100 n.45
Haigh, Christopher   36
Hamilton, A.C.   83 n.10
Harding, Jennifer   14 n.35

Index

Harris, Paul   19 n.51
Hatcher, O.L.   144 n.57
Heal, Felicity   44
Heffernan, Julián Jiménez   169 n.23
Herford, C.H.   187 n.50
Heywood, Thomas   30, 32, 147 n.61
   The Rape of Lucrece   82, 101–5
Hickscorner   28, 56–61, 72
Hillman, David   16 n.43
Hobbes, Thomas   4 n.4
Holbrook, Peter   150
Holland, Philemon (translator) *see* Pliny
Holmes, Rachel E.   15 n.40
Howard, Frances   31–2, 117–22, 126–9,
   134–40, 148–9
Hubler, Edward   150 n.66
Hulse, Clark S.   83 n.10
humanity
   defining qualities of   1–2, 32–3,
      155–9, 163–4, 167–87, 193–4,
      198
   hierarchies of   6, 155, 157, 161, 166,
      168–9, 172, 175, 178, 181, 183,
      188, 193
   proximal humanity   33, 155–7,
      166–8, 173, 177, 179, 184, 186,
      190
   reason/rationality   157–62, 173
humoral theory   16–18
humors *see* humoral theory
Hunt, Maurice   170 n.27
Hutson, Lorna   20, 82 n.8, 91 n.30
Hyland, Peter   139
Hynes, Sam   98 n.40

identity
   collective   1, 2, 21, 37, 42, 166, 191,
      197, 198–9
   individual   1, 21, 34, 163, 164, 196–7
   relational identity   162, *see* proximal
      humanity *under* humanity
inhuman *see* non-humanity
interludes *see* morality plays
intimacy   25, 27, 28, 38–40, 45, 47–8,
   50, 54, 66, 74, 113, 123, 197–8
Io   89

Jackson, MacDonald P.   145 n.58
James, Heather   91 n.30
James, Henry   77
Jayne, Sears   67–8
Jed, Stephanie   100 n.45,

Johnson, Toria A.   15 n.40
Jones, Norman   37, 43
Jonson, Ben
   Bartholomew Fair   33, 187–94
Jordan, W.K.   44 n.30, 49

Kagan, Jerome   14 n.35
Kahn, Coppélia   80 n.7
Kennedy, Gwynne   19 n.51
Kennedy, William   121–2
Kerrigan, William   21 n.56, 130
Kewes, Paulina   101 n.47, 102
kind, definitions of   166, 172, 175–9,
   182, 183, 189, 192, *see also*
   humanity *and* non-humanity
kindness   166, 172, 175–9, 182, 183, 189,
   192, 197
Kirsch, Arthur   160 n.16
Knoppers, Laura Lunger   159 n.14
Konstan, David   6, 199
Kott, Jan   64
Kyd, Thomas   146 n.60

Lacan, Jacques   105 n.51
Lake, David J.   145 n.58
Lancashire, Ian   57 n.57, 59 n.61, 59
   n.62
Landes, Joan B.   159 n.14
Langley, Eric   13 n.31, 73, 106 n.53, 118,
   170 n.25
Latimer, Hugh   46, 47–8
Lawrence, Séan   64
Lehnhof, Kent R.   68 n.89
Lewis, C.S.   128 n.25
Lindsay, Tom   169 n.23
Lipsius, Justus   6–7
literary inheritance   32, 35, 139–52
Little, Arthur L.   80 n.7
Lyly, John   13 n.29
Livy   30, 82, 95, 96 n.34, 97 n.35, 100–1,
   102 n. 49, 112
Lobis, Seth   170
Lodge, Thomas
   Phillis   131
Loewenstein, David   64
Lovejoy, Arthur O.   171 n.28
Lowe, Peter   17 n.44
Lucrece   30, 80–2, 86–7, 89, 95–6,
   99–100, 102, 104, 113–15
   see also Heywood, Thomas, *The Rape
      of Lucrece*
   see also Livy

221

Index

see also Ovid

see also Painter, William, *The Palace of Pleasure*

see also Shakespeare, *The Rape of Lucrece*

Lupton, Julia Reinhard   175–6

Lydgate, John   95 n.33

Lynch, Stephen J.   65

Lyndwood, William   53

Lyons, Bridget Gellert   67 n.83

lyric poetry   31, 117–38, 143–4, 149–52

Mack, Maynard   61 n.67

Marshall, Cynthia   22, 85 n.18, 129, 133–4

Marshall, Peter   43, 44

Marston, John   32

The Malcontent   144

masculinity   7, 119, 120, 125, 128, 130, 150

Mathews, Richard   12

Matt, Susan J.   15 n.40

Martines, Lauro   129 n.26

Maus, Katharine Eisaman   21 n. 59, 35, 107 n.54

Mazzio, Carla   16 n.43

McAdam, Ian   188–9

McEachern, Claire   24 n.70

McIntosh, Marjorie Keniston   44, 49 n.47

Meek, Richard   14 n.35, 91 n.29, 107 n.54

mercy *see under* pity

Middleton, Thomas   95 n.33

Miller, Christopher W.T.   100 n.45

Montaigne, Michel de   11–12, 160

morality plays   28–9, 35, 57 n.59, 61–2, 67 n.83 *see also Everyman* and *Hickscorner*

Moyer, Ann E.   12 n.27, 13

Mueller, Janel   38, 44

Mullaney, Steven   37–8

Mulvey, Laura   98, 105 n.51

Nardizzi, Vin   154

Nashe, Thomas   40, 74, 132

Neely, Carol Thomas   129

Nelson, Jeffrey N.   133

Newman, Jane   87 n.25

Nietzsche, Friedrich   9–11, 196, 199

Nohrnberg, James   61 n.67, 67

Nolan, Michael   144 n.57

non-humanity

animals (invocation of)   154–62, 173, 176–8, 183, 184, 190–1, 194, 195

beasts   156–62, 165, 166, 173, 177, 178

creatures   1–2, 7, 51,154, 158, 159, 162, 165, 172, 173, 180, 183, 184, 198

inhuman   153–4

lack   8, 33, 153, 155, 156–7, 159, 160, 163–5, 168, 171, 173, 176, 182, 187–94

material value of   178, 185, 191

Nordlund, Marcus   106 n.53

Norton, Thomas   75

Gorboduc   30, 75, 81

nostalgia   35, 39, 40, 48, 60, 72

Nussbaum, Martha   4, 10

obligation   1, 3, 9, 28, 33, 34, 66, 70, 121, 134, 135, 154, 156, 167–8, 170, 172, 191, 195, 197

O'Connell, Michael   61 n.67, 62

O'Hagan, Sean   114 n.58

Oakley-Brown, Liz   91 n.30

Oatley, Keith   14 n.35

Olson, Greta   155

Orgel, Stephen   186

Ortony, Andrew   14 n.36

Ovid   82, 88, 96, 97, 98, 99, 101, 110

Painter, William

The Palace of Pleasure   100, 101

Palfrey, Simon   187–8

Park, Katharine   171 n.28

Parker, Patricia   129

Pask, Kevin   188 n.52, 188 n.53

passions *see under* emotion

Paster, Gail Kern   14 n.35, 16 n.43, 160

Patterson, Annabel   100 n.45

Peele, George   82, *see also Titus Andronicus*

Percy, Thomas   56–7

Perry, Curtis   61 n.67

Petrarcha, Francesco   146 n.60

Petrarchan convention   118–20, 122, 125, 129, 130, 133, 140, 142, 143, 144, 145, 146, 148, 149, 150

Petrarchism   31, 121–2, 129, 130, 133, 139, 149

Philomel   30, 87–9, 92

pity

absence of/pitilessness   8, 32, 40, 48, 69, 131

definitions of   3–13

222

Index

modern usage 197–8
related terms
  clemency 11, 12
  compassion 11–12
  fellow-feeling 13 n.29,
  mercy 11, 12
  sympathy 11, 12–13
as a secular concept 10, 27, 28, 35,
  50, 55, 56, 63, 69
self-pity 4
Plamper, Jan 15 n.40
Pliny 13 n.29
Pinch, Adela 16 n.42
Pincombe, Mike 172
Pineas, Rainier 55 n.55
the poor 39, 41 n.18, 42, 45–8, 53, 60, 67
Poor Law 29
Potter, Robert 61 n.66
Pranell, Frances *see* Howard, Frances
Pribram, Deirdre 14 n.35
Prince, F.T. 109
Protestantism *see* religion
Punter, David 4 n.3
purgatory *see* religion
Puttenham, George 23, 118, 127
Pyramus (and Thisbe) 126

Quilligan, Maureen 21 n.60
Quintilian 95 n.33

Raber, Karen 155, 169 n.23, 176
Reddy, William 14 n.35, 15, 19
redemption *see* religion
Reformations (English) 28–9, 34–5,
  36–41, 43–4, 48–9, 63, 66
Reiss, Timothy 23
religion
  purgatory 36, 37, 43, 45–6
  redemption 50, 52–3, 55, 59, 60
  salvation 28, 41–3, 52, 56, 58, 60, 61,
    66–8
  structures of 54, 57, 58, 60–3, 68,
    72, 73
Rhodes, Neil 190
Richardson, Catherine 139 n.50, 144
  n.56, 144 n.57, 147 n.61
Roche, Thomas P. 122 n.11, 133
Rodney, Sir George 31–2, 117–22,
  125–8, 131, 134–40, 142, 147–9
Rosenthal, Joel T. 41 n.18, 42
Rosenwein, Barbara 14–15, 18
Rousseau, Jean-Jacques 7–8, 10

Rowe, Katherine 14 n.35, 16 n.43, 86
Rowley, William 35
  The Thracian Wonder (with John
    Webster) 155
Rubin, Miri 41 n.18, 42, 46
Ryan, Lawrence V. 55
Rycroft, Eleanor 57 n.59

Sackville, Thomas 75 *see also* Norton,
  Thomas
Sanchez, Melissa E. 180
Sartre, Jean-Paul 105 n.51
Schen, Claire S. 41 n.18
Schoenfeldt, Michael C. 21
Schopenhauer, Arthur 9
Scully, Sam 24 n.70
selfhood *see* identity
self-pity *see* pity
Seigel, Jerrod 21
Selleck, Nancy 22–3
Seneca 6–7
Shakespeare, William
  Antony and Cleopatra 24
  As You Like It 95 n.33, 139–43, 149,
    166–8
  King Henry VI pt. 3 163–4
  King Lear 29, 35, 38, 50, 57, 61–74
  The Merchant of Venice 32, 153–4,
    156
  The Merry Wives of Windsor 143–4
  Othello 25
  Pericles 26
  The Rape of Lucrece 30, 82–3, 104–14
  Richard II 25
  Richard III 32, 155–8
  Romeo and Juliet 26–7, 140
  The Tempest 33, 168–94
  Timon of Athens 24–5
  Titus Andronicus 29–30, 32, 82–95,
    164–6
  Twelfth Night 95 n.33, 143
  Two Gentlemen of Verona 25
Shannon, Laurie 160 n.18
Sheehan, Michael M. 41 n.18
Shell, Alison 64–5
Shrank, Cathy 36, 45
Shugar, Debora K. 66
Shupe, Donald R. 156
Sidney, Sir Philip
  An Apologie for Poetry 23–4
  Astrophil and Stella 122–5, 134–5, 148
Sierhuis, Freya 6 n.8

223

Index

Simpson, Evelyn   187 n.50
Simpson, James   55
Simpson, Percy   187 n.50
Slights, Jessica   179
Smith, Adam   8
Smith, Denzell   157
Smith, Helen   77
Smith, Nigel   36 n.1
Smith, William
  Chloris   133–4
Solomon, Robert   14 n.35
society *see* communities
spectacle   26, 30, 67, 84–8, 93, 97, 99,
      104, 105, 109–10, 112, 114, 115,
      127–8, 142, 180
Spinoza, Baruch   7
Sponsler, Claire   51 n.50
Stallybrass, Peter   21 n.60
Stampfer, Judah   63
Stearns, Carol Z.   15–16
Stearns, Peter N.   15–16
Steffes, Michael   66
Stewart, Frances *see* Howard, Frances
St. Hilaire, Danielle   70, 91 n.29
Stockholder, Kay   22 n.62
Stoicism   6–8, 12
Stow, John   39–40, 48, 72, 74
Stradling, Sir John (translator) *see*
      Lipsius, Justus
Stubbes, Philip   38–40, 50
Sullivan, Erin   10 n.23, 14 n.35, 15 n.40,
      16, 19 n.51
Sullivan, Garrett A.   16 n.43
subjectivity *see* identity
sympathy *see under* pity

Taylor, Charles   21
tenderness   1, 7, 70–1, 169, 170, 172, 173,
      179, 180, 185, 191, 192, 197, 198
Thomson, J.A.F.   41
Topsell, Edward   160–2
Tricomi, Albert   84
*The True Chronicle Historie of King
      Leir*   65, 71
Tudeau-Clayton, Margaret   191 n.58
Turner, Terence J.   14 n.36
Tyndale, William   46

van Dijkhuizen, Jan Frans   24
Vaughan, Alden T.   179 n.40
Vaughan, Virginia Mason   179 n.40
Vaught, Jennifer C.   17 n.13

Vickers, Nancy   107, 125, 129
Villeponteaux, Mary   129
violation   96, 99, 107, 109, 111, 115,
      133–4, 166,183 *see also* violence
violence
  against pity itself   195
  aggression   131–3, 168
  emotional   30, 83–95, 106, 124, 126,
      133, 134
  physical   64, 68, 75, 77–9, 83–95
      126–7, 131, 132, 133, 149
  in rhetoric   33, 119–20, 131, 132, 133,
      134, 136, 147, 154
  visual markers of   29, 74–82, 82–95
vision
  aggressive vision   105–6, 108, 110
  communicative vision   87–8, 92, 94,
      103–5
  connection through shared
      vision   110, 113–15
visuality   29–31, 82, 87, 102, 104–5,
      114–15
vulnerability   1–3, 5, 7, 9, 27–9, 34, 43,
      46, 48, 51, 53, 55, 63, 65, 69,
      71–2, 83, 129 159, 180, 196–9

Waith, Eugene   83–4
Walker, Greg   52 n.52, 57 n.57, 57 n.59,
      77
Walkington, Thomas   17–8
Wall, Wendy   75 n.3, 132
Waller, Marguerite   130 n.36
Warkentin, Germaine   125 n.16
Wasson, John   61 n.66
Watkins, John   61 n.66, 61 n.67
weakness   1–2, 6, 8, 47, 53, 127, 130–1,
      186, 191, 196
Weaver, William   82 n.8, 109 n.56
Webster, John
  The Thracian Wonder (with William
      Rowley)   144–5
  Appius and Virginia   95 n.33
Wells, Robin Headlam   172 n.30
Wehrs, Donald R.   180
Wesley, John   87
Whittier, Gayle   140
Wickberg, Daniel   16 n.42
Widdowes, Daniel   158–9
Wierzbicka, Anna   4 n.3
Wiggins, Martin   139 n.50, 144 n.56,
      144 n.57, 147 n.61
Wilkinson, L.P.   96 n.34

Index

Willbern, David 87 n.24, 90–1
Williams, Carol D. 85
Williams, Marilyn 60
Willis, Deborah 174
Wilson, Arthur 121, 127–8, 138–9, 148
Wilson, Dover 83
Wilson, Scott 125

Wiseman, Susan 174
Woodbridge, Linda 159 n.14
Wright, Thomas 18–19, 160
Wulff, Helena 14 n.35
Wyatt, Thomas 123–4

Youth (Interlude) 59

Studies in Renaissance Literature

Volume 1: *The Theology of John Donne*
Jeffrey Johnson

Volume 2: *Doctrine and Devotion in Seventeenth-Century Poetry
Studies in Donne, Herbert, Crashaw and Vaughan*
R. V. Young

Volume 3: *The Song of Songs in English Renaissance Literature
Kisses of their Mouths*
Noam Flinker

Volume 4: *King James I and the Religious Culture of England*
James Doelman

Volume 5: *Neo-historicism: Studies in Renaissance Literature, History and Politics*
edited by Robin Headlam Wells, Glenn Burgess and Rowland Wymer

Volume 6: *The Uncertain World of* Samson Agonistes
John T. Shawcross

Volume 7: *Milton and the Terms of Liberty*
edited by Graham Parry and Joad Raymond

Volume 8: *George Sandys:
Travel, Colonialism and Tolerance in the Seventeenth Century*
James Ellison

Volume 9: *Shakespeare and Machiavelli*
John Roe

Volume 10: *John Donne's Professional Lives*
edited by David Colclough

Volume 11: *Chivalry and Romance in the English Renaissance*
Alex Davis

Volume 12: *Shakespearean Tragedy as Chivalric Romance:
Rethinking* Macbeth, Hamlet, Othello, *and* King Lear
Michael L. Hays

Volume 13: *John Donne and Conformity in Crisis in the Late Jacobean Pulpit*
Jeanne Shami

Volume 14: *A Pleasing Sinne:
Drink and Conviviality in Seventeenth-Century England*
Adam Smyth

Volume 15: *John Bunyan and the Language of Conviction*
Beth Lynch

Volume 16: *The Making of Restoration Poetry*
Paul Hammond

Volume 17: *Allegory, Space and the Material World
in the Writings of Edmund Spenser*
Christopher Burlinson

Volume 18: *Self-Interpretation in* The Faerie Queene
Paul Suttie

Volume 19: *Devil Theatre: Demonic Possession and Exorcism
in English Drama, 1558–1642*
Jan Frans van Dijkhuizen

Volume 20: *The Heroines of English Pastoral Romance*
Sue P. Starke

Volume 21: *Staging Islam in England: Drama and Culture, 1640–1685*
Matthew Birchwood

Volume 22: *Early Modern Tragicomedy*
edited by Subha Mukherji and Raphael Lyne

Volume 23: *Spenser's Legal Language:
Law and Poetry in Early Modern England*
Andrew Zurcher

Volume 24: *George Gascoigne*
Gillian Austen

Volume 25: *Empire and Nation in Early English Renaissance Literature*
Stewart Mottram

Volume 26: *The English Clown Tradition from the Middle Ages to Shakespeare*
Robert Hornback

Volume 27: *Lord Henry Howard (1540–1614): an Elizabethan Life*
D. C. Andersson

Volume 28: *Marvell's Ambivalence:
Religion and the Politics of Imagination in mid-seventeenth century England*
Takashi Yoshinaka

Volume 29: *Renaissance Historical Fiction: Sidney, Deloney, Nashe*
Alex Davis

Volume 30: *The Elizabethan Invention of Anglo-Saxon England
Laurence Nowell, William Lambarde, and the Study of Old English*
Rebecca Brackmann

Volume 31: *Pain and Compassion in Early Modern English Literature and Culture*
Jan Frans van Dijkhuizen

Volume 32: *Wyatt Abroad: Tudor Diplomacy and the Translation of Power*
William T. Rossiter

Volume 33: *Thomas Traherne and Seventeenth-Century Thought*
edited by Elizabeth S. Dodd and Cassandra Gorman

Volume 34: *The Poetry of Kissing in Early Modern Europe
From the Catullan Revival to Secundus, Shakespeare and the English Cavaliers*
Alex Wong

Volume 35: *George Lauder (1603–1670): Life and Writings*
Alasdair A. MacDonald

Volume 36: *Shakespeare's Ovid and the Spectre of the Medieval*
Lindsay Ann Reid

Volume 37: *Prodigality in Early Modern Drama*
Ezra Horbury

Volume 38: Poly-Olbion: *New Perspectives*
edited by Andrew McRae and Philip Schwyzer

Volume 39: *The Atom in Seventeenth-Century Poetry*
Cassandra Gorman

Printed in the United States
by Baker & Taylor Publisher Services